# The 10 Biggest Investment Mistakes
## Canadians Make

# The 10 Biggest Investment Mistakes Canadians Make
## Canadians Make

### And How to Avoid Them

## Ted Cadsby

Published in 2000 by Stoddart Publishing Co. Limited
895 Don Mills Road, 400-2 Park Centre, Toronto, Canada M3C 1W3
180 Varick Street, 9th Floor, New York, New York 10014

*Distributed by:*
General Distribution Services Ltd.
325 Humber College Blvd., Toronto, Ontario M9W 7C3
Tel. (416) 213-1919    Fax (416) 213-1917
Email cservice@genpub.com

04   03   02   01   2   3   4   5

Canadian Cataloguing in Publication Data

Cadsby, Ted
The ten biggest investment mistakes Canadians make: and how to avoid them
Includes bibliographical references and index.
ISBN 0-7737-32721
1. Investments — Psychological aspects.   2. Investment analysis.   I. Title.
HG4515.15.C32 2000      332.6'01'9      C00-931366-4

While the author is an executive of the CIBC group of companies, the opinions and recommendations expressed in this book are exclusively his, and do not necessarily represent those of CIBC.

While every effort has been made to ensure the accuracy and completeness of the information contained herein, the author and publisher assume no responsibility for errors, omissions, or inconsistencies; they also specifically disclaim any liability arising from the use or application of information contained in the book.
Readers should consider personally consulting a qualified investment professional in order to take account of their particular financial situations.

Jacket design: Bill Douglas @ The Bang
Text design and typesetting: Kinetics Design & Illustration

THE CANADA COUNCIL | LE CONSEIL DES ARTS
FOR THE ARTS | DU CANADA
SINCE 1957 | DEPUIS 1957

*We acknowledge for their financial support of our publishing
program the Canada Council, the Ontario Arts Council, and
the Government of Canada through the Book Publishing
Industry Development Program (BPIDP).*

Printed and bound in Canada

# Contents

# Introduction

# Just How Smart Are We Anyway?

Q: *Paul loves to read. He was very studious in school because he had a curious mind — always exploring and researching. He tends to be reserved, introverted, and methodical. Do you think Paul is more likely to be a librarian or a salesperson? Why?*

A: **Most people guess he's a librarian. But there are over a hundred times as many salespeople in Canada than librarians. So the odds strongly favour his being a salesperson, despite the stereotype I described.**

Q: *Do you ever pay top dollar to go to a sports event or play, say $160 for two tickets, but drive around and around the block looking for a free parking spot to save $7 in parking?*

A: **You might be surprised how many people do (including yours truly).**

Q: *Picture 23 people in a room. Of the 365 possible birthdays that anyone could have in a typical year, what do you think the odds are that two of those 23 people share the same birthday?*

A: **Most people badly underestimate this probability and guess somewhere between 5 and 10 percent. It's actually 51 percent — better than even odds!**

Q: *Imagine you are about to purchase a $45 light fixture. But you suddenly remember that the exact same fixture is on sale for $20 at a store that is 15 minutes away. Would you make the trip to get the better price? How about if you were purchasing a $750 television set, and recalled the same set at a store 15 minutes away for $25 cheaper?*

A: **Most people would make the trip in the first case, but not the second, even though the dollar savings in both cases are identical. Shouldn't 15 minutes of your time be worth the same amount in either scenario?**

Q: *For $20, you can buy a lottery ticket where you have to pick six numbers between one and 99. Which series of numbers would you be more comfortable betting on: 1, 2, 3, 4, 5, 6? Or 37, 18, 63, 92, 6, 17?*

A: **Most people believe that the second series is a better bet, even though they know that the two series are equally random — the lottery machine that spits out the numbered balls doesn't know the difference. It's as if they don't believe what they know!**

Q: *If Jill is better than Jack at shooting hoops, would it be better for Jack if they played a game to 11 or 21 hoops?*

A: **Most people believe that Jill will beat Jack in both games with an equally high probability. The shorter game of 11 hoops actually gives Jack a better chance. The shorter game has a higher chance of an unlikely outcome, whereas the longer game is more likely to reflect the likely outcome of their skill difference.**

Q: *Brenda is in her forties, and very outspoken. She majored in environmental sciences in university, where she led campus rallies to protest industrial development on the city's waterfront. Do you think Brenda is more likely to be a teacher, or a teacher who is also an active environmentalist?*

A: **Studies demonstrate that the large majority of people would believe she is both a teacher and an environmentalist. But she is much more likely to be just a teacher, since the odds of being any two things are lower than being just one thing.**

Welcome to the mystery of the human mind. We are strange beings, capable of gross illogic and extreme irrationality — not to mention emotion that borders on melodrama, and supreme overconfidence in our beliefs and judgements. I say "welcome" because most of the time we have pretty big blind spots where our thinking and behaviour are concerned.

There is no shortage of self-help books that address the barriers to our ability to have better relationships, more successful careers, and increased self-fulfillment. But there are too few that address the bizarre human condition as it relates to investing, even though *human psychology is, without doubt, the single biggest obstacle to successful investing*. This fact has been well documented by researchers in the branch of economics known as "behavioural finance."

As someone who works in the investment industry, I have seen investor psychology at work. I have watched astute, educated individuals repeat investment mistakes, and have occasionally caught myself making the same types of mistakes. Intrigued — and concerned — I immersed myself in the academic literature and interviewed behavioural finance specialists and professors. Although I was already aware of the common mistakes that investors make, I learned from behavioural finance that the frequency of certain mistakes is predictable, because they originate from the psychology that we all share. And the errors are costly — detracting significantly from the returns that could otherwise be earned.

But aside from the academic studies, and a few general publications, there is little in the way of general reading material that explores common investing mistakes within the context of the investor psychology that causes them. If investors were more aware of their psychological stumbling blocks, they would have a much better chance of avoiding the errors that prevent them from earning the best possible returns.

That's what this book is about: understanding how investor psychology is the root cause of the 10 most costly investment mistakes, and learning how to avoid them. *Your portfolio returns can be improved forever simply by avoiding the 10 big mistakes.*

Part One of this book covers the following: (i) a brief introduction to the history and concepts of behavioural finance; (ii) an exploration of how our minds work, often in surprising ways; and (iii) the key principles of successful investing. Part Two gets to the mistakes themselves, starting with a summary of the Big 10, followed by a chapter dedicated to each.

The mistakes are not in strict order of importance, and each chapter dealing with a particular mistake is a stand-alone chapter that can be read independently of the other mistakes. But because Part One lays the foundation for understanding the mistakes, I do strongly recommend reading this section first; you will find that throughout the book I allude to all of the concepts that are described there. At the end of every chapter, I've included a "Recap," which highlights the crucial points.

Part Three concludes the book with asset allocation recommendations (including a useful "twist" on the usual method of creating asset mixes), as well as a summary of the important points covered in the book. The appendices relate to more detailed examinations of particular topics that arise in some of the chapters. In the main text, I've separated out some of the more detailed math into "math breaks," in which I delve a little more deeply into some of the concepts. But if you choose to ignore these side-bars, you will not miss any important material. The appendices are essentially extended math breaks.

Throughout much of the book, I will use mutual funds as the investment product of example. This is not because funds are the only way to invest, or even the best way for all investors. However, they are often the most convenient and effective way for many investors to access the stock and bond markets. If you purchase stocks and bonds directly, either through an advisor or through a discount broker, the investment errors I describe are equally applicable.

As I write this very paragraph on Friday, April 14, 2000 — *I kid you not* — the TSE 300 has closed down 5.5 percent from yesterday, for a one-week loss of just over 10 percent. The US market went down by the same amount. I'm confused . . . not because I'm frightened, but because I don't know what to buy — there are so many great bargains in the stock market! Having my savings fully invested to begin with, I only have part of today's paycheque with which to take advantage of the great prices. I decide to remain faithful to what I preach, and stay with my overall asset mix, which means investing some in the TSE 300 index, and some in the US market index. It will be a few months before this manuscript is finalized, so I'll let you know how that decision fared in a postscript at the end of Part Three.

# PART 1

## Human Psychology
## Meets High Finance

# The Origins of Behavioural Finance

*Eye Opener:*
*Fortunately, we're not a bunch of computers walking around with limbs and big mouths. But if we were, we'd make fewer investment mistakes.*

## Investing 101: It's All in the Mix

Asset mix is the most important decision — how we choose to mix the proportions of stocks, bonds, and cash in our portfolio. This is not news to most people. Whether it's really believed, never mind practised — that's another question.

Smart investing begins with an appropriate combination of domestic and foreign stocks, bonds, cash, GICs, and other assets. This is a cold hard fact by which every competent investment advisor lives and dies. Some advisors will add greater or lesser value by choosing the particular securities within each asset class. But the allocation of asset classes within an investment portfolio is the first and most important step.

Harry Markowitz is the father of modern portfolio theory. In June of 1952, at the young age of 25 when he was in graduate school, he published an article that outlined his thesis. He claimed that the only factor an investor can intelligently control is the variability of an entire portfolio — not the ups and downs of its component parts, but the portfolio as a whole. You can't control how the different stocks, bonds, or general markets move, but you *can* control the volatility of your entire portfolio. That control is exercised by *how* you combine asset classes in your portfolio. He published a book in 1959 that expanded this notion and earned him a 1990 Nobel Prize. Today his insights are taken for granted; every time you hear someone espousing the virtues of diversification, you can credit Harry Markowitz.

In outlining his research, Markowitz defined risk in a simple, quantitative way: Risk is the degree to which prices vary around their average. The risk of an asset is defined by its variability, or how far the price of an asset moves away from its average price. Mathematically, this variation from the average is known as standard deviation, which measures the volatility, or ups and downs, of prices. If the average price of a stock is $12, and within a year it goes as low as $11 and as high as $13, it has a low standard deviation because it doesn't move much from its average — it's not very volatile. A more volatile stock, which swings from $4 to $20, has a high standard deviation. Markowitz's insight was that the risk of an entire portfolio — the portfolio's standard deviation — is not defined only by the standard deviation of each of the individual stocks and bonds within the portfolio, but also *by the way the securities interact with one another.* The volatility of the portfolio, therefore, depends on how the securities are mixed together. And because the mix is controlled by the investor, he can have a large degree of influence on the risk of his portfolio.

Markowitz argued that the goal of every investor should simply be to determine the ideal portfolio for him- or herself. This portfolio should have the minimum amount of risk for an expected level of return. The higher the desired performance, the more risk an investor would have to assume. There are many ideal portfolios suited to many different investors. But there is only one ideal portfolio for each investor, since that portfolio will have just the right amount of risk — no more, no less — to achieve the desired expected return.

## MATH BREAK

You may have heard of "mean-variance optimization" — a phrase that describes Markowitz's work in a nutshell. "Mean" simply refers to the average expected return of a portfolio, and "variance" is just volatility or standard deviation. So the best portfolio is one that optimizes the return-risk relationship: You determine what return you need (say 10 percent annually in order to retire comfortably), then you invest in a portfolio of assets (an asset mix) which has the least amount of risk for your required return. Since there's no free lunch, you can't have a 10 percent return objective if you're only willing to invest in GICs and T-bills. But you do have the opportunity to minimize risk to a point, and that point is the exact mix of stocks, bonds, cash, and other assets that will likely earn you 10 percent, with an expected standard deviation that is lower than any other 10 percent–earning portfolio.

So how do you know which asset mix gives you the lowest risk for the highest return? You need a mathematical computer program, called linear programming, to determine the best mix of assets for any required rate of return. The inputs to the program are the expected returns and volatilities of each asset class (which is usually based on their historical characteristics), as well as the correlation between the different asset classes (which measures the similarity or difference in their movements). The program will generate a series of portfolios which all optimize the mean-variance relationships. All of these portfolios will lie on a line called the "efficient frontier." This line tracks all the portfolios that have an expected return for a certain level of risk. The more risk an investor can afford to take, the more return you can expect to earn — her ideal portfolio will lie at a higher point on the efficient frontier. It's all very mathematical and straightforward: a rational investor should simply choose the portfolio that has the minimum amount of expected risk for whatever expected return she needs.

Between 1973 and 1974, the US market collapsed by over 40 percent in reaction to surging oil prices that induced 11 percent inflation, despite high levels of unemployment. The Watergate scandal didn't help either. Not surprisingly, the turmoil meant that Markowitz's theories of risk management became increasingly popular. So it wasn't until the 1970s that his theories of portfolio management became mainstream. At the same time, however, academics began questioning the notion that investors are consistently rational.

In the early 1970s, academic articles began appearing that documented how seemingly irrational people really are. The first works focused on how investors think of risk. Research revealed that people tend to view risk in more complex ways than were suggested by the traditional model used by economists such as Markowitz. Risk, it seemed, was as much a psychological phenomenon as it was a mathematical one. Standard deviation didn't fully capture how investors thought of risk. Throughout the 1970s and into the 1980s, momentum picked up on research that analyzed the ways in which people stray from consistent rational decision making. While these new insights did not invalidate Markowitz's work, they did suggest that investors were not likely to automatically follow his prescriptions, even if they understood them.

At the same time, a concurrent theme of research began to evolve that questioned the rationality, or efficiency, of the market as a whole. Stock prices bounced around, it seemed, between extreme valuations that didn't always represent fair values. If investors are not always rational, and markets appeared inefficient, how was an investor to properly manage risk in the simple way that Markowitz envisioned?

While initially bewildering, the solution to this puzzle is thankfully straightforward and much more widely understood and accepted today than it was in the 1970s. *While investors can be irrational, and markets can move in exaggerated ways in the short term, a long-term and disciplined approach to investing can overcome both of these problems.* The insight within that sentence is so deceptively simple that its significance and power can easily be overlooked. I will have plenty more to say about this in the following chapters. For now it's sufficient to note that it was in the 1970s that psychology and investment theory joined forces, and the important field of behavioural finance was born.

## Behavioural Finance

Up until the early 1970s, economics was generally thought of in purely mathematical terms. The leading school of quantitative economics — the University of Chicago — prided itself on mathematical modelling (called econometrics), intended to predict growth, inflation, and other economic trends. One of the key underlying assumptions of economic predictions is that people are rational — their actions are based on a straightforward understanding of how the world works. This school of thought — known as "rational expectations" — was also championed by the university; it was conceived in 1961 and blossomed in the 1970s. Markowitz's work, which preceded the rational expectations hypothesis, was nonetheless dependent upon the same assumptions: Rational investors should make their portfolio decisions based on an understanding of the tradeoff between risk and reward. If people make mistakes in their investing strategies, it's simply because they just don't understand; otherwise, they'd rationally follow the rules.

But starting in 1970, academic papers began to explore a new way of thinking about economics, one that emphasized the less rational side of human thinking patterns. This new approach rejected the assumption that human beings are consistently rational. Instead, it started from the polar opposite hypothesis — that humans are oddly irrational and unreasonable.

This idea is obvious when we compare humans with computers. Computers have a huge advantage over us in two main respects, especially when it comes to investing; both differences relate to the way they solve problems:

1. Computers are consistently logical — faithful to how they have been programmed. We, on the other hand, are not hardwired to be consistently logical.
2. Computers are not vulnerable to emotions, which can sometimes steer us in wrong directions.

Naturally I'm not suggesting that the only thing that separates us from machines is a bit of emotion and irrationality. But I am pointing out that being illogical, irrational, and emotional weakens our ability to process information effectively. So we're prone to error. What's interesting is that because we all share a common nature, the quirkiness of human behaviour can actually be predicted with some degree of reliability. *We're a quirky bunch, but we're consistently and therefore predictably quirky.*

It was in the 1970s that the study, categorization, and documentation of all the consistent and predictable ways that we are irrational began to expand. This type of psychological research was not new, but it *was* quite revolutionary when researchers began to look at how the systematic errors in our thinking could be applied to the disciplines of economics and investing. This is where psychology meets high finance — in the study of the ways in which we behave oddly when it comes to money, or "behavioural finance," as it's more formally known. Behavioural finance is all about the odd *behaviours* that we exhibit when it comes to our *finances.* Make no mistake — we're odd in myriad other ways, especially when it comes to our romantic lives. But just as we need to temper some of our behaviours when it comes to romance, so too can we benefit from understanding and counteracting our unhelpful financial habits. *The truly successful investors are those who understand their investment psychology so they are able to apply Markowitz's ideas about portfolio asset mixes — and avoid the behaviours that lead to the 10 biggest investment mistakes.*

Successful investing depends on following a few crucial investment rules, all of which are easier to follow, you'd think, than the rules of good health. One of the important investment rules is to not fret and fidget with your portfolio — in essence, just forget about it. You'd think that would be a lot easier to manage than going for a 30-minute workout four times a week. If only human psychology didn't get in the way.

So let's analyze just how predictably irrational you and I really are. This will lay the groundwork for understanding the big investment mistakes, all of which are attributable in various ways to our psychology. I think you'll find the examination of our foibles quite revealing. (Believe me, I'm as susceptible as any investor to the 10 mistakes, and work hard to avoid them by keeping the lessons of behavioural finance at the fore-front of my mind.)

## Recap of Behavioural Finance

1. Investing theory is founded on the Nobel Prize–winning principles that Harry Markowitz wrote about in 1952. His thesis, which still stands today, is that investors can control risk by the way they mix assets within their portfolios. Not only *can* they, but they *should*: Asset mix is the only element of the investing process that they can realistically control.

2. Behavioural finance is an academic field originating over 30 years ago, but only recently becoming mainstream. It marries the study of psychology with the basics of investment theory to understand the way in which human beings make consistent and predictable mistakes with their money.

3. The 10 biggest and most common investment mistakes that Canadians make all originate from a shared investor psychology. The secret of successful investing — of maximizing returns — is to understand and overcome our thinking foibles. And there are plenty of them . . .

# The Limits of
# Our Thinking

*Eye Opener:*
*Most of us are unaware of just how unproductive our thinking*
*patterns can be. This lack of knowledge makes us vulnerable . . .*
*to our own brains!*

## Psychology 101: The human mind is dangerous.

I am not referring to our capacity to wage war or engage in terrorism. I am talking about the ways our brains can work against our best interests in everyday aspects of life. The same capability for complex thought that allows us to be infinitely creative and gives our lives richness and meaning also contributes to less desirable behaviours. In the context of investing, it leads us to make inappropriate decisions that detract from our financial returns. But the good news is that behavioural finance has made significant progress in uncovering some of the never-before-revealed mysteries of investing psychology.

The behavioural finance literature tends to not categorize investor psychology consistently, so I've distinguished four categories of psychological tendencies — or cognitive limitations — that have a bearing on investment mistakes. I've identified each with two descriptions — a type of thinking, and a more colloquial name for the problem:

| Cognitive Limitation #1: | Wrong Thinking, or **"Unawareness"** |
|---|---|
| Cognitive Limitation #2: | Distorted Thinking, or **"Twisted Perceptions"** |
| Cognitive Limitation #3: | Emotional Thinking, or **"Fearfulness"** |
| Cognitive Limitation #4: | Unexamined Thinking, or **"Overconfidence"** |

I'll go through each one of these weak thinking patterns, and give specific examples of each.

# 1. Unawareness

The first cognitive limitation is probably the most inoffensive of the four. It doesn't draw out how odd we can be or make us look weak to the same extent as the other limitations. There are two elements of "unawareness"; I've distinguished them as "lack of knowledge" and "innumeracy."

## Lack of Knowledge

This one is simple: Sometimes we just don't have the information we need to make informed decisions. And we're often completely unaware of the stuff we don't know. For instance, it wasn't until I showed a friend how to bleed the radiators in her home that she understood there was a simple solution to being cold all the time: She didn't know how hot-water radiators worked. And I didn't believe that scrambled eggs could actually be tasty until I was shown not to add milk since it dilutes their flavour.

Investing is no different. Many investors generate sub-par returns because they don't understand some of the investment basics. They simply haven't been educated in the financial fundamentals of how markets work, and how to put the markets' natural characteristics to work in their favour. The problem arises when you cavalierly invest money without the guidance of someone with expertise. You would never put a critical health problem in the hands of someone who wasn't a medical professional. But too many people "self-diagnose" and "self-prescribe" when it comes to their investing strategies.

## Innumeracy

This form of unawareness is more insidious, because it's less obvious to most people. It's most prevalent in the way that most of us unknowingly struggle with basic probability theory. Probability theory plays a much more significant role in our daily lives than most of us realize, and it is integral to the investing process. To give you a simple example, most of us would be hard-pressed to make a good prediction on the probability of flipping four heads or four tails in a row, in a 20-flip coin toss. The term "innumeracy" was coined by John Allen Paulos, a mathematician and author of a book by the same name. Innumeracy describes a cognitive limitation that parallels its more familiar cousin — illiteracy, but it focuses instead on how mathematically illogical we can be.

In the introduction to this book, I presented a few tricky questions. One related to the fact that there are 365 possible birthdays that someone could have in a typical year. Picture a room in which there are 23 people. Of the 365 possible birthdays that any individual could have, I asked how likely it was that two share the exact same birthday.

Most people underestimate this possibility, including myself initially, and guess around 5, maybe 10 percent at the high end. The answer surprises most people because it's over 50 percent (51 to be exact).

## MATH BREAK

If you're skeptical, here's the math: $1 - [(365 \times 364 \times 363 \ldots 343) \div 365^{23}]$. I ask you to trust me on this, to save the three pages of explaining it.

If you're really interested in the math, pick up the book *Innumeracy*, listed in the "Suggested Reading" section at the back of this book.

What's interesting about this problem is that it exposes how badly we underestimate the frequency of randomness, or patterns existing within random numbers. We tend to think of unusual events as unlikely to occur, and when they do occur, we label them as coincidences (or sometimes, even miracles). Because our minds are not computers, they are not adept at handling probability analysis, so our intuitive abilities fail us. The result is that when we're confronted with surprising events, we over-interpret them because we don't appreciate how frequently unusual patterns occur in random events. So we invent stories to explain them, such as "what a coincidence" or "bad luck always comes in threes" or "he has a golden touch since everything goes right for him."

The odds of flipping a coin 20 times and getting four heads or four tails in a row are 50 percent. Once again, most people think the odds are much lower because they do not have a good sense of how easy it is for "coincidences" to occur. How about a more everyday example? You get a call from someone you haven't heard from in over a year. And you were just thinking about them the day before! What a coincidence! The caller must have picked up "vibes" from you when you were thinking about them. Maybe one of you has ESP!

Actually, this "coincidence" is not unusual at all. If you think about the 30 or so people that flutter through your mind on any given day what are the odds that at least once every couple of years, one of those 30 or so people calls you within a week of your thinking about them? The odds are very high that *one* of those 30 people will call — not one in particular, but one of the 30. Consider how many phone calls you get over 10 years — say three each day of the year, to be conservative, for a total of 10,950 calls (or 10,956 if you include leap years). That's a lot of opportunities for you to get a call from someone you've been recently thinking about! In fact, in a given decade, there's about a 67 percent chance of some person calling you soon after you've thought about them, and much higher odds if your popularity commands more than three calls a day.

## MATH BREAK

It's true that there's a very small chance of someone calling you within a short time of your thinking about them — let's say for argument's sake that it's as low as 0.01 percent. That means there's a 99.99 percent chance it *won't* happen for any particular call.

But that's just one call. If there are 10,956 calls in a decade, then we've got a better chance of it happening at some point for *some* call. So the odds of it *not* happening are not as low; in fact, the odds are $0.9999^{10,956}$, which is a 33 percent chance of it *not* happening.

If there's a 33 percent chance of it not happening, then there's a 67 percent chance that it will happen. And a much higher probability if you get five calls a day — about an 84 percent chance of it happening once in a decade. If you get 10 calls from 10 different people every day, which is not unusual if you combine incoming calls at work and home, then the odds are 84 percent that you'll experience this "coincidence" once every *five* years and 31 percent within *one* year.

Now if you're in a job where 20 different people call you every day . . . well . . . you get the picture. What appears to be a coincidence is shown to be mathematically predictable and quite commonplace, once you overcome your intuitive biases and understand probability theory.

We tend to overinterpret random events because our innumeracy inclines us to underestimate how often random patterns occur in nature. We should actually expect patterns to appear frequently within randomness. But we don't and so, for example, we're more impressed with horoscopes than we should be. A horoscope with many vague predictions is likely to be right on a few of them at least, and these predictions are the few that most people focus on, ignoring the others that are meaningless. Same with a psychic, who makes 10 generic predictions, half of which appear to be dead on. We marvel at the "hits," while paying little attention to the other half that make no sense. It has been estimated that there are about 20 times more astrologers in North America than there are astronomers!

The probability of *some* unusual event occurring is high. It's the probability of a *particular* unusual event occurring at a particular time that is very low. The problem is that we tend to badly underestimate how often *some* unusual event or pattern appears in the randomness of our lives.

What has this got to do with investing? We'll get into much greater detail when we look at Mistake #2, "Timing the Market." The markets move randomly in the short term, but most investors don't see it that way. Captive to a psychological disposition to overinterpret random events, they read a lot of meaning into the ups and downs of the market. A few bad days in the market bring out the headlines "Stocks enter bear phase" or "Long-awaited stock correction finally arrives." You don't read headlines like "Random market volatility is ignored by long-term investors." I don't expect you to take it on faith that the markets move randomly in the short term, so I'll be demonstrating that to you in the chapter on market timing. For now, it's important to recognize one of the key psychological factors that interfere with our maximizing investment returns — unawareness. Some of the important stuff we don't know is probability analysis and how frequently meaningless patterns occur within a series of random events. *A lack of awareness makes us vulnerable to our psychological tendency to want to interpret what is fundamentally un-interpretable.* This tendency toward overinterpreting just about everything we perceive is the hallmark of the second cognitive limitation.

## 2. Twisted Perceptions

As if not having knowledge and being innumerate weren't bad enough, we are also very vulnerable to distorted thinking, a good example of which is stereotyping. Sure, we know that not all librarians are quiet bookworms, but we tend to view them that way. We make quick judgements that are often very superficial and unrelated to truth or reality. In the case of distorted thinking, it's not really a matter of not knowing certain things, or not being intuitive about probability theory. It's more a matter of our thinking being, simply put, irrational.

This cognitive limitation is the most broad, and perhaps the most interesting. I've broken it down into five types of distortion, each of which demonstrates the common psychological foibles that have been documented by behavioural economists: Heuristics, Mental Accounting, Endowment Effect, Framing, and Overinterpretation.

## Heuristics

The first category is the most celebrated of all behavioural finance discoveries: heuristics. Heuristics are mental shortcuts — rules of thumb — that our brains develop so they can organize and synthesize information more quickly. They are unconscious methods of simplifying complexity in our decision-making routines. I've already mentioned one common example of a heuristic — stereotyping. "All young men who dress in dark hooded jackets are dangerous." This is a quick and easy rule of thumb that may not be true a lot of the time, but it's a convenient shortcut that preserves our safety in some instances. Stereotyping is an example of a broader classification of heuristics called "**representativeness**." We tend to generalize that like things go with like things. We use representativeness to categorize the world in our never-ending quest to make sense of our surroundings. This technique is very useful much of the time, as hooded men in dark alleys are usually best avoided. But it is the overapplication of this heuristic that can get us into trouble.

Here's a nice example of the pitfall of representativeness. Say a town has two hospitals — one larger and one smaller. The large one delivers 60 babies each day on average, while the smaller one delivers only about 12. As you'd expect, half of the babies are boys and half are girls, in both hospitals on average. But this ratio can vary from day to day, and even over a year. Here's the question: Do you think that both hospitals have an equal chance of delivering more boys than girls over a one-year period? Or would one be more likely than the other to deviate from a 50-50 split?

Most people assume that the odds are the same for both hospitals, because the general population should be *represented* equally in both hospitals. Because they should both approximate a 50-50 split, they are equally likely to deviate from that split over one year. Representativeness fails us here, though; the smaller hospital is much more likely to have a majority of one sex, since the smaller number of babies it delivers allows it to deviate more significantly from the general trend. The 50-50 trend is *represented* better in the larger sample from the larger hospital, over a shorter period of time. The same logic applies to why you want to keep tennis matches or a game of golf short if your opponent is better than you — you'll increase the odds of winning since the longer you play, the more the difference in skills asserts itself.

A common form of representativeness that relates to money is "gambler's fallacy," where we tend to think that after tossing three heads in a row, the fourth toss has a better-than-even chance of being a tail. If you are dealt a string of bad blackjack hands, or the roulette ball keeps landing on red, a good hand or black landing is right around the corner. This thinking stems from our use of the law of large numbers to *represent* a smaller sample. We know that a good prediction of the ratio of heads to tails in a large sample of coin tosses is 50-50, so we generalize from that law that a smaller sample will produce the same outcome since it *represents* the larger sample. We conclude that after a bunch of heads, we have to start seeing some tails to get to the 50-50 split. This conclusion is overapplying the heuristic of representativeness: Every coin toss has a 50-50 chance of being heads or tails on its own, and it's only in advance of a large number of tosses that we're entitled to say that the overall split is likely to be 50-50. When you hear people say, "This bull market can't last much longer since we've already had a few 'up' years in a row," they are invoking logic that probably suffers from gambler's fallacy — a case of overusing representativeness.

There are other heuristics that are equally hazardous. "**Availability bias**" is a technique we often use to make hasty judgements that are inappropriately skewed toward evidence that is readily available or recent in our memory. Most people — around 70 percent — assume that murder is much more common than suicide. The reverse is actually true (generally there are three suicides for every two murders in North America). But the *availability* of murder reportings in the media, compared to the sparse reportings of suicide, leads people to misjudge the frequency of each. Similarly, most people are surprised to learn that dying in a car accident is 40 times *more* likely than dying in a plane crash; plane crashes get a lot of media coverage. Another example: How did you feel about swimming in the ocean after you saw the movie *Jaws* — any different? Availability bias is at work when investors' tolerance for risk mysteriously drops, right after a market correction. All of a sudden, investors perceive that the chance of losing money in the stock market, even over the long term, is much higher than it was the day before the market went down 3 percent.

"**Anchoring**" is a heuristic whereby we tend to let a particular starting point overly influence our estimation or prediction of something. If you are negotiating the buying price for a house, you are likely to be very influenced — or *anchored* — by the list price. One of the key tactics to successful negotiation is to anchor your counterpart to a price, or price range, that is in your favour. Anchoring has been identified as one of the leading reasons why stock analysts tend to be slow to change their estimates of a company's earnings, even as the company's conditions change — analysts tend to get anchored on the historical earnings trend of a company. Investors are equally susceptible to fixating on a particular price of a stock or mutual fund, such as the price at which the security was purchased. This form of anchoring can be very costly if you are waiting to sell a fallen stock or mutual fund until it recovers, just because you anchored yourself to the purchase price.

There are other heuristics we use in assessing problems, but representativeness, availability bias, and anchoring are the three most common and relevant to the investment process. Let's look at other forms of distorted thinking that are not heuristics per se, but are equally hazardous.

## Mental Accounting

This is one of the most amusing examples of distorted thinking. For example, I don't know about you, but I'll treat myself occasionally to a nice night out and spare no expense on a lavish meal including an over-priced bottle of wine, elaborate appetizers and entrees, desserts, and expensive specialty coffees. But on the way to the restaurant, I'll circle around the block a few times in search of a free parking spot, so I don't have to pay $7 to park in a lot. I've been known to drag dates through the pouring rain over a hundred metres, just to save that seven bucks. (FYI: You don't earn any brownie points doing this — take it from me.)

Here's another one: A friend of mine will think nothing of buying premium brand-name laundry detergent instead of a perfectly good (and cheaper) generic label, but will go to great lengths to steam stamps off letters, if the stamps are reusable.

Mental accounting is a psychological trait that virtually all of us are vulnerable to. It describes our irrational way of putting different expenses in different accounts in our head. I don't mind debiting my "restaurant expense account" for a hefty amount once in a while, but I'm much more stingy with my "parking expense account." Same with my friend's "detergent account," which is apparently quite separate from his "stationery and supplies account."

Here's a demonstration that is often used to show how susceptible we are to mental accounting. Imagine you are on your way to see a play (or rock concert, if that's more typical for you). On the way, you discover that you've lost your $80 ticket. Would you proceed to the event and purchase a second ticket to see the show, or would you turn back home to see if there was a good movie on TV? Think about what you would do, and we'll come back to this scenario momentarily; but first another question.

Let's say you hadn't yet purchased the ticket, but had money in your pocket to buy it when you arrived. On the way, you discover that you've lost $80, which must have slipped out of your pocket. Would you proceed to buy a ticket anyway, maybe stopping at a bank machine nearby if you needed to, or would you turn back home?

Most people will turn home and give up on the event in the first example. It's hard to repurchase something expensive just because it was carelessly lost. However, most will proceed to buy the ticket in the second scenario; after all, it was money that was lost, not the ticket. Different responses to different scenarios, *even though the net cash outlay is identical in both situations*. The reason for the difference in responses is mental accounting. Most people are reluctant to debit the "ticket account" twice. But in the second scenario, most don't mind the double cash outlay because the misplaced money will be debited to a different account, such as the "lost money and other miscellaneous expenses account." Our ability to mentally categorize money into different accounts would put the most flexible circus contortionist to shame.

## Endowment Effect

We tend to treat things we own much differently than things we do not. For instance, if you were given a mug that had a $10 value, how much would you sell it for? How much would you pay to buy a similar mug? Most people would not sell the mug for less than $10, but would be unwilling to pay more than five dollars to buy a similar mug. Cute, eh? But a more serious problem arises if the mug is a stock or a mutual fund.

We are very reluctant to treat a security we own the way we would treat one we did not, which is a mistake, and a good example of distorted thinking. If a stock we own has fallen in price, and the prospects for its recovery are not good, we're much more inclined to hold on to it in the hopes that it will recover. But we should be viewing the decision to hold or sell in exactly the same way as if we were deciding whether to buy it or not. If it's not an investment worth buying, then it's not one that's worth holding. The endowment effect tends to distort a rational approach to investments we already own.

## Framing

Framing refers to how our views and decisions are influenced by context — by the way a situation is framed.

Let's say you have $1,600 in your chequing account. If I offered you a 50-50 chance of either losing $250 or winning $400, would you take the bet? According to studies that have assessed responses to this question, most people decline.

Let's say again that you have $1,600 in your account. Would you prefer to keep the $1,600, or take a 50-50 chance of having either $1,350 or $2,000 in your account? Most people take this bet.

The answers should be the same since the questions are basically identical. *But the questions are framed differently.* The first question is framed from a reference point of zero so that the gains and losses appear incremental and the potential loss usually elicits a conservative response. The second question is framed from a reference point of the account balance of $1,600, which makes the potential loss less troubling for most, and the potential gain, more exciting.

If you frame an investment opportunity in a risk-oriented way, such as from the perspective of how volatile the stock market can be from one week to the next, you're inclined to invest too conservatively. But you'll have a different perspective if you frame the same choice in a way that recognizes risk as a function of time, such as the risk of losing money over 10 years, which is very low. An inappropriate frame will incline you toward the wrong decisions.

## Overinterpretation

We saw an example of overinterpretation when we considered how unusual and coincidental most people think it is that two people out of 23 could share a birthday, even though this random event occurs with a high degree of probability. Overinterpretation is probably the most pervasive and perilous of all cognitive limitations.

The mind has a natural but relentless way of keeping itself busy —

our nature is to think and think and think and never stop. Our brains don't even close down when we're sleeping. They are the most incredible perpetual motion machines on the planet, always searching for meaning, always seeking patterns and order — always interpreting things. They relentlessly churn over ideas, thoughts, worries, dreams, interpretations. On and on with no pause. If you close your eyes and try to prevent your mind from wandering to anything, but just keep it focused on nothing at all, or focused on just your breathing, you'll see how hard it is. Most people can't even count to 10 without letting some arbitrary thought or worry float through their mind. Try it! Unless you've been trained in meditation, yoga, or some other thought-discipline exercise, I can almost guarantee you that you can't make it to 10 and remain "thoughtless." I would venture to say that *overinterpretation is the hallmark of our wonderful brains, and to a large extent of what we are as human beings.*

We looked at how innumerate we are when it comes to predicting patterns in randomness. And the consequence is that we overinterpret randomness — we give it more meaning than it has. Let's go back to the coin toss, and look at two series of Hs and Ts, representing a coin toss where "H" represents a head and "T" represents a tail.

*Series #1:* **H H H T T T**
*Series #2:* **H T H T T H**

Most people think that if the first sequence occurred, it would be an unusual coincidence, because the pattern doesn't seem random. But both series are equally likely. Try it: Flip a coin 20 times or more; you'll be surprised how "unrandom" the random flips appear to be. The patterns we see are not unusual and not unexpected to the trained observer; they are just as meaningless as the sequences that contain no patterns.

You may intellectually agree with what I'm saying, knowing that it is true, but still have difficulty internalizing the significance of it. Our minds are incredibly stubborn. They are so stubborn, and the biases we have are so powerful, that we actually have a lot of trouble believing what we know to be true! To return to one of the opening questions in this book, let's say you're playing a lottery and you can choose any six numbers between one and 99 to be your entry ticket. Which series of numbers are you more comfortable betting $20 on?

*Series #1:* 1, 2, 3, 4, 5, 6
*Series #2:* 41, 70, 9, 17, 54, 22

We know that each series has an equal chance of winning in a fair lottery, which generates random winning ticket numbers. But it would be hard to pick the first series, wouldn't it? There's no meaning in the randomness of the first series that would truly influence its chance of winning the jackpot. But our intuitive biases lead us astray. The world and the randomness that is so much a part of it is not easily tolerated by our meaning-making minds, which rush to fill the vacuum of meaninglessness with all sorts of conclusions and beliefs. And the random ups and downs of the stock markets provide fertile ground for this behaviour.

We'll get into the detail of this phenomenon later, especially in the chapter that dissects market timing. Overinterpreting randomness is fundamental to our nature, and responsible for generating some of the biggest mistakes commonly made by investors.

## 3. Fearfulness

Unfortunately, the limits of our cognitive powers don't end there. It gets worse. I'm sure that I don't need to demonstrate how emotional we can be. All you need to do is think back to the last heated argument you had with a loved one about something preposterously insignificant. Or your reaction to the stopped car in front of you at a green light, when the driver was cheerfully talking on a cell phone. Emotions make life so meaningful and rich for us. Yet they can make our lives so miserable if we're not careful. Our capacity to love and experience great joy is no less pronounced than our ability to be unreasonably angry, upset, or fearful.

Money is one of the most psychologically charged aspects of our lives. How did you feel the last time you lost money in the stock market, or at a casino? Or when your furnace broke down and you had to shell out $3,000 for a new one? I don't know about you, but I'm quite unemotional when filling my car up with $30 of gas. But if I run into a 24-hour grocery to grab some milk and return to my car to find a $15 parking ticket on my windshield, I'll rant and rave about the legal system and how unjust the world is until I tire myself out.

There is probably no greater obstacle to successful investing than unmanaged emotions. In fact, successful *living* is largely dependent on emotion management. A healthy and nurturing relationship demands significant management of our emotions — you can't afford to fly off the handle every time your partner leaves the top off the toothpaste, or says something inconsiderate. Most self-help books are geared toward dealing with the challenge of unmanaged emotions in our relationships. But a productive investment strategy also requires emotional discipline. The fear that grips investors when the markets suffer a steep decline often leads them to bad investment decisions. Rational (as opposed to emotional) decision making is a much more reliable approach, which has proven to yield better results. However, it can be difficult for us to subordinate emotional decision making to rational decision making because of our biology — the intimate relationship between the rational part of the brain and the emotional part. The rational part — the neocortex — developed millions of years *after* the emotional part — the amygdala. The root of many problems, investment mistakes included, is the imbalance between an overactive amygdala and a subordinated neocortex.

The neocortex makes us uniquely human: It gives us an extraordinary intellectual edge over other animals, because it is where all high-level thinking occurs. But because all animals, including us, are dependent upon the more rudimentary limbic system, of which the amygdala is a crucial component, the neocortex must work in conjunction with that emotional part of our brains. Every thought we have carries with it an emotion of some sort, no matter how subtle. Thinking and feeling go hand in hand — they are virtually inseparable. But when the emotional part gets a strong hold on us, there's trouble.

## MATH (BIOLOGY) BREAK

The function of the amygdala is to assist the neocortex in its decision making. Biologists believe it does this by comparing incoming sensory impressions to its cache of emotional memories, stored in the form of vague, wordless blueprints, many of which were developed by us as infants before we could speak. It can then "inform" the neocortex as to the emotional meaning of our perceptions. It is the neocortex–amygdala circuit that allows us to streamline decision making. The neocortex plays the analytic role that weighs options and possible outcomes. But it is the amygdala that plays the emotional role and motivates us to action.

If the amygdala is removed, we lack all traces of emotion, and therefore lack the emotional motivation to take action. A very interesting phenomenon, documented at the University of Iowa, involved a gentleman who underwent brain surgery only to have his amygdala accidentally severed from his neocortex. Following the operation, he was capable of cogent thought and dialogue, but couldn't make a decision if his life depended on it. That's because the neocortex couldn't "speak" to the amygdala in order to integrate the amygdala's emotional memory into its information processing. The poor man lost his job, his wife, and his house because his thoughts were emotionless. The neocortex needs emotion to give its thoughts some motivation toward action.

On the flip side, if the amygdala is overactive, the rational neo-cortex gets subordinated and we make decisions and take actions that are neither prudent nor productive. If an emergency is perceived by the amygdala — for example, an attacking bear — it will orches-trate an immediate response on its own, *before* the neocortex is able to complete its processing work to come up with more rigorous and precise conclusions. When you experience a "fight or flight" response to a threat or scare, it's your amygdala that is comman-deering and mobilizing your body. While this emergency response system is occasionally useful, it was much more useful to our pre-historic ancestors: Traffic jams and stock market crashes often elicit emotional responses that are similar to the stress our ancestors experienced from attacking tigers. Unfortunately, the complexity of our daily lives in the twenty-first century often demands more sophisticated responses than the simple amygdala can provide.

We need both the rational neocortex and the emotional amygdala in order to be effective in our lives. But we need them in the right bal-ance. The dominance of emotional thinking over rational thinking is useful when life-and-death experiences confront us and we need our emotional instincts to move us to instant action. But in more common, everyday circumstances, such as coping with stock market volatility, emotional thinking usually steers us in the wrong direction.

The right balance between rational and emotional thinking — skewed in favour of a heavier influence from rationality in most circumstances — is crucial for effective decision making. Investment mistakes originate because money is an extremely emotional thing for us. Specifically, the pain we feel when we lose money is quite poignant — so much so that the fear of losing money can distort our investment decision making, if we neglect a more rational approach.

## The Fear and Pain of Losing Money

Psychologists have given this topic considerable study. They have determined that we actually feel the pain of losing money about twice as intensely as we feel the pleasure of gaining it. Finding a $50 bill blowing in the grass of a deserted park is pretty exciting. But reaching into your pocket to discover you've lost 50 bucks is extremely upsetting — about twice as upsetting as the pleasure of finding the same amount. To have sufficient incentive to gamble, most people will require a potential upside of two dollars before they feel comfortable putting one dollar at risk.

The pain of losing money is so intense for us that the emotion will actually skew our attitude toward risk. Allow me to demonstrate: Envision the following scenario. Suppose you have $85,000 in your pocket. It's dusk and you're rushing to get to the bank to deposit it, so you take a shortcut down a deserted alley. All of a sudden you are confronted by a crook. He's an odd man, though, and doesn't simply insist that you hand over all your money (the amount of which he happens to know). He says he is willing to make a deal with you.

He gives you a choice: You can hand over the $85,000 and be allowed to leave unharmed; or you can play a card game with him where you have an 85 percent chance of losing $100,000, and a 15 percent chance of losing nothing at all. If you agree to gamble, and you lose $100,000, he will accompany you to your bank where you will be forced to withdraw the extra money and give him the full amount.

You're faced with a decision: take the sure loss of $85,000 and walk away that much poorer; or take the gamble where you have an 85 percent chance of losing even more — $100,000 — but a 15 percent chance of getting off scot free. What would you do?

Most people in this situation would take the gamble. In fact, studies have shown that over 90 percent of people would choose to gamble given the choice, because the possibility of not losing any money at all, and avoiding the emotional pain that would otherwise accompany the loss, motivates them to take the risk.

There's no right answer to this puzzle, by the way. Both choices have a mathematical expected value of $85,000. The question merely elicits your preference. And studies have convincingly demonstrated that the vast majority will choose to take the reasonably high risk of losing more (an 85 percent chance of losing $100,000), because that risk entails the small possibility (15 percent) of losing nothing.

I'll come back to this scenario, but first another — this one considerably more pleasant.

This time you're in a mall, walking up to the lottery stand to cash in your weekly ticket. Congratulations! You just won $85,000. But the eccentric lottery agent informs you that this isn't an ordinary lottery. It's an innovative one, where you have two options to choose from. You can take your winnings, or you can play a quick card game that will give you an 85 percent chance of winning even more — $100,000 — but a 15 percent chance of not winning anything at all, which would leave you with no winnings. Which option would you pick? Again, there is no right answer. Just your personal preference.

Just over 80 percent of people faced with the lottery choice would choose the sure gain of $85,000 and pass on the gamble that entailed a small risk of not winning anything.

What's interesting is that in the first dilemma most people are willing to take the substantial risk of losing an extra $15,000, just for a shot at the much lower chance (15 percent) of keeping their money and not losing anything. However, in the second scenario, most people are not willing to take a risk — even when that risk favours their winning an extra $15,000. They stick with the sure win of $85,000 because they are avoiding the possibility — albeit only a 15 percent chance — of ending up with no winnings.

| Scenario #1: Crook in Alley | Scenario #2: Lottery Stand in Mall |
|---|---|
| **Sure Loss of $85,000** | **Sure Gain of $85,000** |
| Gamble with 85% chance of losing $100,000 and 15% chance of losing nothing | Gamble with 85% chance of winning $100,000 and 15% chance of winning nothing |
| ↓ | ↓ |
| **Risk Seeking** | **Risk Avoiding** |

What drives your appetite for risk, therefore, is not necessarily your income, your net worth, your job security, the number of years until retirement, or any of the other things we're always told to consider in assessing risk. What defined your risk tolerance in this case was the location of the potential loss. The intense fear of losing money is so strong that it made you risk-averse in the second scenario, but risk-seeking in the first scenario! Behavioural finance refers to our inconsistent appetite for risk as "prospect theory."

The pain of losing money, and the fear associated with this pain, is an example of the "loss aversion" we all experience. Because short-term market moves can have such a pronounced effect on our feelings about investing, the term "myopic loss aversion" is used to describe how short-sighted we can be in worrying about losing money. By focusing on the risk of losing money in the short term, where the risk is quite high, we can neglect the equally significant risk of not saving enough to meet our long-term goals. If our investment strategies are designed to protect us from short-term losses, they will tend to be very conservative. But conservative investments expose us to the risk of not growing our money aggressively enough over the long term, and ending up with insufficient savings to retire with. The long-term risk of losing money in the stock market is very low, so a long-term focus should be geared toward meeting our financial needs. When we're unduly influenced by myopic loss aversion, we unknowingly take on bigger risks to our long-term financial security than we often realize.

## The Fear and Pain of Regret

The fear of regret is very closely related to the fear of losing money. Although it's usually defined separately from losing money, and I have distinguished it as well, this fear is essentially a function of the same emotional inclination. We not only hate losing money that we have, but we also hate losing money that we *could have had*. Only slightly less awful than actually losing $1,000 is the prospect of losing out on a potential $1,000 that we could have had but didn't get.

Here's an example of the power of regret: Which of the following two scenarios would you judge to be a worse experience? You arrive at the airport 30 minutes late for a flight you were booked on for a European holiday, and now have to wait over three hours for the next flight. Or, you arrive 30 minutes late for the same flight, which you are told was delayed by 29 minutes and just took off 60 seconds ago.

The end result of both scenarios is identical. But I'll bet that you would suffer much more regret in the second scenario.

We fear regretting a decision so much that we'll actually pay to avoid it! Check this out: Mr. Winner is the one-millionth customer at Celebrity Theatre, and wins $100. At a different theatre — Show Time Theatre, which is part of a new and larger chain — Ms. Behindwinner is right behind the one-millionth customer. The one-millionth customer at Show Time is awarded a whopping $10,000. Ms. Behindwinner, because she is right behind the millionth customer, is awarded a prize of $125. Who would you rather be: Mr. Winner or Ms. Behindwinner?

Most people choose to be Mr. Winner, even though he pockets $25 less than Ms. Behindwinner. Studies show that most will pay $25 to avoid the regret of not being the millionth customer. Unfortunately, the fear of regret is not limited to hypothetical puzzles. Regret aversion is responsible for some of our most important financial decisions. We often factor in the degree to which we anticipate feeling regret from the outcomes of our decisions. For instance: "If I don't buy that risky mutual fund my friend owns, and he makes a lot of money, how painful will it be for me if the fund continues to do really well?" If we judge the possibility of regret to be high, this can motivate us to invest imprudently.

In the same way that our emotions can cause us to say and do stupid things in our relationships, our emotions frequently cause us to make foolish investment decisions. This will become even more apparent as we explore the 10 big mistakes.

## 4. Overconfidence

Beyond being vulnerable to illogical, irrational, and emotional thinking, we are also overconfident in most of our judgements and decisions. It's a natural part of our human psychology. Once again, it's a handy survival technique. If we took a lot of time to assess what we needed to do to protect ourselves from an attacking grizzly bear, second-guessing ourselves along the way, we'd get mauled to death long before we jumped into action. We would have perished a long time ago, if it weren't for the quick speed of our brains, and the certainty we have in our beliefs. The

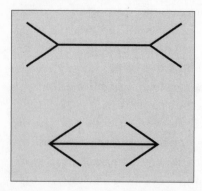

confidence we have in our judgements allows us to avoid being paralyzed as we make our way through the complexity of a typical day.

Take a look at the illustration on the left:

Which line appears longer — top or bottom? Or perhaps they're both the same length? Virtually everyone thinks the top looks longer, although you may try to outsmart me and confidently suggest that the two lines are the same size.

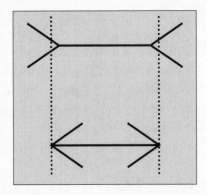

In fact the bottom line is longer. (Fooled you, I hope.)

Yes, this is an optical illusion, and one you may have seen before (except for my little home-made twist, designed to catch the smart-alecks). But the point is that *it's your brain that is fouling up*, not your eyes. Your eyes do the seeing; your brain does the interpreting. The thing about our fancy brains is that they were designed to draw very quick conclusions, often without sufficient information or knowledge. As with the optical illusion, we tend to make judgements very quickly, without any modest acknowledgement that in many cases, we don't have enough information or knowledge to be as confident in our decisions as we are. This habitual overconfidence is very useful if you're being chased by a grizzly bear and don't have a lot of time to contemplate all the possible alternative reactions and choose the best course of action. And it really helps us get through our daily routine as we're bombarded with excessive sensory information that our tireless brains want to interpret quickly.

But the flip side of this survivalist technique is that we often overdo it. Our minds work in such a way that we rarely make any distinction between our *beliefs about things* and *the things themselves*. Our beliefs are usually quick fabrications that may or may not conform to the way things really are, but we rarely differentiate between evidence that suggests a belief *may* be true from evidence that a belief *is* true. It's truly astounding how our minds, in constant motion, draw all sorts of conclusions about people, events, and ourselves, that are barely justified by the thin facts and perceptions we have; yet we treat these perceptions as reality. Think of the glance from a friendly stranger that we misinterpret as mean-spirited. The caring comment from a loved one, which makes us feel condescended to. An innocent question by a coworker that we misconstrue as a challenge to our expertise. Our minds gravitate to simple judgements and conclusions that are usually based on what we've previously experienced and how we've already decided the world works. We tend to overinterpret, overapply heuristics, and misapprehend many things, but that's just our nature — a part of being human — and not really the problem in and of itself. The problem is that we're usually not aware of the unjustified certainty we ascribe to our interpretations. If we perceived our interpretations to be what they really are — hypotheses — we'd be less inclined to act on them so quickly.

Fortunately for them, our prehistoric ancestors, who were adept at escaping dangerous threats on a daily basis, did not have to trouble themselves with complex challenges such as maximizing investment returns. Where overconfidence served our ancestors very well, we are often undermined by our overly quick decision making.

## Confirmation Bias

Not only do we rarely question our preconceptions, but we also tend to naturally seek out confirming evidence for our opinions and beliefs. We can be slow to integrate and accept information that contradicts our initial beliefs, but very quick to absorb information that confirms our thinking. Even more than that, psychologists have demonstrated that we have a bias toward positive confirmation of any kind, even if negative confirmation is just as relevant. Ask a bunch of school children to guess a number between one and 1,000 by asking some questions. Watch how the children cheer upon receiving positive answers, such as "yes, the answer is between 500 and 1,000," whereas they groan to responses such as "no, the answer is not between zero and 500." The information contained in both answers is obviously equally meaningful. But the positive response garners a distinctly excited reaction.

Confirmation bias helps us quicken the process of analyzing and judging. But it increases the odds of arriving at invalid conclusions since we skew our analysis in favour of a predetermined outcome. We have a natural and dangerous tendency to ignore information that does not conform to beliefs we've already established or are already far down the road of establishing. We rarely probe for answers that contradict our beliefs, and are not hesitant to draw far-reaching conclusions from scanty and even unreliable information, if it complements the direction our beliefs were taking anyway.

## Satisfycing

Related to confirmation bias is satisfycing, which means we confidently stop at the first plausible solution that satisfies us, rather than continuing our examination. Satisfycing can be a very helpful strategy for looking for a new home since you don't have time to view every possible alternative. But it can be a dangerous approach to choosing an investment, where the first possible alternative that seems to meet enough requirements isn't necessarily the best. Satisfycing can play a dangerous role when we don't have, or don't use, all the information that is available to us.

## Ambiguity Aversion

Our minds abhor ambiguity. This is especially the case for those of us born and raised in the Western hemisphere, where we are immersed in a culture that values rationality, logic, and answers for everything. Western Christianity, for example, is much less mystical than either the Greek Orthodox or Oriental religions. Our obsession with "the right answers" is admirable in many respects, but so easily leads to simple solutions, which belie the true ambiguity of much that we are confronted by. The problem with ignoring and shunning ambiguity so fervently is that our minds tend to be less open to alternative hypotheses. We rush to simple interpretations and conclusions without sufficient regard to how superficial our analysis is, because of a natural disregard for ambiguity.

Probably the greatest magic trick that humans perform from moment to moment is turning gray into black or white almost instantaneously. Unfortunately, stock market moves are among the most ambiguous and complex phenomena we're exposed to, notwithstanding our black-and-white interpretations of them. Sometimes, there just aren't any obvious or agreed-upon explanations for things.

## Illusion of Control

The last element of overconfidence is the illusion of control. Again, this is a handy survival tactic because it empowers us to act. If we didn't think we had any control over our environment and the world we live in, we would just lie in bed all day eating cookies and watching game shows. But the problem is that we tend to overestimate how much control we really do have. We tend to treat chance events as controllable to an extent, which explains some of the appeal of gambling. This is not surprising, since control and chance are so intimately linked in almost every aspect of our lives. The way our careers evolve, the people we develop relationships with, how our interests and hobbies evolve, and many more fundamental aspects of our lives are a product of both chance and our own influence — so tightly knit together that the two are usually indistinguishable.

But when we treat random events as controllable, we set ourselves up for frustration and often extreme counteractions. We confidently pull our money out of gold stocks when the price of gold falls and invest in oil stocks, just to be disappointed when energy prices fall. We often credit ourselves with far too much skill in picking winning funds or stocks. And we often blame ourselves too much for investments that don't end up being profitable. We fail to recognize just how uncontrollable the markets are.

Investing requires a great deal of modesty. One of the most powerful antidotes to the 10 biggest mistakes is to recognize our natural but unwarranted overconfidence. We usually fail to recognize the limitations of our cognitive abilities, because the way we think is so natural to us — it is hardwired into our brains. *The key to avoiding many investment mistakes lies in developing an awareness of our limitations, which gives us the power to compensate for them.*

So there you have it — the key factors that dominate investor psychology: cognitive limitations characterized by unawareness, twisted perceptions, fearfulness, and overconfidence. You'll see these human foibles weave their way through the exploration of the 10 biggest mistakes. Ignore them at your peril. But understand them, and you will be better equipped to stay faithful to the proven principles of successful investing, which we'll outline in the next chapter.

## Recap of the Limits

1. **Fortunately, we do not operate like computers. But if we did, we'd make fewer investment mistakes. Where we are disadvantaged, compared to computers, is in how illogical, irrational, and emotional we can be. On top of that, we're largely oblivious to these weaknesses and therefore supremely overconfident in many of our judgements — usually unjustifiably so.**

2. **The key psychological foibles that emanate from our not being computer-like have a direct impact on our investment returns. They are:**

   - **Wrong Thinking, or "Unawareness":**
     Lack of Knowledge — *simply not having enough knowledge*
     Innumeracy — *relying on invalid intuitions about probabilities*
   - **Distorted Thinking, or "Twisted Perceptions":**
     Heuristics — *relying on mental shortcuts such as representativeness, availability bias, and anchoring*
     Mental Accounting — *compartmentalizing money in unproductive ways*

Endowment Effect — *allowing ownership to influence our decisions*

Framing — *being influenced by the way a choice is framed*

Overinterpretation — *ascribing meaning to randomness*

- **Emotional Thinking, or "Fearfulness":**

  The Fear and Pain of Losing Money — *allowing potential loss to dominate decision making*

  The Fear and Pain of Regret — *allowing potential regret to dominate decision making*

- **Unexamined Thinking, or "Overconfidence":**

  Confirmation Bias — *exclusively seeking evidence that confirms our beliefs*

  Satisfycing — *accepting the first reasonable option we contemplate*

  Ambiguity Aversion — *fabricating explanations where none is warranted*

  Illusion of Control — *operating as if we have more control than we do*

3. These cognitive limitations steer us away from implementing and maintaining an effective investment strategy. Our psychology usually directly conflicts with what's best for our investment objectives (just as our psychology works against many other aspects of our lives, unfortunately).

4. If we understand how exactly psychology affects our investment decisions, we can overcome the common investment mistakes, which contravene the proven investment principles.

5. But first we have to understand the principles of successful investing themselves . . .

# The Rules of
# Successful Investing

*Eye Opener:*
*Success in investing (as in much of life) is very much dependent upon putting probabilities in your favour — getting them working for you, not against you. And putting market odds in your favour couldn't be easier, because the best investment strategy is basically to do nothing!*

In the beginning, there were few rules. Investors would more or less randomly allocate their money into stocks and bonds. But there were crashes. The big one that lasted from September 1929 until July 1932 was harrowing — the US stock market went down 89 percent over that period. The crash of 1973 that extended into 1974 was only marginally less painful — the stock market went down 43 percent from its highest to its lowest point. Today's investors are the beneficiaries of these crashes, because the turmoil spawned a lot of research into risk and how to manage it, led by the pioneering efforts of Markowitz in the early 1950s. At the same time, governments and central banks have benefited from the research that economists were doing on managing the volatility of economic cycles more effectively through monetary and fiscal policy. That's not to say things aren't as bumpy today as they previously were. Nor does it mean that we won't suffer severe market downturns from time to time. But it does mean that there are now some established rules, accepted by academics and professionals, that make it easier to be a successful investor. Before we get to the rules, though, let's define a few terms to make sure we're speaking the same "investment language."

## Definitions

*Securities:* Stocks, bonds, or money market instruments such as T-bills. Any or all of these assets are securities. Equities and stocks are the same thing — just two different names that refer to the same type of security. Similarly, bonds and money market paper are sometimes both referred to as fixed income products. The word "asset" can have many meanings, but in this book I use it to mean the same as "security."

*Index:* Tracks a large number of securities in a particular market. The most commonly known index for Canadian investors is the TSE 300, which comprises 300 of the largest and most liquid stocks traded on the Toronto Stock Exchange. I will use the S&P 500 index to refer to the US market, since it is the American index that is mostly widely cited by investment professionals. Most of the popular international indexes are structured by Morgan Stanley Capital International, so you'll also see me refer to their indexes, such as the MSCI Europe Index.

*Asset Class:* A broad category of securities that share common characteristics. The three most basic asset classes are stocks, bonds, and cash. But to be more useful, it helps to break down these classes further into cash, Canadian bonds, international bonds, Canadian equities, US equities, European equities, Asian equities, and emerging markets equities (such as Russian and Latin American stocks). This level of differentiation is sufficient for most purposes, but you can get even more specific, for example, by creating categories of investment style such as small- and large-company stocks, or value and growth stocks. Or you can differentiate asset classes by industry sector, such as technology or financial services. Geographic asset allocation, however, is still the most common and effective way of diversifying among different asset classes.

*Portfolio:* The combination of securities that collectively make up the total sum of your investments. A diversified portfolio will consist of securities from each asset class.

*Asset Mix:* The proportions of each asset class in your portfolio. For example, you may have 10 percent cash, 40 percent Canadian and international bonds, and 50 percent Canadian, US, and international equities. Or your mix may be 5 percent cash, 20 percent bonds, and 75 percent stocks. I will also use the term "asset allocation" to refer to asset mix, because it is a popular way of describing the percentage of your portfolio that you assign to each asset class.

Now . . . the important stuff.

## How to "Win" in Investing

There are natural probabilities in life that you can't fight if you want to "win." You may win by fighting the odds, rather than playing with them, but your chance of success is greatly reduced. If you want a high-paying job, your odds are better if you get an education and work hard. If you want to be healthy, you have to eat properly and exercise regularly. If you want to maximize your investment returns, there are probabilities that you need to put in your favour. Some lazy people with no education get rich. And some people live to 100 while smoking and drinking through their entire lives. But those are the exceptions that prove the rule.

Here's a pleasant surprise, though: Unlike many of life's other challenges, putting investment odds in your favour requires very little incremental effort! You don't have to study harder, work harder, or eat better. In fact, the less you do, the better off you'll be! When was the last time someone made you an offer like that?

But there is a catch: In investing, as in other aspects of life, our natural psychology can sometimes pull us away from doing what's right. The unique challenge of successful investing is that many investors don't really understand how investment probabilities work, so they are not able to put them to use. And many don't know how their psychology leads them away from the basic investment principles. I know eating chocolate cake each night for dinner doesn't go a long way toward meeting my objective of health and energy, so I resist (most nights). But you can't resist what you don't understand, so many investors' returns suffer badly — often without their even knowing it! In other words, in the worst possible scenario: (i) investors are vulnerable to their own psychology because they aren't aware of how it works against them; and (ii) this psychology entices them to contravene proven investment principles, which they may not fully understand. The result of these two factors is that their returns end up being less than they could be.

Since investment success depends on putting the laws of probability in your favour, let's lay down the laws, from which we'll derive some basic rules.

## Investment Probability Laws and Their Implications

Three laws define most of the investing process. They begin with two crucial building blocks that relate to the fundamental nature of market returns:

1. *In the short term, the markets move randomly. They are unpredictable because you never know, in advance, what they will do tomorrow, next month, or next year.*
2. *In the long term, the markets are more predictable — they go up.*

And one crucial building block relating to the fundamental nature of portfolio risk:

3. *Portfolio risk is largely defined by the relationship — the correlation — between its component parts. The risk of a particular stock, bond, or mutual fund is not just defined by its own characteristics, but also by the extent to which it either offsets or reinforces the risk of other securities in the portfolio.*

I will pursue each of these laws in greater detail in forthcoming chapters. But for now, I will give a very brief explanation — proof, you might call it — of these three laws, starting with the first two.

### Why Are Markets So Volatile and Unpredictable in the Short Term, but More Reliable in the Long Term?

In answering this question, I'll use stocks as the main example, although most of the concepts that relate to stocks are equally applicable to bonds.

- Stock prices are nothing more than the value of future cash flows that a company is expected to generate for its shareholders. Cash is generated from earnings. Cash benefits shareholders either through the payment of dividends, or by the appreciation of the shares themselves as the company invests its earnings into expansion (or buys back its own shares on the market).

- The price of a stock, therefore, is driven by two principal factors. First, there are the estimates of future company cash flows. Second, there is the value put on those cash flows. A company may have very good prospects for generating cash, but the *value* that investors put on those future cash flows can be affected by a number of factors.

- The factors that affect the value placed on estimates of future cash flows are threefold. First, if interest rates are high or expected to rise, then the value of future cash will be reduced, because high interest–paying bonds become more attractive to investors than stocks. Second, any uncertainty about the future cash will affect its current value: If the company does not have a long history of producing consistent cash, then estimating future cash flows is difficult, so the value placed on the estimates will be reduced. This uncertainty can often be measured by the disparity between different analysts' forecasts of earnings. Third, the emotion of the marketplace can influence the value placed on future cash: If investors are extremely optimistic or pessimistic about a company, or the market in general, their sentiment will strongly influence the value placed on future cash flows.

- The price of a stock will quickly adjust as any new information affecting either the estimates or the value placed on those estimates is reflected in investors' buying and selling of the stock. And the factors that underlie a stock's price, especially the emotion-based factors, can change quickly and unexpectedly. The more abrupt and significant the change, the more violent the shift in stock price.

- All of the factors that drive a stock's price are largely unpredictable because they are random. They occur instantaneously and often without any forewarning. Even the elements that analysts do attempt to predict, such as future profits, interest rate changes, etc., are only "educated guesses." And if you're right about interest rates falling by half a percent, or company earnings increasing by 5 percent, how do you know precisely what the impact will be to the stock's price? What if market sentiment changes — everyone becomes increasingly pessimistic about technology stocks, for example — making the stock's price go down, despite rising profits and falling interest rates? Do you see how difficult it is to account for all the complex drivers of a security price? No computer program has been built (or is likely to be built) that is mathematically rigorous enough to factor in all the possible elements that drive the market at any given moment in time, such that consistent and profitable predictions can be made of its short-term moves. Such a program would have to reliably predict not only what changes might affect a company's future cash flows, but also how any changes will alter the value that investors place on those cash flows. The mechanism of a stock price change is similar to many systems found in nature, such as avalanches, weather patterns, and even human relationships — they are inherently "chaotic." That's not to say, however, that stock price moves are uncaused. More on this when we explore market timing.

- Bond prices are subject to the same chaotic system of random movements. The cash flows of bonds are their interest payments. Actual and anticipated changes in interest rates have the greatest impact on the current value of a bond's future cash flows. But there is a degree of irrationality or emotion in the bond market as well.

- Despite this unpredictable chaos, most securities do generate positive returns over the long term. Stocks reflect the fundamental economics of a company over a longer period of time, after all irrational and short-term influences have been eliminated, just as a marriage or relationship, for example, will reflect its underlying health in the long run, despite the occasional emotional conflict. Ultimately, a stock's value has to reflect the actual growth in the company's profits, or else no one would invest in it (except a few gamblers). In fact, all companies combined have to reflect the growth of the overall economy, which is positive in the long run. If long-term economic growth were negative, the world's economy would shrink and the world's growing population would be increasingly unemployed. But as productivity increases with technological innovation, and as more developing countries embrace capitalism, economic expansion will flourish for a long time to come. If it didn't, we'd all have bigger problems to deal with than our investment returns.

The volatility of the market is one of the most misunderstood elements of the market; I've expanded this topic in Appendix #1 at the back of this book.

## Portfolio Risk Is About Combining

Risk is a complex concept that I'll discuss in a separate chapter (see Mistake #1). But for now I'll point out something about risk that is mathematically undeniable:

- The risk of a portfolio of securities is *not* equal to — and in fact is usually lower than — the sum or average of each security's risk. This is because the risk of each security offsets, to an extent, the risk of other securities. For example, the stock of an umbrella company and the stock of a sunscreen company are likely to move in opposite directions. The risk of a portfolio holding both stocks will be much lower than either stock on its own. So the risk of a portfolio is largely a function of the correlation between the securities.

## Implications of the Three Laws

The three investment laws — that markets are unpredictable in the short term, but go up in the long term, and that risk is largely a function of how securities are combined — have important implications.

The first implication is:

- *You have limited control over the* returns *that your whole portfolio generates. But you have substantial control over the* risk *you take within your portfolio.*

You can't dictate what the market will deliver to you. Even if you put your money in a GIC, you have no control over what the GIC rate will be when you renew. You do have some limited control over your returns, insofar as you're likely to earn higher returns over time if you invest in the stock market rather than exclusively in GICs.

You have greater control, however, over the risk that you take. The decision to invest exclusively in GICs, rather than exclusively in technology stocks, has a very large *predetermined* impact on risk. More important, your investment risk can be lowered or raised by how you mix your assets, no matter how risky the individual assets are on their own. For example, adding a volatile technology or Latin American fund to your portfolio can actually *reduce* the risk of your overall portfolio.

This revelation about risk leads us to another implication, which happens to be the all-time best trick of investing. While the expected risk of a portfolio is not equal to (and is in fact less than) the average of each security's risk, the expected return *is* equivalent to the average of each security's return. So:

- *You don't have to give up returns to lower your risk!*

For example, the umbrella and sunscreen companies could each have expected returns of 10 percent, but when one's up, the other's down, so your risk is reduced without having to settle for the 5 percent returns of a GIC or money market fund. How's that for magic?

Most individual investors have a simple financial objective: to maximize their wealth. In some circumstances, an investor's objective may not be to maximize wealth, but to generate a reliable stream of income in order to pay daily living expenses. But this is not the common case. Most of us, no matter our age, want to maximize our returns and therefore our net worth. Even retired investors usually want to ensure they have plenty of money to allow them to live comfortably into their nineties, and leave generous estates to their heirs.

If most investors want maximum returns, and the factor that they have most control over is risk, then the only thing that truly differentiates one investor from another is the amount of risk each can afford to take. Another implication of the laws:

- *Risk tolerance is what differentiates most investors from each other. Therefore, risk management should be the dominant focus of every investor.*

So let's take the laws and their implications and derive some basic investment rules.

## Investment Rules

1. The best you can possibly do to maximize returns — the objective of most investors — is to put probabilities in your favour. This means using the nature of the market itself to your advantage: exploit its long-term upward trend and avoid its short-term unpredictability.
2. Your returns will ultimately be determined by your asset mix; however, given the unpredictability of markets, you can't predetermine which asset classes within your mix will outperform over any period. So it's best in most cases to have exposure to all of them, in appropriate proportions.
3. The proportions that you own of each asset class are determined by your risk tolerance.
4. Risk tolerance is determined by a number of factors including the amount of time you have to invest, the security of your job and

income, and the extent of your financial responsibilities. For instance, if you are saving for retirement in 20 years and have a very stable income and no children, you can take on more risk than someone who has an unstable income and is saving to send a child to university.

5. With few exceptions, your asset mix should stay constant. We'll see in the chapter on Mistake #3 that changes should only be made to reflect alterations in your risk tolerance, your return objective (which is usually a constant — maximizing wealth), or a fundamental long-term economic shift in the markets themselves.

6. One other rule is not directly related to the laws or their implications, but I'll be discussing it in some detail later in the book (see Mistake #4). Security selection — which bonds and stocks you choose within each asset class — is a secondary consideration, after the mix of the asset classes themselves has been determined. It's secondary because you can, in theory, avoid this step altogether if you index each asset class. Indexing removes the decision of which particular securities to purchase by simply tracking a stock market index. By contrast, in an actively managed fund, the money manager attempts to add value above the returns of an index, by choosing outperforming securities within each asset class. Only the most skilled active managers are able to achieve this.

It's interesting to note that the natural laws of the markets, and their implications, lead to the same end point: the importance of asset mix.

Here's how the logic flows:

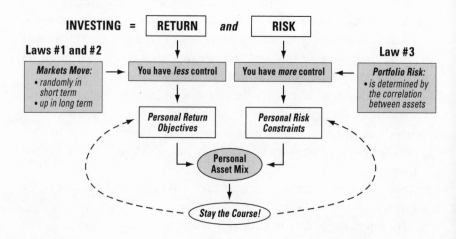

## Does It Really All Come Down to Asset Mix?

No. It doesn't *all* come down to asset mix. But *most* of it does. Asset mix is the one thing you have the most control over. You can't control what the markets will do and when they'll do it (although you can guess). And you can't control which stocks and bonds will outperform (although you can guess this as well).

You've probably read or heard that "asset allocation is responsible for over 90 percent of a portfolio's returns." The often-quoted "90-percent factor" originates from a study that has been misinterpreted ever since it was first published. The study originally examined the main drivers of short-term volatility, and discovered that the starting asset mix of a port-folio accounted for 94 percent of the *volatility* of returns from one quarter to another (i.e., over successive three-month periods). The degree to which asset mix was altered over each period, as well as the security selec-tion within each asset class, contributed the remaining amount. The study was later updated and used to demonstrate that asset mix explained 92 percent of quarterly *volatility*. This conclusion is barely interesting to an investor with a five-year or longer time frame. Unfortunately, the study has since been misinterpreted by well-meaning marketers, who have spread the word that asset mix accounts for over 90 percent of *returns*.

Subsequent studies have demonstrated more convincingly that asset mix does indeed account for a large part of the actual returns generated by a portfolio — typically between 82 and 132 percent. Asset mix can account for more than 100 percent in the case where fees, security selec-tion, and market timing all detract from portfolio returns. And even when timing and security selection are adding value to your total returns, the asset mix still dominates — driving 82 pecent of the end result.

Having said that asset allocation is by far the largest determinant of portfolio returns, I don't want to mislead you into thinking that the choice of securities, or of mutual funds, is not important. Over longer periods of time, different mutual funds within an asset class can generate very different returns.

## Asset Mix Compared to Security Selection

Let's compare the range of returns of asset allocation to the returns of security selection. If you had invested in the best asset class in 1999, you would have had your money invested in emerging markets stocks: the Morgan Stanley Emerging Markets Index earned 60 percent in Canadian dollar returns. The worst asset class in 1999 to have invested in was international bonds, which generated negative 11 percent in Canadian dollar returns. The difference between the best and worst asset classes is enormous: 71 percent.

**One-Year Returns**

| Best-Performing Asset Class | Worst-Performing Asset Class | Difference |
|---|---|---|
| Emerging Markets: 60% | International Bonds: −11% | 71% |

Let's say you got the asset mix call right, but not the security selection. The best-performing emerging markets fund available in Canada in 1999 returned 87 percent, while the worst-performing emerging markets fund returned 30 percent. The difference between the best and the worst was 57 percent.

The best performing international bond fund generated negative 5 percent while the worst one returned negative 16 percent. So the difference was 11 percent in the worst asset class category.

**One-Year Returns**

| | Best-Performing Fund | Worst-Performing Fund | Difference |
|---|---|---|---|
| **Emerging Markets** | 87% | 30% | 57% |
| **International Bonds** | −5% | −16% | 11% |

The asset class call was the more important decision in 1999 since there was a bigger spread between the best and worst asset classes than between the best and worst funds within each asset class. Even the worst security selection within emerging markets funds still generated 30 percent. Meanwhile, the best security selection within international bonds still returned a negative number. In any given year, the big rewards are in *guessing* which asset class will outperform (I use the word "guessing" purposefully, as we will explore later in Mistake #3, "Overusing Tactical Asset Allocation"). If you're invested in the best asset class in any year, you're likely to be in good shape, no matter what fund you've chosen within that asset class. But over longer periods of time, fund selection can become increasingly important.

If we move to a five-year period ending on December 31, 1999, the best and worst asset class returns converge a bit, which isn't surprising since over longer time periods, the general asset classes revert to their long-term averages, which aren't that far off from one another.

**Five-Year Returns**

| Best-Performing Asset Class | Worst-Performing Asset Class | Difference |
|---|---|---|
| US Equities: 29% | Asian Equities: 2% | 27% |

But interestingly, the fund returns still diverge quite a bit:

**Five-Year Returns**

| | Best-Performing Fund | Worst-Performing Fund | Difference |
|---|---|---|---|
| US Equities | 46% | 9% | 37% |
| Asian Equities | 17% | – 10% | 27% |

Here are a few more asset class categories, along with their best and worst returns over the five years ending in 1999:

**Five-Year Returns**

| | Asset Class | Best-Performing Fund | Worst-Performing Fund | Fund Difference |
|---|---|---|---|---|
| Canadian Equities | 17% | 29% | 1% | 28% |
| Canadian Bonds | 10% | 12% | 3% | 9% |
| International Bonds | 7% | 8% | 1% | 7% |
| European Equities | 23% | 31% | 9% | 22% |
| Emerging Markets | 2% | 11% | – 3% | 14% |

The range between the best and worst asset classes in a given *year* is usually greater than the range between the best and worst funds within each asset class. But over *many years*, the choice of funds within an asset class becomes increasingly relevant.

Here's a graphical representation of returns over five years, comparing different asset classes and the range of fund performance within those asset classes:

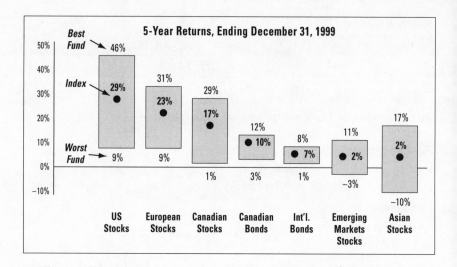

**5-Year Returns, Ending December 31, 1999**

Looking at the graph you can see that picking the wrong funds could have a disastrous effect on your returns, even if you pick the right asset classes. Although the asset class decision is the most important one, if you load up on underperforming funds, your returns will be badly penalized. (Note how the index return appears closer to the top of each range — there is more downside below the index than upside above it. I'll have more to say about this in the chapter relating to Mistake #4.)

*So how do you pick the right asset classes, and then the right securities within each asset class?* The answers to both questions are easy. Let's take one at a time.

## How Do You Determine Asset Mix?

There are three major considerations in determining your asset mix: your financial objectives, your practical risk tolerance, and your emotional risk tolerance.

*Financial Objectives:* These are goals you want to achieve with your money. You probably have multiple goals that all need to be addressed by your investment strategy, such as a new home, children's education, and retiring comfortably. As I've mentioned, most goals can be captured by the objective "maximizing wealth," or "maximizing returns." Occasionally, maximizing wealth has to take a back seat to earning a consistent income, for example, to pay for living expenses. But even the need for regular income can usually be accommodated by a portfolio designed to maximize wealth, as we'll explore in Mistake #9, "Underestimating the Impact of Tax."

*Practical Risk Tolerance:* This refers to how much risk you can afford to take to meet your goals. For instance, you may want to invest for the purpose of buying a new home in five years. The five-year time horizon will limit how much risk you can afford to take. You'll want a very small weighting in stocks — probably zero percent — for a holding period of less than five years. The same goal — buying a home — within a longer time period of, say, 10 years, can accommodate more risk and therefore a higher allocation of equities. Another example of practical risk is the security of your job and income level. Let's say you are an independent consultant, working on your own. You want to buy a home in six years, but you're fearful that the economy may turn recessionary and your practice will therefore suffer fewer billable hours. You are supporting a family of three, and you only have a modest amount of savings. You probably can't afford to hold many stocks, if any, because your circumstances imply a low practical risk tolerance, even over a six-year period. Other elements of practical risk tolerance are your net worth, which provides a cushion of safety, and debt obligations, which may limit your risk tolerance if you have fixed loan and interest payments you have to cover.

*Emotional Risk Tolerance:* This is an indication of how you feel about risk. Even with a long investment time horizon, you may not be able to get a whole meal down when the market gyrates because it upsets you so much. Or maybe you're uncomfortable with stocks because you don't have a high level of investment knowledge.

Your asset mix must reflect your objectives and risk tolerances, if it is to do the job you want it to do. Sounds easy in theory, but a problem arises when one or both of the risk tolerance constraints do not jibe with your objectives. Perhaps you want to save to buy a cottage in 10 years, but can't take too much risk since you'll need the same money to fund your children's education if you don't get the annual bonuses at work that you are counting on. Or maybe you want to have a large nest egg to retire on so you can do a lot of travelling, but you just can't stomach the volatility of the market. *If the three elements are not all aligned, how do you reconcile them to arrive at the right asset mix?*

*The first two have to be in sync.* You simply can't save for a new home over a three-year period, investing exclusively in technology stocks. This strategy might pay off, but the likelihood of ending up with less than you started with is too high. *Your practical risk tolerance, especially your time horizon, must constrain your objectives.* Practical risk is fixed, so some or all of your financial goals have to be modified to accommodate the inflexibility of practical risk considerations. Even if you have a long-term time horizon of 12 years in which to save for a new cottage, you may have to lower your expectations of how luxurious that cottage can be, if you are planning on having four children and have no savings but a large mortgage. In this example, it wouldn't be prudent to take a lot of risk in the stock market — say more than 50 percent — even over a 12-year period. Your objectives must take into account the lower practical risk tolerance that is imposed by the financial obligations of a family and mortgage.

The good news is that your emotional risk tolerance is more flexible. At least it should be. That's because it's purely psychological. If you are attempting to maximize your retirement nest egg, and have a number of years to reach your goal, but are terrified of the stock market, then . . . well . . . get over it. I know that sounds insensitive. But I can't find any other way to make the point. Some tradeoffs are unavoidable, such as when your objectives conflict with your practical risk considerations. But other tradeoffs we can avoid, such as when the conflicts arise from emotional reactions rather than from real risk factors.

Life involves tradeoffs. Unfortunately, whoever engineered the master plan made sure we can't have it all. Some people are lucky enough to earn a lot of money while not having to work very hard; but for most of us, there is a correlation between how hard we work and how much income we are capable of earning, so we have to trade off our leisure time to make money. Same with emotional risk. If you want the big returns over the long term, you have to put up with some discomfort in the short term. You don't get rich by investing exclusively in GICs, so if you really can't get over your feelings about market ups and downs, then you'll likely have to reconsider your objectives. If you are prepared to give up some luxury at retirement for emotional peace of mind today, then so be it. If that's the tradeoff you want to make, there's nothing fundamentally wrong with that. But make it with the knowledge of what you're giving up.

I should qualify this last point by saying that there *is* something very wrong in trading off long-term growth to have peace of mind today, if you end up taking on the risk that you will outlive your money and spend your last few years in poverty. Most investors are better off maximizing their long-term savings in a prudent but not overly conservative way, and accepting the short-term bumpiness which has psychological, but no other, meaning.

When I say "get over it" in relation to emotional risk, I'm not saying anything more meaningful than if someone were to tell you to get over a fear of flying in order to take a trip to Europe. You may have an exaggerated fear of airplane crashes. But you're better off to subdue your fear. No matter how many newspapers have recently reported stories about plane crashes, the odds of crashing are still remote.

There are many advisors who suggest that investment knowledge plays an important role in determining your risk tolerance. I do not believe that to be true. Most people don't have a clue how their car operates, but they are quite comfortable driving over 100 kph on the highway, because it gets them where they want to go. If you want to save for a comfortable retirement that includes travel and a generous estate to leave to your children, do you have to have a deep understanding of how the stock markets work? The rules are the rules, and whether you have a shallow or deep understanding of them, they still work — and they're there for you to take advantage of, independent of your particular knowledge level. It's not only doctors who take aspirin for headaches, even though they're the only ones who understand why and how it works!

## How Do You Determine the Right Securities Within Each Asset Class?

The answer to this question is dealt with to a large extent in the chapter on overestimating active management — Mistake #4. Suffice it to say that given the large range between the best and worst funds within each asset class, you want to make sure you end up with the better, and not the worse, returns. If it were easy to pick the better-performing funds, more people would be rich. And in fact it's not that complicated, so more people *should* be rich!

When we looked at the graph showing the ranges of best and worst returns in each asset class over five years, I commented on how consistently high the index appeared to be within those ranges. If there is a secret to increasing the odds of getting the best returns within those ranges, indexing is it. If you're skeptical, I hope you're unequivocally convinced by the end of the chapter on Mistake #4.

For now, the answer to picking the right securities within each asset class is "don't" — just buy the index. Don't, that is, unless you have a high degree of confidence in a seasoned money manager to be near the top of those ranges. And even then, I'd start with the index and build on it. We'll address this in much more detail later on.

The problem with human psychology is that it encourages us to contravene the basic rules of successful investing. And that's what this book is all about — getting a grip on how our thinking messes up the potential for good investment returns. More than half of the big mistakes that investors make can be traced to problems with asset allocation — because the right mix isn't defined initially, or because the mix is changed too radically from time to time, or both. The reason investors don't implement and persevere with the right asset allocation is because certain human psychological traits lead them astray. For instance, investor psychology overemphasizes the role of picking stocks and funds, as well as making asset mix changes; but these are the wrong elements to focus on. Overemphasizing the wrong elements reduces your returns, and I will be demonstrating that throughout the book.

The key to successful investing really comes down to *understanding* and *counteracting* your natural psychological tendencies to thwart the rules. The task is easy, because the best investment strategy is basically to do nothing except sit tight. The only real work is setting up the right asset allocation. In fact, the more you do after this step, the more you're likely to subtract from your returns. Too bad staying healthy, earning a good living, and meeting countless other challenges in life aren't as easy as that!

If you put market probabilities in your favour with the right asset allocation, you can stop worrying (at least about your money).

## Recap of the Rules

1. **You increase the odds of living longer by exercising and eating right. You increase the odds of having a successful relationship by being self-aware and communicating well. And you increase the odds of maximizing your investment returns by**

   - **establishing an appropriate asset allocation (the mix of cash, bonds, and stocks in your portfolio) and,**
   - **being disciplined (staying the course, despite enormous psychological temptations to do otherwise).**

2. You have very little control over what returns you'll earn, but quite a bit of control over the risk you take. So risk should be every investor's primary concern, and risk tolerance is what differentiates one investor from another.

3. Asset mix drives a large part of the overall returns you earn on your portfolio. Although the initial asset mix decision is crucial, the picking of mutual funds (or stocks and bonds) can have a large impact on your long-term returns — often a negative result.

4. How do you get the right asset mix? There are two basic rules:

   • Since you can't predetermine which asset classes will outperform in any given year, it's usually best to cover them all, in some form.
   • The precise mix of asset classes should be determined primarily by your financial objectives, constrained by your practical risk tolerance.

5. The only reason you would change your asset mix is to accommodate any shifts in your circumstances that alter either your financial objectives or your practical risk tolerance, or both. You can also shift your mix to reflect changes in long-term economic trends.

6. Emotional risk tolerances, such as your personal taste for, or knowledge of stocks, should not play an important role in your asset allocation decisions.

7. What do you do about security selection within each asset class, to ensure it doesn't detract from your potential returns? Go easy on security selection. Treat it as a complement to owning the market as a whole. More to come on this topic when we examine Mistake #4. But let's see exactly what happens when human psychology thwarts the principles of successful investing . . .

# PART 2

## The 10 Biggest Mistakes

# Introducing the Big 10

*Eye Opener:*
*Start with the fundamental principles of investing. Throw in human*
*psychology, which encourages investors to contravene these rules in*
*bizarre, but entirely human ways. You'll end up with the 10 biggest*
*and most common investment mistakes that Canadians make.*

As we saw in Part One, the keys to successful investing are simple and unambiguous.

First, you implement an appropriate asset allocation that reflects your investment objectives, constrained by the practical risk tolerance that is unique to you. And second, you stick with it, making only modest changes when your personal circumstances alter your practical risk tolerance. Once in a while, you can modify your mix a bit to reflect worldwide changes in long-term economic trends.

The single biggest impediment to implementing these simple strategies is human psychology. How our minds work makes us vulnerable to illogical, irrational, and emotional thinking, all of which stem from the natural cognitive limitations of our brains. To add insult to injury, we are also slow to recognize the thinking errors that we're prone to, and this lack of humility makes us even more vulnerable to them.

The 10 most common investment mistakes can be traced to one or more of the four cognitive limitations, or psychological foibles, that

I outlined in Part One. These foibles are closely related in many cases, so many of the investment mistakes originate from a combination, or even all, of them. We will see, for example, that the investment mistake of market timing is based on both twisted perceptions and the overconfidence we have in our misguided beliefs about how the market works. And you'll see that every mistake involves unawareness, at least at some level.

Ladies and Gentlemen: Without any further delay, may I present to you the 10 biggest investment mistakes made by Canadians, along with the psychological foibles that are to blame:

| | Unawareness | Twisted Perceptions | Fearfulness | Overconfidence |
|---|:---:|:---:|:---:|:---:|
| #1 Misunderstanding Risk | ✔ | ✔ | ✔ | |
| #2 Timing the Market | ✔ | ✔ | | ✔ |
| #3 Overusing Tactical Asset Allocation | ✔ | ✔ | ✔ | ✔ |
| #4 Overestimating Active Management | ✔ | ✔ | ✔ | ✔ |
| #5 Succumbing to Home Bias | ✔ | ✔ | | ✔ |
| #6 Not Knowing What You Own | ✔ | ✔ | | |
| #7 Not Knowing How You're Doing | ✔ | | ✔ | ✔ |
| #8 Underestimating the Power of Compounding | ✔ | | | ✔ |
| #9 Underestimating the Impact of Tax | ✔ | ✔ | | |
| #10 Overpaying for Guarantees | ✔ | ✔ | ✔ | |

Note that six of the mistakes — #1, #2, #3, #5, #6, and #7 — relate to a direct contravention of the two key fundamentals of successful investing: asset allocation and staying the course. The other four mistakes can be equally damaging, but for different reasons.

On to the mistakes themselves. For each one I'll describe the error, cover the "Behavioural Explanation" that causes the mistake, and then define the solution to the problem.

# MISTAKE #1

## Misunderstanding Risk

*Eye Opener:*

Q: *Which is riskier: one very volatile stock, or two very volatile stocks?*

A: *One is almost always riskier, because the two stocks will usually offset each other to an extent, as we saw briefly in the chapter "The Rules of Successful Investing."*

It's ironic that two of the most common and damaging investment mistakes — misunderstanding risk and market timing — stem from polar opposite psychological tendencies. The first mistake usually originates from our timidity — our vulnerability to irrational fears. The second mistake stems from the opposite problem — an all-encompassing overconfidence that emboldens us to attempt the impossible. We humans are an odd combination of fearfulness and arrogance. Poor decision making results from both.

We'll explore how overconfidence gets us into trouble in the next chapter. But let's first look at the enormous impact our emotions have in our thinking about, and behaviour toward, risk.

# The Problem

Emotions encourage many investors to think of risk in this way:

- *The volatility*
- *of the stock market*
- *over the short term*
- *as described by the headlines*
- *which cause them to lose sleep at night.*

Each of these five components reveals a flaw in thinking that can lead to unproductive decision making. Risk is not just volatility, as we will review in this chapter. And it's certainly not the volatility of just one or two stock indexes, such as the TSE 300 or the Dow Jones. For an investor with a five-year time horizon, risk is not related to what an investment is doing on any given day or even year. And someone who is properly invested should not only sleep peacefully through the night, but find the newspaper headlines very entertaining!

The problem is this: *since there is no commonly accepted definition of risk, investors are overly susceptible to the influence of their emotions in their thinking about it.* Many investors associate risk with market volatility, so they put too much emphasis on the risk of losing money. In fact, a US survey of over 600 mutual fund investors found that over 50 percent defined risk as the chance of losing money. While losing money is a legitimate risk, it is not the only one that investors need to consider.

There are many examples of poor investment decisions that arise from this particular misconception of risk:

- Altering a portfolio's asset mix because the stock market goes down for three days in a row. This drop can cause an investor's risk tolerance to suddenly decrease (only to mysteriously increase when the market recovers).
- Postponing the sale of underperforming stocks or mutual funds because of the reluctance to convert a paper loss to an actual loss. Or postponing a planned move because the value of a house has fallen and the owner is reluctant to sell at a lower price than he or she originally paid.
- Investing too conservatively, by giving too much portfolio weight to GICs, money market funds, and savings accounts, because of the fear of losing money in the stock market.

The last example is one of the most common mistakes, and one worth examining in a bit more detail, since it reveals the difficulty of defining risk exclusively as the potential to lose money. Let's compare two individuals, both 40 years old, and both with portfolios valued at $150,000. The first individual, Mr. Safety, invests exclusively in GICs for the next 25 years because of his strong fear of the stock market. Mr. Safety views risk as equivalent to market volatility, and he wants no part of it. Ms. Diversified, on the other hand, invests in a diversified portfolio, which includes GICs as well as stock and bond mutual funds. We'll assume that the first portfolio generates 6 percent on average each year, whereas the second portfolio generates 9 percent — not a big difference, and an underestimation of the historical long-term gap between the two.

Here's what each investor has upon retirement at age 65:

**$150,000 RRSP Invested at Age 40:**

|  | Savings at Age 65 | Number of Years Savings Last |
|---|---|---|
| **GICs @ 6%** | $644,000 | 12 years |
| **Balanced Portfolio @ 9%** | $1,293,000 | 25 years or more |

Ms. Diversified has twice as much after 25 years. But does it matter? Isn't Mr. Safety's $644,000 plenty to retire with? Unfortunately, if you take into consideration some very conservative assumptions about inflation, Canada Pension Plan payouts, taxes, and the income required to live comfortably, you'll find that Mr. Safety's portfolio is likely to last 12 years at the very most, whereas Ms. Diversified's portfolio will last at least 25 years and probably much longer. And even if you tinker with the assumptions, you'll find that it's virtually impossible to give the GIC-only portfolio a life span of longer than 12 years.

You can see that Mr. Safety's view of risk was too narrow. His fear of losing money was so immediate and so powerful that he ignored the severe risk of retiring without enough money. With a better definition of risk, he would have been able to manage it more effectively.

Risk is something of a holy grail in the investment world, and it's one of the most elusive concepts in finance. There are almost as many ways to define it as there are people who write about it. Here is a sample of risk definitions, from a much larger group I could have listed:

- standard deviation of returns (commonly known as volatility)
- probability of loss, and probability of inflation-adjusted loss

- tracking error (underperforming a predetermined index)
- probability of underperforming a risk-free asset, such as a T-bill or GIC
- probability of expected shortfall (chance of not meeting a required return)
- value at risk (probability of exceeding a predefined loss)
- semi-variance (downside risk)
- regret

I'm going to briefly describe the first and last of these terms — volatility and regret — since they each demonstrate a different but equally unproductive view of risk. They are both popular definitions, even though they are starkly different from one another. They represent the oldest and newest ways of describing risk — the purely mathematical approach and the purely psychological approach.

## Volatility (a.k.a. Standard Deviation)

Volatility is a mathematical measure of risk described by the statistical term "standard deviation." It is a dry, emotionless definition of risk. Volatility was the centrepiece of the portfolio theory developed by Markowitz in the early 1950s, and its popularity has persisted into the twenty-first century. Volatility is what you'll see measured in your monthly mutual fund section in the national newspapers.

Volatility measures the degree to which a security's value goes up and down, compared with its average value — it's the difference, over a period of time, between the *expected* return of a security (based on its long-term average), and its *actual* return. If you tell me I can expect a 10 percent return from an investment, my question to you is, "How likely is it that I'll get either less or more than 10 percent?" Standard deviation answers that question by measuring how far from the average the actual returns are likely to stray over a period of time. If you tell me that the standard deviation is 6 percent, then I know that around two-thirds of the time, the annual returns of my investment will be between 4 and 16 percent, which is simply 10 plus or minus six. If instead you tell me that the standard deviation is 12 percent, then I know that two-thirds of the time my returns will be between negative 2 and positive 22 percent. An investment with a standard deviation of 12 percent is obviously a lot more volatile than one with a standard deviation of 6 percent.

# MATH BREAK

## How Exactly Do You Interpret Standard Deviation?

It works like this: one standard deviation refers to 68 percent (two-thirds) of all possible returns; two standard deviations encompass 95.4 percent of all possible returns; and three standard deviations encompass 99.7 percent.

So if a stock has a long-term expected return of 10 percent and a standard deviation of 12 percent, we know that 68 percent of the time, the actual returns will be somewhere between negative 2 and positive 22 percent. We also know that 95.4 percent of the time, the returns will be within two standard deviations of the expected return, or between negative 14 and positive 34 percent. And almost all of the time — 99.7 percent of the time — the actual returns will range between negative 26 and positive 46 percent. (Four standard deviations represent 99.9 percent of the time, where the returns will be between negative 38 percent and positive 58 percent).

Standard deviation is popular because it can be interpreted in a variety of meaningful ways. Using the same example, we can say that there is a one-in-six chance of getting a return that is worse than negative 2 percent. How did I get those odds? Simply by using the same numbers and tossing them around a bit: since 68 percent covers one standard deviation, 32 percent of the time the returns will be *outside* of the range of negative 2 to positive 22 percent. Half of 32 percent will be positive and half will be negative, so 16 percent will be negative. That means that 16 percent of the time (or one year in six), we'll get a return that's worse than negative 2 percent. Here's yet another way of looking at it: If you're considering a fund with an expected return of 10 percent and a standard deviation of 12 percent, then you should expect a loss of 2 percent roughly every six years.

You can see why standard deviation is used so commonly — not because it's easy to calculate or even easy to understand on its own, but because you can use it to formulate risk statements that are not too difficult to comprehend. Whether they are accurate or convey meaningful information is another question, though. A question worth pursuing . . .

There are several problems with defining risk as standard deviation. First, volatility implies the chance of losing money, but doesn't incorporate the risk of not earning enough on your money. You can eliminate volatility entirely by stashing your money under a mattress, but that doesn't protect you from inflation, which reduces the value of your cash as it sits earning no returns. Second, the volatility rankings listed in the newspapers are based on three- or five-year standard deviations, even though an investor's time horizon is often much longer. A three-year volatility ranking isn't too meaningful for a 10-year investment time horizon. Finally, it treats both types of deviation from the long-term average — both the ups and the downs — exactly the same way. Two funds can have the same volatility rating, but one might be volatile because its returns have been recently much higher than its average, while the other is volatile because its returns have been lower. Although standard deviation doesn't differentiate the two types of volatility, we certainly do. Volatility on the upside is good news since it means that returns are higher than expected, whereas volatility on the downside is trouble.

Here are two funds with the same returns, and the same long-term standard deviations.

| | 10-Year Return | 10-Year Volatility |
|---|---|---|
| Safer Fund | 10% | 12% |
| Riskier Fund | 10% | 12% |

What is not obvious is that Riskier Fund is much riskier than Safer Fund. Suppose I told you that you had a choice between the two funds, both of which had expected returns of 10 percent and standard deviations of 12 percent. The difference is that Riskier Fund has a higher probability of having a really bad year once in a while, but many good years that offset the year of big losses. Safer Fund will likely have a really high return once in a while, which will offset its more frequent years of average returns. Which would you consider more risky?

Safer Fund is unlikely to ruin you financially, even though there's a good chance it will underperform in a few years. Riskier Fund has a better chance of outperforming its expected return, but in one year it could generate a huge negative return that could wipe you out. The tradeoff is typical of many investment decisions: If you want to play it safe and avoid an unusually large loss, you have to give up the high probability of doing better than 10 percent. Most investors would prefer Safer Fund since the prospect of unlimited losses on Riskier Fund represents too high a downside to accept. The true risk of each fund is not fully described by its standard deviation.

## MATH BREAK

To get a little more technical, the problem with volatility is that it does not account for skewness, which is a measure of how *asymmetrical* the actual returns are around their long-term average.

Let's go back to the two funds with identical returns and volatility measures. I've charted their expected returns and the probability distribution of all their returns. I've also shown a neutral fund that does not suffer from any skewness, since the likelihood of returns being above or below the average is identical.

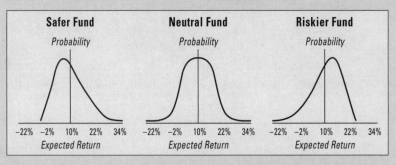

| Safer Fund | Neutral Fund | Riskier Fund |
| Probability | Probability | Probability |
| −22% −2% 10% 22% 34% | −22% −2% 10% 22% 34% | −22% −2% 10% 22% 34% |
| *Expected Return* | *Expected Return* | *Expected Return* |

Both funds have an expected return of 10 percent, and a standard deviation of 12 percent. But they are very different. The expected return of each fund is measured along its horizontal axis, and the probability of achieving a particular return is measured along the vertical axis.

The returns of Safer Fund are less likely to be far above the average expected return of 10 percent, but the occasional above-average returns could be extremely high. Statisticians refer to this distribution of returns as being skewed to the right since there are a lot of possible above-average returns, represented by the "tail" that stretches to the right.

The returns of Riskier Fund are the opposite: The distribution of returns in this case is skewed to the left, as illustrated by the "tail" to the left of the expected return. This means that the possible downside is practically unlimited — the worst possible returns, while carrying a low probability of occurring, are way below the expected returns.

Skewness reveals the weakness of standard deviation, which only has relevance as a risk measure if the expected returns are normally (symmetrically) distributed, as they are in the Neutral Fund. Even then, as we've already noted, standard deviation doesn't differentiate between bad and good surprises. As it happens, stock markets don't always generate returns that are normally distributed. In fact, they are symmetrically distributed only about 50 to 60 percent of the time, and over longer periods of time — greater than five years — they are symmetrical only about 30 percent of the time.

We can try to get around the problem of return distributions that aren't normal by complementing standard deviation with a measure for skewness, but then we lose a lot of user-friendliness. If I told you I owned a fund that had an expected return of 10 percent, a standard deviation of 12 percent, and a skewness of 1.1, would you have a clear picture of the fund's risk? What if I told you that in addition to a skewness of 1.1, the fund's expected return distribution suffered from severe positive kurtosis? Unless you were a statistics major in university, you'd probably end up running for GICs, and I wouldn't blame you.

Clearly, standard deviation, despite its venerable stature in the investment industry, is not nearly robust enough as a definition of risk. That's not to say it's useless; we'll come back to it later in this chapter since it can be useful in analyzing how different securities interact with one another within a portfolio. But using volatility to assess the risk of a stock market or mutual fund is only really useful when it is combined with other statistical measures, such as skewness, which gets complicated. We obviously need a more user-friendly way of describing risk.

## Regret

No definition of risk is more user-friendly than one based on "regret." What are the odds that you will regret the outcome of a certain decision? If you invest only in stocks with the intention of buying a car in two years, the odds are very high you'll regret the outcome, given the potential of stocks to lose money over a two-year period. Regret can do something that volatility cannot: It can accommodate the notion that there is risk in not earning sufficient returns to meet your financial objectives. If you have a modest retirement nest egg, and invest exclusively in

GICs yielding 5 to 6 percent annually, you are likely to regret how much money you'll have to retire on. Regret is useful not just because it's simple, but also because it can be personalized: You may regret investing in a fund that doesn't beat a market index, but your retired neighbour may regret losing money in stocks. The advantage of thinking of risk as regret is that it can be customized to each individual's unique circumstance. But that advantage is also its weakness.

Because the concept of regret is so flexible, it is vulnerable to distortion by individual preferences. Mr. Safety, for example, can argue that he does not want to invest in stocks because there's a strong possibility he'll suffer regret every time the market goes down. He may make this argument even if he requires double-digit returns to ensure a comfortable living standard upon his retirement in 20 years. You can appeal to the cold, hard mathematical facts that demonstrate that the likelihood of losing money over 20 years is very low, and that he may regret not investing in stocks because of the returns he'll miss out on. But that won't dissuade him. Every time he sees a frightening headline in the newspaper about markets going down, he will be relieved that he successfully avoided the pain of regret that he would have otherwise suffered. Should his emotions have that much prominence in his decision-making process?

No. If emotions were the only factor governing our day-to-day decisions, then most of us would eat more cake and fewer vegetables, watch more TV and exercise less. Mr. Safety needs to be educated on the tradeoffs he's implicitly (and possibly unwittingly) making. His emotional aversion to stock market volatility is not entirely irrelevant, but it should not be the overriding factor in his investment plan. Suffering the short-term ups and downs of the market is just as necessary as turnips and jogging. Where volatility as a definition of risk was too hard and unaccommodating, regret is too soft and situation-dependent. We need a way of thinking about risk that is as logical and rational as standard deviation, but as simple and intuitive as the notion of regret — a rigorous definition that will prevent our psychological foibles from getting the better of us.

## The Behavioural Explanation

- *Fear and Pain of Loss*
- *Fear and Pain of Regret*
- *Mental Accounting*
- *Lack of Knowledge*

Imagine reading these headlines as your day begins; they are real clippings I took from the newspaper:

**"Another massive sell-off devastates Wall St."**
**"It's 'Armageddon,' stock analyst says as panic continues"**
**"Traders push panic button as sky falls on markets"**
**"Biggest stock markets in free-fall"**
**"Gates of hell open wide . . . investors fall in, never to be heard from again"**

Okay, I made the last one up. But it's not that much more dramatic than the others, is it? And the others are all taken from the national newspapers after the October 19, 1987, crash.

How do they make you feel? A tad uncomfortable? Emotions often cause us to do some pretty stupid things, and the domain of investing is no exception. Emotions are among the greatest perks to being human, inspiring great achievement and self-fulfillment. But they can also ruin relationships, families, and careers, and subvert our best intentions.

As I outlined in the chapter "The Limits of Our Thinking," behavioural psychologists have determined that the most prominent emotion to influence our investment decisions is the pain we feel when we lose money. And this feeling is so pronounced that we experience it twice as intensely as we feel the pleasure of receiving money.

**We feel the *pain* of loss TWICE as intensely as the *pleasure* of gain**

This imbalance has an enormous impact on our investment decisions. The intense discomfort of losing money looms so largely in our minds that our rational thinking about risk can be distorted.

I also demonstrated very concretely in "The Limits of Our Thinking" how emotions alter our perception of risk, and our appetite for taking it.

*Take Risk to Avoid Loss*

Sure loss of $85,000 or 85% chance of losing $100,000 combined with 15% chance of losing $0

Sure gain of $85,000 or 85% chance of gaining $100,000 combined with 15% chance of gaining $0

*Avoid Risk to Avoid Loss*

We are generally willing to take a big risk even for a small opportunity to avoid losing money (as in the first scenario). But we'll shy away from a good chance of winning more money, because of the small chance of losing money that accompanies it (in the second scenario). Our separate choices are not irrational. It's not foolish to choose to gamble for a 15 percent chance of avoiding being robbed of $85,000; nor is it nonsensical to avoid gambling because there's a 15 percent chance of losing our winnings. What is irrational, though, is that our risk tolerance — our willingness to gamble — is not *consistent* across different situations. *It is the imbalance between our fear of losing money and the pleasure of winning it that underlies the inconsistency in our tolerance for risk.*

Unfortunately, this irrational behaviour can have greater implications in the real financial world. Here's an example of how our emotions focus our attention on the trees, at the expense of the much more important forest. Below is a graph of the range of annual returns of a stock, a stock market, and a diversified portfolio. The range depicts the best and worst annual returns over a 10-year period ending December 1999.

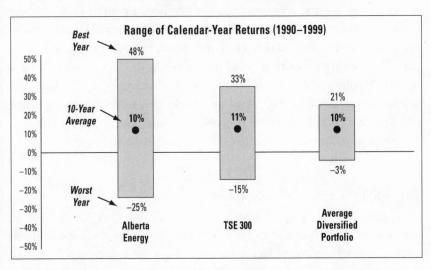

You can see that the range of one stock's annual returns (I'm using Alberta Energy as an example) is much broader than the range of annual returns of the Canadian stock market. And the TSE 300 in turn covers a much wider range than the returns of a diversified portfolio (I'm using the average returns of an aggressive balanced fund as a proxy). The best year for the stock was 48 percent and the worst year was negative 25 percent. The best for the TSE 300 was 33 percent, and the worst was negative

15 percent. The diversified portfolio had a tighter range of returns, ranging from 21 to negative 3 percent.

Even though the average 10-year returns of each were similar, the stock and index had much less predictable returns in any given year. The problem arises from the attention that the media give to the first two bars. The newspapers, periodicals, and TV and radio programs always highlight the risk of certain stocks, or the stock market as a whole, over very short periods of time.

You never read headlines such as "Diversified portfolios make it through stormy markets unscathed" or "Markets go down, but diversified portfolios hold their own." After all, those headlines wouldn't sell newspapers. What sells is "Markets plunge. Armageddon at hand," because those headlines cause people to think, "I'd better pick up this paper and see what's going on."

Dramatic headlines induce fear and this emotion focuses our attention on the wrong types of risk, such as the volatility of stocks over a very short period of time. Even within a diversified portfolio, emotions tend to encourage mental accounting: Most investors associate risk with the individual parts of their portfolio, rather than the overall portfolio itself. We tend to compartmentalize each part of our portfolio — the safe cash part, the income-producing bond part, the volatile stock part — which makes us vulnerable to panic when our stock account falls because of a market correction. But the risk of our stock, or one stock market, is not the type of risk that a long-term investor should be concerned with. *The only risk that matters is the risk that characterizes an entire portfolio* — not its component parts.

## The Solution

The solution is a productive definition of risk that protects us from the sway of our emotions. In fact, we need to suck the emotion right out of our thinking about risk, so we can manage it more productively. The emotional way of thinking about risk can be very costly, because it motivates a change to your predetermined asset allocations — a deadly mistake that we'll explore in more detail in the following two chapters. By removing emotion from your thinking about risk, you can be faithful to a more logical and more rewarding way of contemplating it. Let's contrast the emotional but costly way of thinking about risk with the logical and rewarding way:

| COSTLY | | REWARDING |
| --- | --- | --- |
| Emotional Thinking | | Logical Thinking |
| *focused on:* | | *focused on:* |
| Today's headline | ⬅———➡ | Investor's time horizon |
| Stock market | ⬅———➡ | A portfolio |
| Short-term volatility | ⬅———➡ | Assessment with advisor |
| Not sleeping well | ⬅———➡ | Maximize your returns for retirement |
| *Risk is bad* | ⬅————➡ | *Risk is rewarding* |

The logical way reveals how rewarding risk can be. *If it weren't for risk, you wouldn't be able to earn 10 percent or more on stocks!* Equity returns are higher because they compensate for higher risk. In order to take advantage of risk, though, you have to take the emotion out of your assessment of it — that's the only way you can prevent it from unreasonably intimidating you.

You may think that your emotions are a crucial component of assessing risk. After all, many advisors will ask you questions such as "Can you stomach a 20 percent drop in your portfolio?" or "Would you rather go hang-gliding or canoeing?" These questions have merit, since a portfolio that is only theoretically sound won't serve you well if you can't get food down every time there is a change in your net worth from market moves. But giving too much weight to your emotional reaction to volatility undermines the importance of both your financial objectives and your practical risk tolerance. As we explored in "The Rules of Successful Investing," your objectives (such as maximizing wealth for retirement) and practical risk tolerance (defined by, for example, your time horizon) should dominate the construction of your asset allocation; neither of these drivers should be affected by your feelings.

So let's get "logical" and come up with a productive definition of risk. Let's start with a logical look at the risk of losing money, since emotion tends to exaggerate this particular element of risk.

## Risk of Loss

The risk of losing money in stocks is not a function of their price fluctuations while you're holding them. It's the chance of actually losing money over a specific time period. The time period relates directly to your financial objectives. If you buy a good Canadian equity fund for 10 years, its value before the tenth year is not the least bit important. It's only upon selling the fund that its value is important. So how do we judge this time-specific risk?

If we go back to 1956 when the TSE 300 index was established, then we can see what percentage of time periods suffered negative returns:

**TSE 300: Percent of Periods with Positive Returns**

| 1-Year Periods | 3-Year Periods | 5-Year Periods | 10-Year Periods |
|:---:|:---:|:---:|:---:|
| 72% | 94% | 99% | 100% |

The only negative five-year period was 1969 to 1974, where the five-year loss was 2.2 percent, largely because of the oil crisis at the time. Neither Canadian stocks nor Canadian bonds have suffered a 10-year period of negative returns since 1956, although bonds have come close to being flat — producing less than one percent in the 10-year periods ending in 1959 and 1960.

Here's an eye-opening puzzle that illustrates the significance of the time periods used to assess gains or losses:

Q:  *Over the past 70 years, the average stock market decline has been as large as the average rise, but the gains occurred more frequently, since stocks went up around 70 percent of the time. It is also true that over that same period the average gain was about 1.7 times bigger than the average loss, and stocks went up around 90 percent of the time. How can both of these statements be correct?*

A:  **The first statement analyzes stock returns over one-month periods, whereas the second statement refers to returns over five-year periods. While monthly gains have been more frequent than monthly losses, they have been about the same size; five-year gains have been much larger than five-year losses, and even more frequent.**

Historically, the average stock market decline has lasted around eight months, which is only 13 percent of a five-year time horizon. To put that figure into perspective, think of stubbing your toe on the way to get the newspaper — it hurts for about a day, and is entirely forgotten by the end of the week (13 percent of a week is just less than one day). While eight months is the *average* length of a stock market decline, there have been some very short drops, such as the summer decline of 1998, which lasted only six weeks in the US and 10 weeks in Canada. For an investor with a 10-year time horizon, that represented less than 2 percent of the total investment period. That's equivalent to a day in which you suffer the inconvenience of misplacing your keys and look around for them for 10 minutes until you find them. Too bad it happened, but it doesn't have much of an impact on your day!

*Risk of loss is meaningless, except in the context of a specific time period.* The following numbers are not carved in stone, since for every study that assesses the risk of loss, there are different estimates. However, estimates of potential loss are generally within a tight range, so these numbers, which are a compilation of many studies, are reasonable:

**Estimated Percent Chance of Losing Money**

|          | Stocks Only | Diversified Portfolio |
|----------|-------------|-----------------------|
| 1 year   | 30%         | 15%                   |
| 5 years  | 10%         | 5%                    |
| 10 years | 5%          | 2%                    |
| 20 years | 2%          | 0.5%                  |

You will not find a single study of loss probabilities that does not demonstrate that the chance of loss declines dramatically (i) over time and (ii) as a portfolio is diversified beyond just one asset class.

Starting with the "Stocks Only" column, the more time you have to invest, the more you can benefit from the long-term appreciation of the market. So even if the market goes down over a short period of time, the odds are high that your portfolio will recover, since the long-term trend of the markets is up. If the stock markets don't go up in the long term, it can only be because companies' cash flows are not growing. And if company cash flows are stagnant, it's because there is no economic growth, and therefore no new jobs are created, which means a lot of unemployed people in the long term. This is precisely what happened during the Great Depression, when the US market collapsed 89 percent from September 1929 to November 1932 and generated a 10-year stock market loss of 6 percent, ending in 1938.

But that scenario is not likely to recur. Governments and central banks have a much better handle on how to manage domestic economies with money supply and fiscal policies than they did in the 1920s. And as Latin America, Africa, and Asia (especially China, India, and Russia, with their enormous populations) continue to develop and industrialize, there will be hundreds of millions of new consumers with buying power that will fuel worldwide economic growth for a long time to come. At the same time, advances in technology are doubling economic productivity.

The most recent long-term market decline has been in the Japanese market, which declined by about 2 percent for Canadian investors in the 1990s (it declined by 5 percent in Yen, so Japanese investors suffered more — our fall was cushioned by the concurrent fall in the Canadian dollar). Again, this was a unique circumstance that could repeat itself, but not as a normal course of events. Even if one market does suffer an unusual 10-year decline, as Japan did, an investor is protected by the fact that it is highly improbable that all stock markets around the world would decline over the same 10-year period.

Stock prices will always jump up and down a lot, as new information comes out about a company and investors' trading activity immediately reflects that information. The price of a stock in the short term is dependent upon many factors that influence the company's future earnings and the value that investors place on those earnings. Anything new — new information, or a shift in investor sentiment — will alter the price, sometimes marginally and sometimes quite dramatically. But here's the catch, and the reason why risk is not about short-term volatility: although prices can swing a lot in the short term, they tend to be more stable in the long term, since a company's fundamental economic health drives its stock's long-term value. This is much like a career, which can have a lot of ups and downs over a day, month, or year, but will have a long-term trend that generally reflects a person's professional skill. So if you have a long time horizon, whatever happens to the price of a security between when you buy it and when you sell it is irrelevant. In fact, if the price goes down in the interim, it can be a great buying opportunity if you have spare money to invest, just as losing your job can often open up new opportunities that were previously unexplored.

I've sketched out a lot more detail about market volatility in Appendix 1, if you're interested. The important idea is that *the risk of loss is a function of the time over which an investment is held.*

The chart on the previous page shows that the risk of loss declines dramatically over time, but it also reveals something else. The diversified portfolio, in the right-hand column, enjoys a much lower chance of loss than the stocks-only portfolio. That's because the characteristics of combined securities are much different from the characteristics of each security on its own.

Earlier in this chapter we explored how stock and fund returns are not always distributed evenly (or "normally," in statistical terms) around their average, which makes volatility a less useful measure of risk when analyzing individual securities. But the returns of diversified portfolios do tend to be more symmetrically distributed around their average. So volatility can have some use in describing the risk of a portfolio, especially in explaining why the chance of loss on a diversified portfolio is much lower.

Here's one of the questions I opened this chapter with. Let's say there are two stocks: stocks of tech.com and Bluechip Corp. The expected return of both is 12 percent. But tech.com has a much higher volatility — 20 percent, meaning that its average annual return varies, between negative 8 and positive 32 percent most of the time. Bluechip Corp. has a volatility measure of only 10 percent, so its return is generally between 2 and 22 percent. Which is the less volatile investment: tech.com, Bluechip Corp., or both stocks combined?

Intuitively, it might seem that Bluechip Corp. by itself is the less volatile investment since it's hard to see why both stocks together — a very volatile stock and a less volatile one — could be less "bouncy" than the less volatile one on its own. But the answer is that the least volatile investment will usually be a combination of the two stocks. The reason that intuition fails us is because we don't tend to consider how the two stocks move *in relation to each other*. If one goes up while the other goes down, and vice versa, then the volatility of the two stocks combined will be lower than the less volatile one on its own.

Here's another way of looking at the "umbrella and sunscreen" analogy we used in "The Rules of Successful Investing." This time a single company sells both umbrellas and sunscreen, which means that the volatility of its earnings will be dramatically lower than if it sold only one or the other. If one product isn't selling, the other is likely to be. The company still has expected returns of 10 percent based on solid earnings each year, but some years the sunscreen business will make up most of its earnings, while other years it will rely on umbrella sales. A portfolio of different assets works in exactly the same way.

On the infamous "Black Monday" of October 19, 1987, when the US market collapsed by 21 percent, gold stocks went up by as much as 10 percent! That's why a diversified portfolio has a lower chance of suffering a loss than does a stocks-only portfolio. The standard deviation of a portfolio is not the sum of the individual assets' volatilities, but a function of both the sum and the way the assets interact to offset each other, as measured by their covariance. The magic of covariance — how two volatile assets together create a less risky combination — is demonstrated mathematically in Appendix 3. I use two stocks as an example in that appendix, and also show how the markets of two countries — Italy and Canada — can be less volatile when combined.

If you understand the umbrella–sunscreen analogy, then you understand that two volatile assets produce a less volatile portfolio when combined. So a second important notion, adding to the idea that risk is a function of the investment time period, is that *the risk of loss is a function of the combination of assets within an entire portfolio.*

## A Productive Definition of Risk — More than Just Loss

We know that risk is not equivalent to the random volatility of any given stock market or mutual fund on a given day, week, or year. The risk of loss is a function of both time and the covariance of assets within a portfolio. But even that doesn't tell the whole story. Remember that Mr. Safety let the chance of losing money dominate his investment decisions, and unknowingly exposed himself to the risk of not earning enough money. Risk reflects both the chance of losing money and *the chance of earning less than is possible.* Losing money is a risk only because it reduces your ability to consume. But not earning enough on your investments is a risk that also reduces your ability to consume. The end result of both risks is the same — your purchasing power has not been maximized.

That's why investment risk is best thought of as two distinct risks — the risk of losing money and the risk of not generating adequate returns:

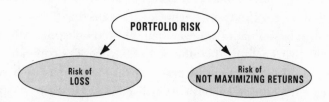

In fact, risk is the imbalance between these two. There are two conflicting tensions in the investing process: the desire to avoid losing money and the desire to maximize returns. Risk is not getting the balance between these conflicting tensions right. If you invest exclusively in GICs, you'll cheat yourself out of better returns, but if you invest only in technology stocks, you could end up going bankrupt. If your asset mix is appropriate, then it will balance the two risks against each other, in such a way that your overall portfolio risk is reduced. You will not only prudently avoid loss, but you'll also maximize your returns. We've already seen that practical risk tolerance is what constrains your objectives. Since the objective of most investors is to maximize their returns, and since practical risk tolerance is focused on avoiding a possible loss that cannot be accommodated by your personal situation, we can summarize the balance this way:

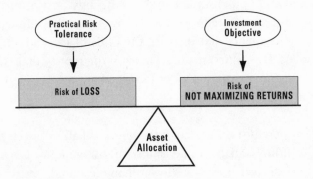

When your practical risk tolerance is balanced against your objectives, your portfolio will be based on the right asset mix, and the risk of loss will be properly balanced against the risk of not generating good returns. In Part Three, I will recommend some asset allocations that balance these risks, for different sets of practical risk tolerances.

## The Right Balance Minimizes Both Types of Risk

At the opening of this chapter, we saw how different investments lead to very different end results, in the example of Mr. Safety and Ms. Diversified. Let's reintroduce Ms. Diversified and look at the value of diversification a different way. Over 25 years, she invested in five asset classes. Even though the expected return of each investment was around 10 percent at the beginning of her time horizon, her actual returns on each varied quite dramatically:

| Initial Investment | Rate of Return | Ending Value |
|---|---|---|
| $25,000 | (100%) | $0 |
| $25,000 | 0% | $25,000 |
| $25,000 | 4.5% | $75,136 |
| $25,000 | 8% | $171,212 |
| $25,000 | 16% | $1,021,856 |
| $125,000 | 9.8% | $1,293,204 |

Interesting to see that Ms. Diversified's portfolio consisted of one investment where she lost *all* her money, one where she earned *nothing* at all, another where she earned a paltry 4.5%. The other two investments were more successful, especially the last one. And ta-dah . . . Ms. Diversified lives happily ever after. That's the power of diversification — you can afford to have some investments wiped out completely and others earn nothing, and still come out ahead of a GIC-only portfolio. Time and diversification not only reduce possible losses, but they allow for more aggressive investments that increase the odds of maximizing returns. That's why Ms. Diversified made so much more money than Mr. Safety, without taking on a great deal of extra risk. That's the magic of diversification, and magical it truly is:

- A portfolio's return is the sum of the returns of all the assets in it.
- But, a portfolio's volatility and chance of losing money is *not* the sum of the risks of each asset — it's lower than the sum.
- So, a diversified portfolio can *simultaneously* minimize both the risk of loss and the risk of not generating maximum returns.

You *can* have your cake and eat it too! How often does that happen in life?

You just have to watch out for your emotions. Emotion will throw the balance off — usually by placing too much emphasis on the risk of loss while neglecting the risk of not maximizing returns. The solution to misunderstanding risk is to remove emotion from the equation, so that you keep the two competing risks in balance, and therefore keep the overall risk of your portfolio minimized. A logical perspective of risk allows you to free yourself from the natural human inclination to let emotion take the driver seat in your investment strategies. If emotion comes for the ride at all, it should be locked up in the trunk. And don't let it out, even after you've retired!

## Mitigating Retirement Risk

*How much do you need to retire comfortably?* The answer is about 20 times the pre-tax income you want each year. You'll only need about three-quarters of that if you're willing to forgo an estate and die with nothing in the bank. Most retirees can live comfortably on an annual income that is between 50 and 75 percent of their pre-retirement income. So if you want to retire with a pre-tax income of $60,000, you'll need savings of $1.2 million, or only $900,000 if you plan to die penniless. This ballpark estimate takes into account inflation and assumes that the value of your home is *not* included in your nest egg (since you'll need it to live in!). It also assumes that you remain invested in a diversified portfolio containing some equities through your retirement.

*What should you invest in when you've retired, and how much can you withdraw each year?* These two questions are closely related. Most retired people should have some equities in their portfolio. A 65-year-old person has better than even odds of living past 80, and a better than 20 percent chance of living past 90. That's a long time to rely on GICs or bonds exclusively and not outlive your money. In any given year, stocks have proven to have about a 60 percent chance of beating bonds; over five years, that figure is 80 percent. So the best way to mitigate outliving your savings is to invest in some stocks, and never withdraw more than 10 percent of your portfolio each year for living expenses. Studies have shown that withdrawing about 6 percent of your portfolio each year generates a very high probability of preserving your savings for at least 25 years, but only if the portfolio consists of 25 percent stocks and 75 percent bonds. The lower the portion in stocks, the lower the probability that a 6 percent withdrawal rate will allow your assets to last 25 years. A portfolio that is 100 percent bonds has a less than 20 percent chance of lasting 25 years, if 6 percent is withdrawn each year.

## Don't Get Carried Away
Research has demonstrated that seatbelts encourage people to drive more aggressively. So just a final caution about long investment time horizons: Don't assume that time diversifies away all the risk of investing in stocks. In fact, the probability of suffering a loss in the stock market falls as more time expires, but the *potential size of the loss* increases. As time unfolds, the chance of the market being negative decreases, but in the rare circumstance that it does drop, the accumulated loss can become bigger. This is especially true if your portfolio suffers in the early years of your time horizon, when losses reduce the capital you have to build on. All of which is to say that you still need a properly diversified asset mix to ensure you're both minimizing risk and maximizing returns.

The unemotional, logical approach to assessing risk focuses on the risk of your entire portfolio, including, but not limited to, stocks. Risk is the tension between avoiding loss and not maximizing your returns. That's the only prudent way to think about risk; any other way, especially the emotional way that focuses on scary headlines about loss, will cost you.

# Recap of Mistake #1: Misunderstanding Risk

1. Understanding risk is a crucial part of the investment process. Unfortunately, while there are many ways to define risk, the most common is volatility, which is not always the most useful measure. But a less statistical definition, such as "regret," leaves too much room for individual preference, which should not be a major determinant of asset mix.

2. Because many investors do not evaluate risk properly, they allow their emotions to skew their thinking about risk: There is a natural imbalance we all experience between the intense pain of losing money, and the weaker pleasure of gaining it. We generally feel the pain of losing money twice as intensely as the pleasure of gaining it. The mental accounting of investment portfolios makes investors especially vulnerable to this imbalance, and so our emotions tend to get us overly focused on the risk of losing money in the short term.

3. The solution is to think of risk in logical terms, taking emotion out of risk assessment. The logical approach acknowledges that a productive definition of risk is two-fold: the risk of losing money, and the risk of not earning as much as possible. Portfolio risk arises when these two risks are not in the right balance. Your practical risk tolerance (which dictates your tolerance for losing money), and your objectives (which usually involve maximizing returns), must be properly balanced against each other.

4. The two elements of portfolio risk are kept in balance with the right asset mix, which can be different for every individual. But it is the distinct *practical risk tolerance* (and less often the distinct investment objectives), that determine the mix — not an individual's *emotional risk tolerance*, which tends to pull an investor away from an appropriate asset allocation.

5. By removing emotion from your perspective, you can use time and diversification to maintain the perfect balance between minimizing the risk of loss and minimizing the risk of not earning enough. Time and diversification work to both minimize loss and maximize gains — a rare occasion in life where "you can have it all!"

# MISTAKE #2

## Timing the Market

*Eye Opener:*

Q:  *If you toss a fair coin 20 times, what are the odds of flipping five heads in a row?*

A:  *Twenty-five percent, which is much higher than most people think. (The odds are 50 percent for four heads and 10 percent for six heads.)*

Q:  *After you have flipped those four heads in a row, what are the odds of flipping a fifth?*

A:  *Fifty percent. Each flip is entirely independent of the flip before it. Try telling that to an optimistic gambler who's sure he's going to win the next spin of the roulette wheel because the ball hasn't landed on a red square in a while!*

> "The market's too high. It's definitely overvalued."
> "It doesn't make sense to invest now, with the markets hitting all-time records."
> "It's better to stay out of the market while it's going down . . .
> wait until it hits bottom."

I hear versions of these comments every single day. And I always give the same response: "Says who?" The best money managers in the world would not hazard a guess as to where the market will be next week or next month. In fact very few will predict with any confidence where it will be in a year. They will determine a 12-month range for market values, and they may guess what the actual values might be 12 months in the future, more for fun than anything else. But they know that ranges and guesses are the best they can realistically come up with.

It's true that stock markets can get ahead of themselves from time to time. There's a certain amount of emotion in the market that exaggerates price changes and leads to overvaluation. But even if the market does get ahead of itself, it's never truly apparent until *after* it corrects. So you don't have the benefit of prior knowledge, and you can lose out on a lot of returns while waiting to see if you're right.

The problem with market timing is that it brings together the worst aspects of our psychology (especially overconfidence) with the worst aspects of the market itself (its randomness). Combined, these two factors have a dramatically negative impact on returns — easily cutting portfolio performance in half, as we'll see.

## The Problem

We'll start with a little game I call "Let's Time the Market." I'm going to show you how an actual market — the S&P 500 — unfolded over a certain period of time; I ask you not to look ahead to the charts after this one, if you can resist.

The all-time high point in the history of the S&P 500 occurred at the

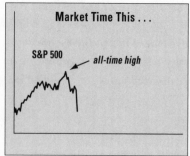

Market Time This . . .

S&P 500 — all-time high

peak in this chart. Then came a nasty little dip, which engendered the following actual headlines:

**"Stash cash to be prepared for bear market"**
**"Markets plunge as investor fears rise"**
**"No sign of bottom"**
**"It's a mad, bad, dangerous market"**

Try to imagine how you might have felt, if you were an investor at the time, and what you might have done. How tempted would you have been, as many were, to pull all your money out of the market? Or perhaps some of it? Would you have been courageous enough to invest more?

Let's go back to that point in time and see what happens next:

Now you may be tempted to cut your losses, since the market has given back some of the money you lost from its high. Or maybe you'll breathe a sigh of relief and relax. Looks like the worst is over. Let's see:

At this point, the headlines don't help. The consensus of analysts is that the market attempted to recover but couldn't break through a crucial resistance level on its way up, so it is heading back down as a result. Who knows how far down it will go this time?

Well, well. A very nice recovery, back to the all-time market high. A new record, in fact. But not so fast. The pundits are cautious: The market has attempted to surpass its former record but didn't get very far. In fact it appears to have topped out. At best it may just stay flat, and at worst, it will come crashing down again. The consensus is clear: The probability of its coming down is much higher than the probability of its staying flat. Very few analysts are courageous enough to predict more gains in the immediate future. So you probably won't be surprised at what ensues:

Surprised? A very bumpy, but steady rise. When did this occur? It was the two-year period from January 1998 to January 2000. You can see the first nasty dip was the summer of 1998 when all of those apocalyptic headlines were published.

The market timing game is not easy to win!

## The Studies on Market Timing

There have been many studies on the effects of market timing on investors' portfolios. Most research is based on US data, since the academic community in the US is much larger than in Canada. One of the most highly regarded studies covered the 10-year period from 1985 to 1995 and compared the returns of the average US equity fund to the returns earned by the average US equity fund investor.

While the average US equity fund generated a compound annual average return of 12 percent, the average US equity fund investor earned only 6 percent each year. Half as much! How could this be? There's only one difference between the average fund and the average investor. The fund was invested in the market the entire time, while the average investor was not fully invested the whole time, but put money in, and pulled money out, reinvested, and then withdrew, over and over again. As the stock market went up and down in its typical way, it tempted US investors to try to outsmart it by timing their investments.

When I first read this study, I thought to myself, "That's surely an exaggeration. I get the point, but I can't really believe that the average equity fund investor earned only half of what the average equity fund generated." I was skeptical. So I charted the S&P 500 over that period to see if it could shed any light on what happened.

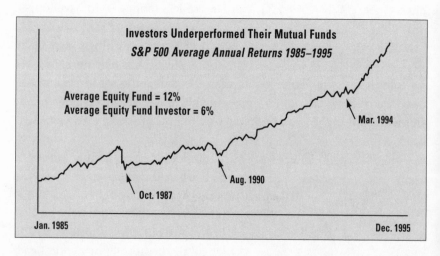

The first thing you'll notice is the notorious crash in October 1987. Many shaken investors took their money out of the market for a good while, waiting for things to settle down. But they missed the recovery if they did that. It ended the year up 4 percent in Canadian dollars. Naturally nobody remembers the recovery and positive return of that year, only the terrifying headlines that accompanied the fall:

**"Another massive sell-off devastates Wall St."**
**"Panic selling hits markets around world"**
**"Wealth of investors took trouncing as value of Canadian stocks fell $37 billion"**

The year of 1990 wasn't too pretty either: the Gulf War accompanying a recession. Most of us completely forget just how frightening the Gulf War really was, because it "ended" so quickly. At the time, there were widespread fears of possible nuclear escalation, chemical warfare, and serious misgivings about the allies' ability to stem Saddam Hussein's aggression. The US market dropped 21 percent over the summer and into the fall. Here are just two token headlines from 1990:

**"Is Saddam Hussein clinically insane?"**
**"Gulf war raises danger of global recession"**

Many of the investors who had re-entered the market after the crash of 1987 were confronted by this global chaos and decided to pull their money out of stocks. But those who did pull their money out missed the quick market recovery that followed, as you can see in the graph. It took only six months for the market to recover to its July pre-crash level.

Less conspicuous in the graph is early 1994. The analysts were largely in agreement about the market at this point: It was overvalued. It was unrealistic, they claimed, to assume that future company earnings would ever be robust enough to justify the prices reflected in the market at that time. At best, the market would remain flat for a while, to let earnings catch up to "inflated" stock prices. But the risk of a market correction was very high — a fall of 10 percent was likely, possibly more.

**"Get ready for the stock slump"**
**"Stock markets downturn expected"**
**"Why the stock markets will be stormy"**
**"Lessons of Black Monday: Worried that the market is overinflated?"**

Many investors believed what they read, and why not? These were experts after all. So money came out of stocks and parked on the side in GICs, money market funds, and savings accounts. But look what happened. The market roared ahead despite concerns of being too high. Interest rates declined by about 2 percent because economic growth appeared to be slowing and inflation was very low, thanks to the high rates of the early 1990s. The falling rates gave stock values a strong boost in 1995.

Analyzing the graph, you almost wonder how the average investor managed to squeak out even a 6 percent return! Investor psychology was a strong deterrent to maximizing returns in this 10-year period. But this period is not unique. *The volatility of the market continually tempts investors to react — almost always to their detriment.*

A study released in the year 2000 on Canadian mutual fund investors looked at the decade of the 1990s. It showed that investors earned about 7 percent annually on their Canadian equity mutual funds compared with the TSE 300 return of 11 percent. This pattern is strikingly similar to results of the US study mentioned earlier. Some of this 4 percent difference was attributable to the underperformance of the average fund compared to the index and the fees investors pay on their funds. But even when you adjust for these factors, you're still left with about a 2 percent gap. Two percent a year is a lot of return to give up on market timing. The study also showed that the average holding period of Canadian investors in their equity funds was about three years, which equates to more than three switches in a decade.

## The Challenge of Market Timing

First of all, there are costs to market timing: transaction costs — commissions to get in and out of the market — as well as capital gains tax on gains realized within a year. Both of these costs pose a significant disadvantage to market timing, because they have to be overcome before you're ahead of a buy-and-hold strategy. You might be able to avoid transaction costs if you're using no-load mutual funds to get in and out of the market, but only with limited activity, because most no-load fund companies will either charge you for, or stop you from, excessive trading. Taxes are obviously not an issue within a registered account — an RRSP or RRIF.

To add value with a market timing decision, you have to get both the "in" and "out" decisions right. Getting out of the market before it falls is one thing, but you have to get back in before the market regains its ground; otherwise, you will wipe out whatever benefit you got from getting out early. Research suggests that your "in" and your "out" decisions have to be correct about 70 percent of the time, if you are going to add value to your portfolio with market timing. In fact, since the market goes up more often than it goes down, you only have to get half your timing decisions right when the market goes down, as long as 80 percent of your "back in"decisions are right before the market recovers. But on average, you have to be about 70 percent right.

Is a 70 percent success rate doable? What do you think the odds are of making the right "out" decision, followed by the right "back in" decision? How about extremely low. The reason the odds are stacked against you is that the market jumps around without much advance notice. If you're going to get out of the market before it goes down (i.e., before everyone else starts selling), then you are going to have to know something that others do not. Or you'll have to be a superior analyst of information, so you can draw conclusions before anyone else does. You see, *successful market timing depends on being a brilliant contrarian* — buying stocks when everyone else is selling, and selling when everyone else is buying. Otherwise you're just buying with the trend, buying when prices are rising, and selling when they are falling.

Even if you do have an unusual ability to interpret the information that is available to everyone, in a way that gives you unique predictive power, you'd still be hard-pressed to beat the market. That's because the market moves very abruptly. Remember that stock market prices reflect future company earnings. The price of a stock is nothing more than the value of the company's future earnings, adjusted for interest rates that could have otherwise been earned if an investor invested in a bond instead of a stock. The stock market as a whole simply reflects the value of all companies' earnings. So you don't really know if the market is over-valued until after the fact, when its future earnings have materialized, and you can assess whether the previous prices were justified by the earnings that the companies actually generated. When the market falls, it's a reflection of revised values of earnings projections based on new information that investors are factoring into their projections. For example, prices may not be overvalued today based on all of the information that's available. But if tomorrow, interest rates were to shoot up unexpectedly, or unemployment data were released to change everyone's perception of the state of the economy, the market would quickly reflect this new information; the price of their stocks would change to reflect the altered projections.

You can see that the window of opportunity to use your special predictive powers is very small. Probably the most oft-quoted studies in the investment industry are those that demonstrate that if you are out of the market for just a few crucial days, you'll miss most of the market's gains.

Let's say you were in cash, having exited the market because you feared it was going down. In the two decades spanning the 1980s and 1990s, if you missed the best-performing 40 days in the US market, your returns would have been cut almost in half. If you missed the best 30 days of the 1990s, you would have also cut your returns in half. If you missed the best 40 days in the 30 years between 1963 and 1993, your returns would have been cut in half as well. Over some five-year periods, *all* of the gains occur in less than 4 percent of the trading days! The few days that account for spectacular gains more than make up for flat trading and losses in the other 96 percent of the trading days. See the pattern here?

All of the studies are dependent on the time period they cover — how many years and which years exactly. But they all, without exception, demonstrate the same general conclusion. Most gains occur in a small number of trading days. The least compelling research period shows that 57 percent of gains occurred in 8 percent of trading days. The most convincing research period shows that 84 percent of gains occurred in 0.2 percent of trading days. So we are safe to make the generalization that 75 percent of market gains occur in 5 percent of the time. And around 50 percent of market gains occur in 2 percent of the time.

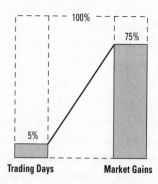

You can see that the opportunity to outsmart the market (i.e., everyone else) is very small. Remember that you're likely to underperform the market if you get either the "out" or the "back in" decision wrong. And since the market goes up more often than it goes down, it can be very costly to be sitting on the sidelines in cash.

So we know from documented research that

- a small percentage of trading days are really big gainers, responsible for a majority of the market's long-term gains;
- about 70 percent of actual trading days are "up" days in the market.

We can draw some interesting conclusions from these two facts:

- if you miss the few big "up" days, your returns will badly suffer;
- if you are a brilliant market timer, the value you are able to add to your returns is not that significant.

The two conclusions together paint an interesting picture.

Starting with the second conclusion, if the market goes up more than down, a buy-and-hold strategy is difficult to compete with, since there aren't that many "down" days to exploit if you're attempting to generate superior returns. Many studies have examined how much you can earn in higher returns assuming correct market timing decisions can be made. If we compare what you would have earned in the 1990s by sitting in cash and buying at the market bottoms each year, you would have added less than one percent per year to the returns you would have had by simply buying and holding. And that doesn't take into account the higher transaction costs of active trading and more frequent capital gains tax payments in non-registered accounts, which, when combined, add up to at least one percent. So the value added by *perfect* market timing calls in this case is practically nothing! Over the past 20 years, an investor who timed the US market perfectly by buying at the lowest point in every month, in each year, earned 20.3 percent on average. An investor who put money in the market on January 1 of each year earned 19.7 percent. The difference between the perfect timer and the invest-right-away person is practically negligible. Once again, these quoted returns are before trading costs are taken into account, so the real difference is even smaller, and possibly even reversed in favour of the non–market timer on an after-tax basis.

Combining the conclusions suggests that *the upside to market timing is limited, while the downside can be significant*. The downside has been shown to be almost twice as big as the upside. For every $1 that you might be able to generate with good market timing calls, there's a risk of losing $2. This makes sense when you consider that the market goes up more often than not, and goes up a lot in short spurts. If you miss the "up" spurts you lose, but if you catch the spurts and miss the fewer "down" days, you're not likely to add a lot of extra value. That's why if you do not have a high percentage of correct bull market calls, you have to make disproportionately more correct bear market calls to compensate for the returns you missed out on.

In general, the best you can do with correct market timing is squeeze out a bit of extra return. But this assumes that you have great timing skills and are right at least 70 percent of the time. If you're right less than 70 percent of the time, you can detract from your returns quite substantially.

## What About the Pros?

Interestingly, many professional money managers became famous after the crash of October 1987 because they were out of stocks at the time. The problem was that most of them missed the ensuing recovery because they stayed out of stocks. If you think the pros have better track records at market timing, think again. If you want some entertainment, look at all the market forecasts that come out in the papers at the beginning of the year. Clip them and pull them out in December to see how accurate the "experts" were.

A tactical asset allocation fund is one whose manager shifts the asset weights based on market timing calls. Canada's most popular tactical asset allocation fund has a mandate to weight different asset classes on the basis of the manager's forecasts. It's interesting to note that cash levels in the fund reached one of the highest levels it ever had — about 20 percent — in October of 1998. That was a few months *after* the market fell in the summer. Between July 17 and August 31, 1998, the US stock market fell 19 percent. It recovered, starting in September, to end the year with a 38 percent return. But the fund raised cash and lowered US stock holdings after the summer market correction (presumably because the manager was getting nervous about the value of US stocks). As it became increasingly obvious that the market was recovering and moving higher, the manager dramatically lowered cash to 10 percent by January 1999. So this popular tactical asset allocation fund moved money from stocks to cash *after* the market corrected, and moved back into stocks about three months *after* the market turned up. Here's a month-by-month rundown of what happened in the US market and how the fund moved from cash to US stocks and back. Note the lag between how the market performed, and how the manager reacted to it:

**Tactical Asset Allocation Fund Holdings**

| | July 1998 | Aug. 1998 | Sept. 1998 | Oct. 1998 | Nov. 1998 | Dec. 1998 | Jan. 1999 |
|---|---|---|---|---|---|---|---|
| S&P 500 return | 1.40% | −11.2% | 3.8% | 9.6% | 4.9% | 6.2% | 2.5% |
| Percent cash in fund | 14% | 14% | 17% | 19% | 19% | 12% | 10% |
| Percent US equities in fund | 11% | 10% | 9% | 5% | 5% | 9% | 12% |

This fund wasn't alone. Let's look at how many managers of Canadian equities became bearish *after* the summer debacle. I'm defining bearish by their action of raising cash in their funds, and reducing equity exposure. This chart shows the monthly return of the TSE 300 over most of 1998 and the percentage of managers holding a lot of cash (more than 10 percent) in their funds.

**Percent of Canadian Equity Funds Holding More Than 10% Cash**

| | May 1998 | June 1998 | July 1998 | Aug. 1998 | Sept. 1998 | Oct. 1998 | Nov. 1998 | Dec. 1998 |
|---|---|---|---|---|---|---|---|---|
| TSE 300 return | −0.9% | −3% | −6% | −20% | 2% | 11% | 2% | 3% |
| Managers with 10%+ cash | 29% | 29% | 31% | 35% | 38% | 44% | 41% | 34% |

See how the market started to decline in May and really took a tumble in July and August? The percentage of Canadian equity managers who got nervous and raised cash above 10 percent in their funds rose dramatically *after* the market went down. Over 40 percent of managers were still raising cash in the fall. By the time things looked more settled, the percent with high levels of cash dropped in December. To be fair, some of the increase in cash holdings is attributable to the market decline itself, which would make the cash holdings in all funds have a higher weight relative to the fallen market values. But this doesn't account for the size of the jump in the proportion of managers who hold a lot of cash (from a usual 25 or 30 percent to more than 40 percent), especially after September when the market started to recover. Equity managers always have the opportunity to invest the cash anyway. Note that the percentage of managers who increased cash jumped way up *after* the market corrected, then fell dramatically *after* the market recovered. It appears that many got both the "out" and "back in" decisions wrong!

The pros don't have impressive track records on market timing, and most don't even attempt it because they know how futile it can be. The *Globe and Mail* publishes a "bulls and bears" survey every two weeks, where they survey money managers, analysts, and advisors and ask them where they expect the market to be in six months. Over a two-week period, the survey results can vary dramatically. For instance, let's look at the survey in early September 1998 because that was just when the market began to recover from a very nasty summer drop of 20 percent. On September 7, 69 percent of the professionals were bullish on the prospects of the US stock market, and two weeks later, on September 21, only 41 percent were bullish. Did much happen in two weeks to justify such a dramatic fall in optimism? No. Two weeks after that, on October 5, only 29 percent were bullish. Apparently the experts were quickly losing faith in the US market and were skeptical of its ability to stage a strong recovery after the rough summer. Given what you know about market timing, it probably won't surprise you that the US market roared ahead with a gain of 33 percent in the 12 months after the summer of 1998, ending August 31, 1999.

If the pros either don't attempt to market time or don't do it well, why do investors attempt the impossible? Why do so many people have opinions on where the market is going, and make investment decisions based on these beliefs? It's because *we're overconfident in our ability to predict the market.*

## The Behavioural Explanation

- *Framing*
- *Confirmation Bias*
- *Ambiguity Aversion*
- *Illusion of Control*
- *Overinterpretation*
- *Innumeracy*
- *Lack of Knowledge*

The problem with market timing, as far as our psychology is concerned, can be explained by three main factors:

1. our overconfidence;
2. our limited ability to assess probabilities and base predictions on them; and
3. the structure and behaviour of the market itself.

Let's look at each of these parts of the problem separately.

## Overconfidence

Overconfidence is probably the most consequential, yet most overlooked, component of investor psychology. By definition, overconfidence implies that we're unjustifiably certain — confident beyond what is reasonable. We make judgements with a degree of assuredness that we're not entitled to.

As we explored in "The Limits of Our Thinking," overconfidence is a fundamental survival technique. If we walked around second-guessing ourselves all the time, we'd barely make it from one side of the street to the other, never mind negotiate our way through the overwhelming amount of information our overloaded senses are exposed to every day. It's so much easier to make quick judgements about the world and other people. It's easier to believe we've got things pretty much figured out (if only others would see the light, of course), and to confidently make our way around, dealing with ambiguity in quick and superficial ways that belie the complexity of the world we live in.

The problem is that the overconfidence that makes our lives run relatively smoothly gets us into trouble from time to time, and investing is a perfect example. Remember the optical illusion I tried to catch you on in Part One? Let's look at another drawing of lines:

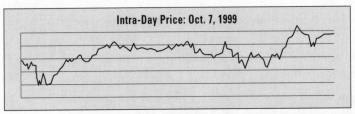

**Intra-Day Price: Oct. 7, 1999**

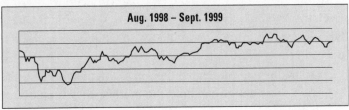

**Aug. 1998 – Sept. 1999**

The top chart tracks the TSE 300 over the course of one day, whereas the bottom chart tracks it over an entire year. Surprisingly, the intra-day trading chart from October 7, 1999, looks a lot like the 12-month chart. That's because they are both the product of random market moves which don't have a lot of meaning. Where most people are quite confident in their ability to project the index's future moves if they're told they're looking at a year's trend, they are usually inclined to say that you cannot predict the index's moves based only on a single day's data. Even though the charts look so similar, people differentiate their meaningfulness by the context they're given. Behavioural finance labels this phenomenon as "framing" because the answer you provide to the problem depends on how the question is framed. In this case, the framing relates to the time period that you are told you are viewing.

Because I talk to so many people about investing, I see firsthand how confident people are in their judgements about the market. They are pretty self-assured, based on what they may have read in the paper, or the view of a "knowledgeable" friend who "watches the market carefully." If you read the paper every day, you'll see that there's a definitive headline for every insignificant move in the market, explaining why it did what it did. It's easy to become accustomed to perceiving the moves of the market as eminently interpretable, when you are subject to market stories each day. The frame you have when you read the headlines is the underlying assumption that the short-term ups and downs of the market are always meaningful. And it's not as if the headlines are averse to expunging every element of ambiguity out of market moves. Here's a headline that popped up after a down week in the market was followed by a modest recovery:

**"Be worried: This stock shakeout is not over"**

Columnists don't write their own headlines. There are headline writers whose job is to do just that. They work on tight deadlines at the end of the day when the stories are filed, so they'll skim the article, often reading only the first and last few paragraphs, to come up with something catchy, to entice readers into the article. If you're skimming the headlines, you'll be subjected to many unambiguous statements that easily invoke confidence in the market's predictability.

If someone has conducted their investment strategy for a long time by believing that they could time the market, they aren't likely to give up that belief too easily. This is especially true when they are vulnerable to "confirmation bias," seeking out evidence that confirms their beliefs, and ignoring evidence that contradicts them. It has been documented that men are generally more overconfident than women, as in the "I don't need to ask for directions" phenomenon. Men actually trade about 45 percent more than women: Research has shown that men, on average, turn their portfolios over 77 percent annually, whereas women turn their portfolios over 53 percent each year. Not surprisingly, this excessive trading has been documented to reduce men's returns by 2.65 percent, compared with the trading that reduces women's returns by 1.72 percent.

We are strikingly overconfident when it comes to making estimates of the probability of something happening. I say "strikingly overconfident" because we have so little basis for being confident at all where probability analysis is concerned. It is difficult for many people to accept just how unintuitive we are when it comes to probability analysis. Let's take a look at a specific example of overconfidence, because it directly relates to the problem of market timing. It has to do with our ability to formulate good predictions.

## Predictability

Predictability is based on probability analysis. Predictions are nothing more than the assignment of probabilities to certain events; in other words, assessing the likelihood of something happening.

Remember the problem I posed in the Introduction, where you had to estimate the probability of two people in a group of 23 having the same birthday? Most people assume it's somewhere between 5 and 10 percent, and they have a high degree of confidence that it's below 15 percent, even though the answer is actually 51 percent. The same degree of underestimation is evident in the coin-tossing question at the beginning of this chapter.

Why do people habitually guess so low? Because we're particularly challenged when it comes to estimating probabilities involving random events. Tasks such as estimating the chance of people sharing a birthday in a random sample, or the randomness of 20 coin tosses, are subject to the natural limits of our cognitive abilities. Math is not intuitive for most of us. Probability theory is even less intuitive. So what? So we underestimate randomness — what does it matter?

It matters a great deal because the result is that we overinterpret random events by seeing patterns in them when none exist. It doesn't just stop with underestimating the frequency of randomness. The result of this underestimation is that we concoct interpretations to explain events that are just random and meaningless occurrences. In "The Limits of Our Thinking," we looked at the situation where you get a phone call from someone you were just thinking about, and how this is usually interpreted as a coincidence, or evidence of ESP. Because we underestimate the frequency of randomness, we confidently ascribe an interpretation to an occurrence that is unjustified because it's just random chance operating in a way that is not unusual. It's not "coincidental" that two people in 23 share a birthday; it's the mathematically predictable randomness that we'd expect. Do you see how we tend to invent stories about random events and give them more importance than they really have?

Here's the crux of the investment problem: Investors do not fully appreciate that the market is fundamentally random in the short term. Its moves are abrupt and volatile. Even though the market moves abruptly, investor psychology doesn't deter us from interpreting market moves as predictable. We confidently see patterns in the market where none exist, and explain every little random rise or fall as if it were truly meaningful. So let me finally demonstrate how truly random the market is in the short term.

## The Market Itself

Most investors don't really understand or appreciate the true nature of short-term market behaviour.

Take any six-week period and I would bet that you could find headlines that bounce from optimism to pessimism almost daily. Watch the headlines over the next couple of weeks; I'll bet they follow a pattern similar to the one I am showing below. These are actual headlines, taken from Canada's largest newspapers in the first few months of the year 2000. Note the chronology:

Feb 3 — **TSE SOARS TO RECORD**

Feb 6 — *Markets show signs of heading for a fall*

Feb 9 — TSE and Nasdaq Hit New Records

Feb 19 — Stock sell off hits Toronto, N.Y. on rate worries

Feb 23 — TSE 300 due for a downturn

Feb 25 — **Nasdaq Hits Record**

Feb 27 — More Market Losses Ahead Analysts Say

Feb 29 — Toronto rides high as New York rallies

Mar 2 — Experts can't explain TSE's wild ride

Mar 3 — Broad-based Rally Takes TSE To Record

Mar 4 — N.Y. markets rally sharply, best week since July

Mar 7 — Fed Rate Stance Clobbers U.S. Stocks

Mar 8 — **CHAOS HITS MARKETS**

Mar 9 — **Bargain hunters help Wall Street recover**

Mar 14 — Bay Street Succumbs to Global Stock Slide

Mar 15 — **Nasdaq Nosedives**

Mar 16 — Dow Gains from Nasdaq Pain

Mar 17 — Market swings likely to persist

Mar 17 — More Ups and Downs Foreseen for Markets

Mar 17 — Fear makes markets stop making sense

Mar 17 — Volatility has market players wondering when to get in, when to get out

Mar 17 — BEWARE – A BEAR MARKET COMETH

Now you tell me that the market is not random in the short term!

Look at the ups and downs, the sporadic and frenetic bounces. I deliberately threw in a lot of headlines from March 17 since they conveniently captured my point about market randomness.

It's important to note here that by "random" I do not mean "uncaused." I do, however, mean "unpredictable." This is a very important distinction — one that is easy to confuse.

## What Does Random Mean?

There are causes for every market move. The market does not have a life of its own, independent of the influence of investors who are trading in it. But the causes of market moves are not necessarily discernable in the short term. The market is principally driven by news. Because the price of a security represents the value of the future cash flows that it will generate for investors, any news that affects the estimation of those cash flows will affect the price of the security.

If, for example, earnings are reported for three big companies on the same day, their stock prices will fall if they all have profits that are lower than expected. If the three companies have a heavy weight in the TSE 300, the index itself will likely be dragged down.

Let's look at a more complicated, yet equally common, example. Say a report is released that indicates that the unemployment rate has fallen. Try to guess how this news is likely to affect the stock market.

Here is a common sequence of events:

i) Falling unemployment means that fewer people are looking for work,

ii) which means that working folks can demand higher wages since they're harder to replace,

iii) which means that inflation will be pushed up,

iv) which means that the Bank of Canada is likely to increase interest rates in order to "cool" off the economy so inflation doesn't get out of control. (Higher rates mean borrowing money becomes more expensive, which slows down corporate and consumer borrowing. Less borrowing means corporations invest less in expansion and consumers purchase fewer goods. This reduced investment and purchasing slows down economic growth.)

v) Stock values fall as a result, for two reasons. First, the slower economic growth that is predicted to result from the higher rates will reduce company earnings' growth. Second, the higher interest rates make stock dividends less attractive because higher-rate bonds are available as an alternative investment.

The interrelationships are very straightforward, albeit a bit circuitous. When news breaks, in the form of an unemployment report, for example, investors factor in the new information and prices adjust accordingly.

Here's the important point: When new information comes out, the market absorbs it very quickly, so prices change almost instantaneously. There are thousands of analysts around the world, as well as retail and institutional investors, scouring the news each day, all day. So it doesn't take long before the new information is reflected in trading prices.

So where's the randomness?

It's in the fact that the news is "new." New information will either confirm or contradict previous predictions. Sometimes the news is so new that analysts are unprepared to predict its effects, as in the case of a sudden and unexpected war, or a surprise oil discovery. So the random effects of news on the markets are "hard to anticipate," but are not "uncaused."

Think of an avalanche: It doesn't start for no reason. One little snowflake lands in just the right spot to trigger a series of movements that cause piles of snow to start tumbling. The timing of the avalanche is completely unpredictable. In fact it may never even occur. Meteorologists can make some judgements about the likelihood of some avalanches occurring, but they can never be certain they will occur, nor can they predict when or how they will occur. And many avalanches occur completely unexpectedly.

Avalanches are a great example of Chaos Theory, whose origins stem from late nineteenth-century mathematics and expanded in the 1960s with the development of computer modelling. Chaos Theory is a concept that scientists use to describe systems that are so complex that they appear chaotic to us — unpredictable. The stock market is very "avalanche-like," or chaotic (or "stochastic" as statisticians would say). Each move is unpredictable on its own because you simply can't anticipate all the complex factors that will influence it at any given moment in time.

Remember the coin-tossing scenario where the probability of four heads or tails in a row is 50 percent? Coin flips are another good example of randomness. There are a number of causes that result in the coin toss being a head or tail: the balance of the coin itself, the angle and speed at which it leaves your thumb, the air that pushes against it as it twirls, and the timing and angle of your catch. Chaos Theory suggests that a sufficiently sophisticated computer using a sufficiently complex series of mathematical formulae could, in theory, capture all the factors in a coin toss that create either a head or a tail result. The same equipment could, in theory, capture all the elements that combine to create the avalanche. So if you had the theoretically perfect computer, and fed it with all of the possible inputs, it could predict what the coin toss or avalanche outcome would be. But in the absence of having such a powerful computer, the coin toss appears totally random, chaotic, and unpredictable. Just like the market.

You can be fooled by all of the explanations that are offered by the experts *after* the market responds to some news. They make it sound like everything the market does is predictable, because there always appear to be good reasons for any changes. For instance, tech stocks defied gravity and interest rate hikes until the spring of 2000 when they came crashing down, at which point everyone "agreed" that the stocks had been overvalued because so many tech startups had no earnings. This after-the-fact analysis didn't explain why tech prices remained so high for so long. Economists refer to that sort of explanation as *ex post* because it was made *after* the fact. But market timers are interested in *ex ante* explanations — insights that explain price moves *before* they occur. If you are subject to enough *ex post* analysis (as you are every day when you read or hear the experts explaining why the market went up or down), you'll be vulnerable to the illusion that they are offering *ex ante* analysis that is reliable and consistent. If they seem to know so well why certain things happened, then surely they must have known beforehand. The fact is that many of the *ex post* explanations are attempts to understand random occurrences that often defy simple explanation, never mind prior prediction.

Randomness comes from not knowing all the factors behind a market move, and it also comes from the suddenness of unexpected events. For example, everyone expected the Canadian dollar to appreciate in the first half of the year 2000. It was below its true value (what's referred to as its purchasing power parity value) and the Canadian economy was strong, growing, and deficit-free. But no one counted on the Quebec premier to start making "referendum noise," as he did in April of that year, in anticipation of calling a Quebec election. The Canadian dollar got hit and stayed comfortably below 70 cents as nervous foreign investors became less optimistic about our currency. All the sound rationale that supported a strengthening Canadian dollar was obviated by an unforeseen event.

There is another important part of the market's random behaviour that I have not yet described. That's emotion. Unpredictable, chaotic, but powerful human emotion.

## The Chaos of Emotion

The direction of the wind can change radically without much notice, and make the difference between an avalanche and a light shifting of snow in the mountains. Similarly, human emotion can make the difference between the market taking a move in a certain direction, and a violent swing up or down. Every investor — the individual day trader, the well-schooled pension fund manager, the neighbour next door who always seems to know what stocks are hot — is subject to emotion. Being human means being emotional; we need our emotions to motivate us to action.

The market is not a purely rational reflection of the true value of stocks or bonds at every moment in time. Emotions can exaggerate the moves of the market quite significantly. And why shouldn't that be the case? Stock market prices are nothing more than a reflection of the thinking behind the trading decisions of imperfect individuals like you and me. *And we are as vulnerable to emotion between the market hours of 9:30 and 4:00 each weekday as we are when someone cuts us off in the passing lane on the way home from work, or when we misplace our car keys in the morning before we leave.* The irrational elements that drive the markets in the short term are as unpredictable as anyone's reaction on a given day to losing their keys. Some days you respond calmly: "Oh well, let me think about where I had them last." Other days you respond as if you had been inflicted with the greatest injustice imaginable.

Emotions don't usually precipitate market moves on their own, although studies have confirmed that in the absence of any news (such as overnight or over a weekend), the market can move in ways that can be attributed only to sentiment. More commonly, though, emotions exaggerate market moves that are initially triggered by specific news. Stock prices are anchored to specific economic drivers, but vulnerable in the short term to unpredictable emotional pulls. And these pulls can be extreme. Witness the S&P 500 (in Canadian-dollar returns) in 1987 — the notorious market crash:

**October 19, 1987:**  –21%  *worst one-day decline in history of the US market*

| October 21, 1987: | 9% | *fourth-best one-day rise in history of the US market* |
| 1987: | 4% | *not bad, but not as good as best year ever — 1915 at 82%* |

Most people forget that the market bounced back and returns for the calendar year were positive (although it did take about 15 months for the market to recover to its October 16 pre-crash level). But more interesting to note is how extreme the market moves proved to be. It's also worth recalling the combination of events that led to the one-day drop of 21 percent. The American Congress was threatening to tax corporate mergers to slow down acquisition activity. The US budget deficit had widened, as had the US trade deficit. There was talk of possible tax increases. US interest rates had risen from 9 to 10.5 percent over the previous two months. The stock market had already fallen 20 percent in the months leading up to October 19, including a 5 percent drop on Friday, October 16. During the weekend before Black Monday, James Baker — then Treasury Secretary — made pronouncements that he would not allow the US trade deficit to widen. He suggested that he would encourage the US dollar to fall in order to shrink the trade deficit (a lower US dollar makes US imports more expensive and exports cheaper). This announcement made foreign and domestic investors very nervous. Did this weekend "news" really warrant a huge drop in stock prices on Monday? No, it did not. That's why the market partially self-corrected on October 21. Investors generally realized that the market had overreacted, just as an angry spouse may say something stupid when provoked, and later apologize after cooling off.

You think October 1987 was bouncy?

| October 28, 1929: | –13% | *second-worst one-day decline in US market history* |
| October 29, 1929: | –12% | *third-worst one-day decline in US market history* |
| October 30, 1929: | 12% | *second-best one-day rise in US market history* |
| 1929: | –17% | *not as bad as worst year ever, which was 1931, at –53%* |

The market return of 1929 was sandwiched between two very interesting years: the third-best and the third-worst. The third-best year in the history of the US stock market was 1928, which generated a 48 percent rise. But the year following — 1930 — was the third-worst year in the US stock market, racking up a loss of 34 percent.

If we look at the ups and downs of the market in just one day, the irrational elements that influence the market can be very powerful. Let's compare the highest point and the lowest point of the TSE 300 in some of the most "emotional" days of its history. What were the percentage changes from low to high on some on these volatile days?

**Percent Change of TSE 300 Within One Day**

|            | Oct. 19, '87 | Oct. 20, '87 | Oct. 27, '97 | Aug. 27, '98 | April 4, '00 |
|------------|--------------|--------------|--------------|--------------|--------------|
| **Low**    | 3,191        | 2,859        | 6,599        | 5,648        | 8,691        |
| **High**   | 3,525        | 3,084        | 6,966        | 5,968        | 9,354        |
| *Difference* | *10%*      | *8%*         | *6%*         | *6%*         | *8%*         |

Do you think there was enough new information within those days to warrant swings in the market of 6 to 8 percent? Absolutely not. Do you think that misplacing your car keys logically entails getting all worked up and angry, as if that would help the search for your keys? Uh-uh. Emotions are a part of who we are, and they can wreak havoc in the short term. How, and by how much, emotion will affect stock prices is very hard — I would argue impossible — to predict. Same with the snowflake, whose effect on the piled-up snow is not easy to anticipate.

The market moves in fits and starts. It moves in reaction to news and the emotions that investors experience when they react to the news. It moves haphazardly, chaotically, randomly, and fundamentally unpredictably, because of the factors that drive security prices, which are never static. Appendix 1 covers the topic of stock market valuations and the cause of their chaotic movements in greater detail.

## The Solution

So how do we get around our overconfidence in our beliefs about the market, and our tendency to overinterpret random events? As we've seen, the market is random, and no investor can possibly know, synthesize, and anticipate all the complex causes that drive the market in the *short term*.

Why do I say "short term"? Take a look at these graphs of the stock market. Note how truly sporadic the market is over a short period and

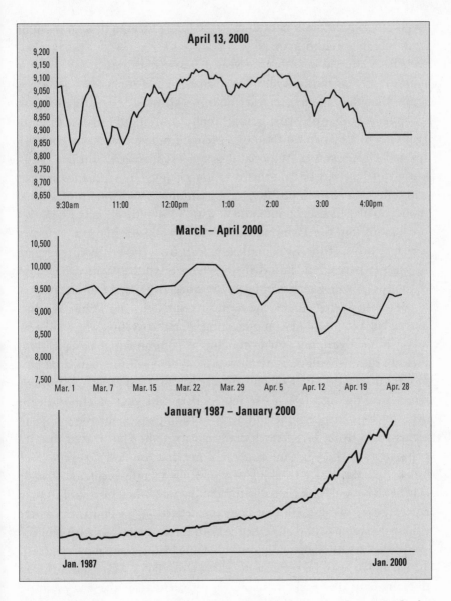

**April 13, 2000**

**March – April 2000**

**January 1987 – January 2000**

how meaningless its ups and downs are; but note also how much the market is dominated by an overriding long-term trend.

In the long term, the stock market reflects the underlying value of corporate earnings. Emotions are largely squeezed out of the long-term trend. That's not surprising when you consider human nature. We can be quite irrational from time to time, but most of us manage to get through our lives without doing too much irreparable damage. Most of our big goofs get corrected one way or another. Similarly, the market generally levels out to reflect rational values in the long run, even though it can be irrational in the short term.

What's short term? About a year or less. That's not to say that the market can't sustain a level of irrationality for a longer period. Many argue that the Japanese market was unreasonably overvalued for an extended number of years, before finally coming back down to earth (with about a 60 percent thud of a decline from its peak to its bottom). It's debatable just how irrational the Japanese market was in the 1980s, but it can generally be said that over longer time frames, market returns will reflect the growth of the general economy. That's why professional money managers usually look out at least 12 months in making market predictions. But the 12-month time frame is still too short a period in which to invest in the stock market. At least five years are required for an investor to have confidence that stock returns will be positive, based on economic growth, which is unlikely to be negative over a five-year period.

Here's an analogy that I find useful. Presumably, you would be reluctant to bet a lot of money on predicting what the weather will be like on July 1 of next year, but you'd probably be comfortable making a wager that the summer will be generally warm. Where will the market be next month or even next year — who knows? Is it likely to generate a positive return over the next five years? Yes. So next time your neighbour leans over the fence in early June and declares triumphantly that he pulled all of his money out of the stock market because he's convinced that it's going to go down, you can calmly respond that you find that very interesting. Tell him you're thinking of cancelling a family picnic on Canada Day because you think it's going to rain that day. When he responds with a perplexed look, explain that both predictions — his and yours — are equally meaningless because they're both forecasting short-term random events that are fundamentally unpredictable by their very nature.

The market can be risky in the short term. But it's very rewarding in the long term. The trick, therefore, is to *ignore the short-term noise in the market, but exploit the long-term trend.*

Market timing favours the market, not the investor. The odds are highly stacked against being able to consistently predict random short-term market moves. And as tempting as it may be to try to interpret and place bets on the market, be aware of your natural psychology, for it will lead you down a costly path. As corny as it sounds, it can honestly be said, "Buy and hold, and your returns will be double-fold!"

# Recap of Mistake #2: Timing the Market

1. Many investors confidently base their investment decisions on predictions of where they think the market is going. This habit has been shown to cut investors' returns by as much as half.

2. Market timing predictions are made despite a general human fallibility in assessing probabilities and basing predictions on them.

3. Our weakness in making realistic judgements about probabilities is aggravated by the natural working of our minds, which like to oversimplify and jump to conclusions quickly and confidently, often without sufficient knowledge or information.

4. To top it all off, the market is fundamentally random, or unpredictable, in the short term. The market is nothing more than a reflection of human activity. It represents all that is rational and all that is irrational in human psychology. Market moves are not uncaused; but the causes of market moves are so numerous, complex, and essentially chaotic that they cannot be consistently predicted over a 12-month period, never mind shorter time frames.

5. Market timing is virtually impossible — you need to have a 70 percent accuracy rate or better to win the game. The marginal incremental benefit to your returns of getting market calls right is overshadowed by the potential losses, which can be twice as large. So not only is market timing difficult, but the downside is bigger than the upside.

6. The solution to market timing is to ignore the short-term ups and downs of the market, which tempt us to overinterpret their randomness as meaningful. The solution is to buy and hold — and take advantage of the long-term trend of the market, which is up.

# MISTAKE #3

## Overusing Tactical
## Asset Allocation

*Eye Opener:*

Q: *Two scenarios: You arrive 30 minutes late to catch a flight for a vacation and have to wait five hours for the next flight. Or you arrive 30 minutes late to catch the same flight, are told that the flight was delayed by 29 minutes but just departed, so you have to wait five hours. Do you suffer equally in both cases?*

A: *Even though the outcomes are identical — a five-hour wait — almost everyone agrees that the feelings of regret in the second scenario are much more intense. Kind of like the intense regret of investing in bonds and getting a minus one percent return, when you could have earned 60 percent in an emerging markets fund.*

At this point, I hope you are convinced that market timing is not only futile, it's very costly. Pulling your money out of the market when you think it's going down, and reinvesting when you think it will go up, is a strategy that reflects a fundamentally mistaken view of the predictability of short-term market moves. But what implications does that have, if any, on another common practice, which is making sure that you own stocks in the countries that are outperforming?

Let's say the consensus of commentators is that investors should over-weight US stocks since the US economy is performing better than the Canadian economy, with less inflation. How do you know the extent to which it would be prudent to buy more US stocks or equity funds, while reducing your holdings in Canadian equities? There's a big difference between market timing, where you go in and out of stocks based on short-term market predictions, and simply overweighting the stock markets that are expected to outperform. Or is there?

Yes, there is a difference. But before we get into this difference, let's back up and look at how tactical asset allocation works.

When you establish your portfolio, there are three main levels of asset mix–related decisions you have to make:

1. How much should you put in stocks, compared to bonds, compared to cash?
2. How much should you put into Canada, compared to the US, Europe, Asia, and emerging markets?
3. Which stocks and which bonds should you buy in each of these countries?

There's also a fourth decision level that's a little more esoteric, but still important:

4. Which currencies do you want your assets denominated in?

We'll leave this last decision to the side and come back to it in the discussion of Mistake #5, which relates to how much to invest outside of Canada.

As we reviewed in "The Rules of Successful Investing," the best way to start building your portfolio is by allocating your money to each of the major asset classes on the basis of your financial objectives and practical risk tolerance. Then you can allocate countries and securities within those asset classes. After this, you have a few choices. You can leave the allocations the way they are and simply rebalance back to the original mix when it drifts too far from the starting point. This "stay-the-course" approach is called "strategic asset allocation" because it relies on a long-term strategic perspective of the markets. Alternatively, you can change the allocations periodically to take advantage of markets you or your advisor think will outperform. For example, if everyone seems to think that US equities are poised to generate the highest returns in the next year, you might increase your holdings of US equities and decrease holdings in other countries. This "change-as-you-go" approach is called "tactical asset allocation" because it is based on shorter-term judgements, which are the basis for tactical changes. This example of tactical asset allocation probably sounds familiar — it is similar to market timing in that you are changing your asset mix based on judgements about different markets. In fact, market timing is an extreme form of tactical asset allocation.

Here's the difference: Tactical changes involve modest changes to the asset class mix in a portfolio, whereas market timing involves big swings in and out of the stock market. Tactical changes are usually based on a medium-term view — usually a 12-month outlook or longer. A tactical assessment is made of which markets offer the best returns for the least amount of risk. Market timing, on the other hand, is based on shorter-term predictions — usually just a few months — on a particular market. The result of a market timing decision is not just a shifting of assets from one market to another, but a large swing in and out of stocks — trying to avoid the downturns and capitalize on the upturns. The ambition of tactical asset allocation is less dramatic — trying to add a bit of extra value by overweighting some asset classes and stock markets while underweighting others.

Most mutual fund managers do not engage in market timing to any great extent because they are cognizant of just how difficult it is to add value by trying to predict where the market is going over the short term. They certainly don't want to be sitting in cash when the market surprises them and goes up 10 percent over just a few days. Most know that investors are not paying mutual fund fees of 2 to 3 percent on their equity mutual funds just to have their cash managed. But many fund managers will engage in some form of tactical asset allocation, particularly within funds that have broad mandates to cover many asset classes. Global equity funds and balanced funds are good examples of funds where managers attempt to add value by making ongoing adjustments to asset allocations within the fund. The difference between tactical asset allocation and market timing is subtle, but important:

| Market Timing | Tactical Asset Allocation |
| --- | --- |
| • Generally attempted by individual investors moving in and out of the market based on short-term predictions with limited information. | • Generally used by professional managers making marginal changes to asset allocations based on a 12-month outlook with fundamental risk/return analysis. |

So that brings us to the central question of this chapter: Should you engage in tactical asset allocation, or is it better to leave your asset mix the same, and simply rebalance back to the original allocations? How difficult is it to add value to a portfolio by employing tactical asset allocation?

If it were easy, it wouldn't be Mistake #3!

## The Problem

In "The Rules of Successful Investing," I showed that while asset mix is not the exclusive determinant of your portfolio returns, it is the most important decision you make. I demonstrated that you need to get the asset mix call right. Putting aside the disastrous strategy of market timing, the most common asset allocation errors involve not starting off with the right mix, and changing the mix too frequently in an attempt to guess which markets will outperform.

When you consider how many changes people make to their allocation of bonds, as well as Canadian, US, and international equities, it's no surprise that portfolio returns are undermined. In the table below I've included the best- and worst-performing asset classes in each of the last 14 years. Given how much variation there is from one year to the next, consider the likelihood of being overweighted in the best asset class in each year.

| 1986 | | 1987 | | 1988 | | 1989 | | 1990 | | 1991 | | 1992 | |
|------|------|------|------|------|------|------|------|------|------|------|------|------|------|
| Best | Worst | Best | Worst | Best | Worst | Best | Worst | Best | Worst | Best | Worst | Best | Worst |
| Japan | Canada | Japan | Europe | E M | Int'l. Bonds | E M | Japan | Int'l. Bonds | Japan | E M | Japan | US | Japan |
| 99% | 9% | 43% | −2% | 64% | −4% | 49% | 2% | 12% | −36% | 31% | 9% | 18% | −21% |

| 1993 | | 1994 | | 1995 | | 1996 | | 1997 | | 1998 | | 1999 | |
|------|------|------|------|------|------|------|------|------|------|------|------|------|------|
| Best | Worst | Best | Worst | Best | Worst | Best | Worst | Best | Worst | Best | Worst | Best | Worst |
| E M | US | Japan | Cdn. Bonds | US | E M | Cdn. Bonds | Japan | US | Japan | Europe | E M | E M | Cdn. Bonds |
| 76% | 15% | 22% | −4% | 34% | −12% | 28% | −15% | 39% | −24% | 38% | −18% | 60% | −1% |

What are the odds of picking the right asset class in each year? Low. Very low. In fact at the beginning of 1999, the overwhelming majority of experts — money managers, commentators, mutual fund writers — were convinced that the emerging markets were not a place you wanted to be for the end of the millennium. Their reasoning was sound: whatever havoc the Y2K computer bug was going to have on developed countries, the problem would be tenfold in the emerging markets, where virtually no investment had been made in upgrading technology, as far as anyone could tell. Not only was this hypothesis compelling, the year started off with emerging markets looking very shaky. But the numbers tell the story: emerging markets is *exactly* where you wanted to be invested in 1999. This example is not unique. In fact it's almost uncanny how the most logical arguments for overweighting and underweighting an asset class are continually proven wrong as events unfold, in their surprising and unpredictable way.

## The Pros

*Barron's* is probably the most venerable US investment publication. Each January they host a roundtable with the most well-known market gurus, to solicit their predictions.

In January of 1998, the august group convened and what follows are some excerpts from their discussion. To be respectful, I won't attribute the comments to the individual speakers.

*"We are not going to have any earnings growth and the market is going to go down."*

*". . . the US and Europe really haven't gotten hit yet. And they are going to get hit . . . You are going to get a major hit on the world banking system from bad loans in Asia."*

*"I think the Japanese stock market will eventually go to a new low."*

*"The US market is the most vulnerable . . . Expectations are unrealistic. So a 20 to 30 percent decline from the top is possible."*

*"European stock markets will also come down."*

You wouldn't have felt very optimistic at the beginning of 1998 after reading their comments, would you? Here is what a Canadian investor would have earned in the three major markets in the year that the predictions were made:

| | |
|---|---|
| S&P 500 | 38% |
| MSCI Europe | 37% |
| Japanese Nikkei | 5% |

Do you think their comments were any more prescient in 1999? Here are some excerpts from the January 1999 roundtable.

*"I see probably a down S&P, maybe by 20 to 25 percent."*

*"We see the US as overvalued . . . So a flat market to one down 10 percent or 20 percent, I could easily see happening."*

*". . . we'll still end the year with the market down 5 percent."*

*"Do I own Japan? No, not really. But if you have to be somewhere, I think Japan is a pretty safe place to be that will outperform if we have a bear market — go down less."*

*"I would like to have 20 percent cash, which is the maximum we can have."*

Interesting. Even more interesting when you consider how the markets did for Canadian investors in 1999:

| | |
|---|---|
| **S&P 500** | 14% |
| **MSCI Europe** | 10% |
| **Japanese Nikkei** | 45% |

Be wary of anyone — no matter what their credentials — who tells you exactly where the markets are going in any given year. The more certain they sound, the more skeptical you should be. In 1995, the S&P 500 posted an impressive 38 percent gain (in US dollars). The following year it posted a 23 percent gain. The American expert analysts agreed that it was overdue to "take a rest" and deliver flat returns in 1997. But in that year it generated 33 percent, which was the first time in the history of the US market that three years in a row enjoyed returns greater than 20 percent. "That's it," declared most experts, "There was no way the US market could deliver good returns for an unheard-of fourth year." In fact, many were predicting a down year, maybe even a crash. They looked like they might have been proven correct in the summer of 1998 when the market started to collapse. But 1998 ended up being a banner year for the US market, returning 29 percent in US dollars, and 1999 wasn't too shameful either, at 21 percent. So much for forecasts!

There is a large discrepancy in a manager's ability to add value with tactical asset mix calls. The best way to demonstrate this is with the range of returns in tactical asset allocation and global equity funds. The difference between the better and worse funds is quite substantial.

First let's look at two of the most popular Canadian tactical asset allocation funds, with returns ending in December 1999:

**Two Large Canadian Tactical Asset Allocation Funds**

|  | 1-Year Returns | 5-Year Returns |
|---|---|---|
| **Better-Performing Fund** | 15.5% | 18.5% |
| **Worse-Performing Fund** | 5.7% | 7.8% |
| *Difference* | *9.8%* | *10.7%* |
| *Avg. Cdn. Balanced Fund* | *8.7%* | *11.1%* |

Note how widely the two popular funds differ; and the gap is even larger in the global equity fund category, where a manager can invest in any stock market around the world.

**Two Large Global Equity Funds**

|  | 1-Year Returns | 5-Year Returns |
|---|---|---|
| **Better-Performing Fund** | 60.4% | 33.1% |
| **Worse-Performing Fund** | 5.6% | 9.3% |
| *Difference* | *54.8%* | *23.8%* |
| *Avg. Global Equity Fund* | *26.6%* | *15.3%* |

Getting the tactical calls right is not easy for the pros; the range around the average is very wide.

## How Does the Upside Compare to the Downside?

Countless studies have assessed how much tactical asset allocation can add to overall portfolio returns, compared with security selection. Which is more important: Changing asset mixes to take advantage of the best markets in any given year, or picking the right stocks or bonds within each asset class?

Picking the right country can be very rewarding, but how easy is it to get that decision right? On average, tactical asset mix calls *subtract* about 0.4 percent from portfolio returns. This contrasts with security selection which seems to *add*, on average, 0.1 percent. These statistics represent the amalgam of many Canadian and US studies.

While the average value added by security selection was a modest 0.1 percent in the studies, the lowest value was 2.1 percent of value *subtracted* and the highest value was 2.3 percent of value added. So security selection appears to be very symmetrical — you can add as much value as you can lose. This is not the case with tactical asset mix calls. While the average tactical call subtracted 0.4 percent, the range was a subtraction of 1.4 percent on the low side, and a 0.6 percent addition of value on the high side. You can see that with tactical calls, unlike with security selection, *the downside is larger than the upside.*

This makes sense when you consider the large influence that a country has on the stocks traded within it. If the Canadian market is up higher than most markets, your Canadian equity fund is likely to do relatively well, even if it's not managed by the best stock picker. We saw in "The Rules of Successful Investing" that asset classes generally have broader ranges of returns than the funds within them.

Since market timing is an extreme form of tactical asset allocation, similar logic applies: Investors are tempted to chase after what they perceive to be the best-performing markets, which, in their judgement, are usually the previous year's winners.

## The Behavioural Explanation

- *Same behavioural factors that generate the mistake of market timing*
- *Plus a bit more emotion — fear of regret*

The psychological factors that are responsible for market timing are the same culprits that encourage tactical asset allocation.

The starting point of the error is the illusion that there is a high degree of short-term predictability to the markets that allows investors to determine which asset classes are the best to overweight and which are best to underweight. Then add in our predilection for reading meaning into randomness and basing predictions on these feeble interpretations, as if we had all the information we needed to make reliable forecasts. Our overconfidence in judging which market will do well adds fuel to the fire.

It's not that we're completely illogical. After all, the Y2K bug looked as if it was going to be a significant problem, possibly causing worldwide havoc and economic catastrophe. If this had happened, the already shaky emerging markets would have been severely hit, since the less developed countries had made very little technological progress in addressing the bug. But as it happened, there was not a better market for Canadians to have been invested in that year!

How'd that happen? It turns out that the risk of Y2K was overblown. Rising commodity prices helped the export businesses of Latin American countries. Fiscal and monetary stimuli helped Japan to turn an economic corner, which helped the export businesses of many Asian countries. And the surprisingly strong US economy continued to import goods from these countries, strengthening their economies. Who would have known? Presumably all the commentators and money managers who were cautioning against investing in emerging markets in January of 1999 should have known . . . *if* all of these factors were knowable in advance, which clearly they were not.

Changing an asset class in anticipation of events that can't be accurately predicted is one thing. But even more illogical is the tendency to change allocations based on last year's returns. Many Canadians turned their backs on Canadian stocks in 1999 because the TSE 300 returned minus 2 percent in 1998. Moving away from the Canadian market, if for the wrong reasons, isn't such a bad thing, since most Canadians are over-invested in Canadian stocks in the first place, as we'll see in Mistake #5. But those who did it in 1999 found their timing wasn't great, since the Canadian market delivered a 32 percent return in 1999.

The final contributor to the problem of picking the future outperforming asset classes is emotion, specifically our fear that we will regret missing out on big gains. If the experts are all saying emerging markets are going from bad to worse, why would you want to risk putting money into them, only to end up looking back on December 31, 1999, to see that you missed out on great returns on North American equities? At least if you follow the experts' advice, you won't suffer from the intense regret of going it alone and blowing it. You can be comforted by knowing everyone else blew it too!

They're all there — the worst elements of human psychology — all conspiring to undermine investment returns. Which is precisely what happens to many investors.

# The Solution

The best portfolios are ones that are

1. *Diversified across all markets, and*
2. *Reflect individual objectives and risk constraints.*

Let's go back to one of the first principles: Successful investing is based on putting probabilities in your favour. What are the probabilities of predicting the best asset class in a given year? Low. Very low. What are the probabilities of maximizing your long-term returns by investing in a broad mix of all asset classes? High. Very high. Does this mean you'll maximize your returns in each year? Clearly not, since you'd have to have invested all your money in emerging markets in 1999 to do that. But it does mean that over the long term, the odds are in your favour if you are exposed to all the major asset classes, without trying to guess (note I say "guess") which markets will outperform in any given year.

We saw in "The Rules of Successful Investing" that establishing the right mix of asset classes is based on your financial objectives, and the risk that you are capable of taking to meet those objectives. Is that to say that nobody can add value by making tactical asset mix calls? And that you should never revisit your mix once it's established? The answer to both questions is "no."

## When Can Tactical Calls Add Value?

Some professional money managers have good long-term track records of adding value by making adjustments to asset mixes. What they don't do is make decisions based on the current day's headlines, the most recent economic report, or the views of some talking heads on TV. The good money managers make well-researched comparisons of the risk/reward relationships among different asset classes. For instance, they'll determine the potential best- and worst-case results from investing in Canadian bonds. Then they'll compare the bond scenarios to the possible outcomes of investing in other securities.

The money managers who have *consistently* been able to add value *over time* by making these tactical asset allocation decisions are few and far between. The extra annual returns that a very talented money manager can generate, using a tactical strategy, is at best up to 2 percent above the returns of a portfolio whose asset allocations are strategically fixed.

But we've seen how large the difference is between the best and worst asset classes in a given year, so a manager can very easily subtract returns from a portfolio with the wrong decisions. And the detraction can be much more than 2 percent, depending on the size of the bets the manager makes. So you have to pick your fund managers carefully if you expect consistent value-added tactical calls. More on picking managers in our discussion of Mistake #4, "Overestimating Active Management."

Your advisor may suggest a "wrap" or asset allocation program, which is managed by professional managers who make the tactical calls on your behalf. But if you don't have 100 percent confidence that changes in your asset mix are being driven by the rigorous research of highly qualified investment managers, you're better off keeping your asset allocation unchanged. Why end up losing 5 percent on your portfolio, just for a possible extra one or 2 percent? When the downside is greater than the upside, probabilities are not in your favour.

Assuming you do have confidence in your money manager's ability to make tactical calls that add value, you should nonetheless make sure the calls he makes are limited to marginal tweaks only, so you're not vulnerable to big bets. Big bets are wonderful if they're right. But there's no point in going bankrupt trying to double your money over a few years. Be suspicious of anyone who wants to change your asset mix more than two to three times in a year. If the world is changing that much every few months, it's highly unlikely that anyone can keep ahead of the changes, so the odds favour staying put, in a well-diversified portfolio that is not subject to constant tinkering.

Excessive asset mix fiddling can also have serious tax consequences outside of a registered account. You have to pay capital gains tax on any gains that are realized from selling one asset class to go into another; this tax liability would otherwise be deferred until you sell out yourself. A skilled manager has to add substantial value in tactical calls to more than offset the lost tax deferral — not an easy challenge, and one that suggests you can't go wrong by minimizing tactical calls in non-registered accounts.

Finally, satisfy yourself that whoever is making tactical calls for you is assessing markets over about a 12-month time frame. If they indicate that they are reducing Canadian equity exposure because of their fear that interest rates are going up in the next month, they are getting dangerously close to market timing, and the chance of being wrong is much higher. Don't forget that the market is a more reliable reflection of true economic activity in the long term than it is in the short term, where it can be unduly influenced by irrational elements.

## What About Funds That Use Tactical Asset Allocation, such as Global Equity Funds?

Some mutual funds make use of tactical asset allocation. Notable among them are many balanced funds and most global equity funds. Balanced funds usually allow their managers to change the mix of cash, bonds, and stocks. And foreign equity funds almost always allow their managers to weight countries differently based on their forecasts. A balanced fund can substitute for a diversified portfolio, and global equity funds can take the place of foreign stock funds in your portfolio. But for investments of $5,000 or more, you're usually better off in a diversified portfolio, which allows you to access the best bond managers, and the best Canadian and international equity managers. For example, if a global or international fund reduces its Asian equities, but has a heavy weighting in Europe, you could unknowingly be taking a bigger bet than you realize on certain markets.

The bottom line is that it is usually a mistake for investors to undertake tactical asset allocation, because they rarely have sufficient information to make good tactical decisions: Unfortunately, a few newspaper and magazine articles, and some commentary on TV, do not qualify as sufficient. Tactical calls should only be attempted by qualified professional money managers, who spend their time doing nothing other than assessing world economic factors. Even then, their calls should be limited to marginal and periodic changes only. As a general rule, you're safe in changing your asset mix rarely, if at all.

## When Is It Appropriate to Revisit Your Asset Mix?

Changing your asset mix for reasons other than tactical market calls can make a lot of sense. First, your portfolio will get out of whack over time since some parts will grow faster than other parts. If US stocks outperform European stocks over a one-year period, then you'll end up with a heavier weighting in US stocks and less in European stocks at the end of the year. So you'll want to occasionally rebalance your portfolio back to the original asset mix. Second, your circumstances will change. You'll experience your share of unexpected changes, such as divorce, losing a job, or getting a huge promotion. And you'll experience more gradual and anticipated changes, such as aging. These changes will alter your practical risk tolerance, so you'll need to change your mix to reflect your new circumstances.

Finally, the risk–reward characteristics of the world's markets do change over time and it is not unreasonable to change your portfolio periodically to reflect these fundamental changes. These changes are legitimate, regardless of whether or not you want your investment manager to make tactical changes. Strategic asset allocation still needs to be dynamic.

## Strategic Asset Allocation Is Still Dynamic

A strategic asset allocation, which is geared toward a long-term view of asset classes, does not mean that you look at the market only once, at the time you set up your portfolio. The world may change over the course of a few years, and your portfolio may need to reflect these large changes. For instance, some Latin American countries such as Chile and Mexico — which are currently considered emerging economies — are likely to become more developed over the next few years. You may want more exposure to them a few years down the road, not because you think they are going to outperform other markets, but because they have already become a more significant part of the world economy. When the *long-term* risk–reward relationships change in certain asset classes, as they undoubtedly will in Latin America, Asia, and eventually Eastern Europe and Africa, it's important to integrate these changes into your portfolio. There are solid reasons to believe that China, India, and even Russia will slowly but surely evolve into more developed economies.

Here's a good demonstration of why you want to make changes from time to time to reflect worldwide economic shifts: This table shows how the major worldwide stock markets have changed over the last 30 years. It tracks the percentage of total world stock market capitalization represented by each asset class:

**Percent of World Stock Market**

|                   | 1970 | 1980 | 1990 | 2000 |
|-------------------|------|------|------|------|
| Canada            | 5    | 5    | 3    | 2    |
| US                | 69   | 50   | 30   | 51   |
| Europe            | 20   | 25   | 23   | 28   |
| Japan             | 4    | 15   | 38   | 10   |
| Asia (excl. Japan)| 2    | 4    | 3    | 4    |
| Emerging Markets  | 0    | 1    | 3    | 5    |
|                   | *100*| *100*| *100*| *100*|

You can see that it would be naive to never revisit your asset allocations, given how dramatically the world can change from decade to decade.

## How Often Should You Make Strategic, Non-tactical Adjustments?

The first type of change — rebalancing back to your initial asset mix — is adequately addressed on an annual basis. Semi-annually is fine, but usually not necessary. The more often you rebalance, the more transaction costs you're vulnerable to incurring. It is a good idea to rebalance early in the year so that any realized capital gains tax will not be paid until the following year; if you rebalance in December, you'll have to pay tax in April of the following year. The best way to lessen taxes is to use new money to rebalance your portfolio. By adding to the asset classes that have fallen below their allocation, you can avoid the selling of other securities that might generate a taxable capital gain.

The second type of change — in response to shifts in your life circumstances — should be made as soon as the event occurs, so your portfolio immediately reflects your changed objectives or risk tolerance.

The timing of the third change — long-term fundamental economic shifts — is less clear-cut. You shouldn't have to make adjustments more often than once every two to three years in order to capture any long-term evolving trends. Changes that are made more frequently, such as once a year, are likely to be tactical calls masquerading as changes driven by fundamental economic long-term shifts.

Here's a summary of what changes are appropriate, and when to make them:

| Type of Asset Mix Change: | Tactical Asset Mix Call | Life Change | Long-term Economic Shift | Strategic Rebalancing |
|---|---|---|---|---|
| Timing: | 2–3 times each year at most | When it occurs | Every 2–3 years | Once each year |

Whereas the first change — tactical asset mix calls — should be directed by a professional money manager, the other changes should all be done in consultation with your financial advisor.

Adding value with tactical asset allocation is a big mistake for investors who (i) do not delegate it to seasoned professionals with proven track records of adding value; (ii) do it far too frequently; and (iii) make very large bets, instead of marginal ones that limit the room for error. Adding value with tactical calls is challenging at best, and potentially disastrous at worst. That's precisely why one well-known American academic who specializes in behavioural finance told me, "I don't allow changes in my asset allocations, and I don't buy lottery tickets either."

# Recap of Mistake #3: Overusing Tactical Asset Allocation

1. Most investors are tempted to adjust their asset mixes to ensure they are heavily invested in the markets they think will outperform. Market timing is just an extreme form of tactical asset allocation.

2. A *minority* of professional money managers are able to add value by changing asset mix, based on their predictions of different markets. But individual investors are almost certain to subtract value with tactical asset changes.

3. The temptation to move investments around is very strong. At work are the same psychological factors that underlie market timing, plus the added fear of regret, which investors experience if they are not following the consensus views of forecasters.

4. What is the probability of consistently adding returns to a portfolio by making adjustments to the mix throughout the year? Very low. What is the probability of maximizing returns by staying the course and not fiddling? Very high. Additionally, there is more downside than upside to tactical asset allocation, so investing probabilities do not favour it.

5. The best asset mix is one that is reasonably static, and consistent with your overall objectives and practical risk tolerance. Adjustments should be made for three reasons: to rebalance back to the original mix (annually); to accommodate changes in your circumstances (when they occur); and, less frequently, to accommodate larger economic shifts among worldwide economies (every couple of years).

6. If you have faith in a particular money manager's ability to add value with asset mix calls, limit them to at most two to three changes each year, and only marginal changes. The high probability of getting a call wrong, and the size of the potential downside, are reasons enough to limit tactical asset allocation activity in your portfolio.

# MISTAKE #4

## Overestimating
## Active Management

***Eye Opener:***
Q: *What percentage of Canadian equity fund managers beat the*
   *TSE 300 for the five-year period ending December 31, 1999?*
A: **Eighteen percent.**

Q: *How about US equity funds that beat the S&P 500 over the same*
   *time period?*
A: **Nine percent.**

Q: *Canadian bond managers beating the SCM Universe Bond Index?*
A: **Twenty-two percent.**

If you've read *The Power of Index Funds: Canada's Best-Kept Investment Secret*, this chapter will be a quick refresher on how to avoid an *overreliance* on active management by indexing part of your portfolio. There is an important role for active management in a portfolio, as you'll see, but active management is best used as a complement to a core holding of index product. This is because indexing is *the* best form of "performance insurance."

One of the most common ways to index is with index funds, which simply mirror the performance of the index they track. A Canadian index fund, for example, usually tracks the performance of the TSE 300. Because the index fund manager buys and holds the stocks in the index, indexing is often referred to as *passive* management; this is in comparison with *active* management, where the manager buys and sells whichever securities she thinks will outperform the index. If you aren't familiar with the arguments showing how indexing can be so powerful, then be prepared to reconsider some of your beliefs and assumptions about investing.

## The Problem

Most of the time, in most markets, most actively managed mutual funds underperform the index for their markets.

That's a fact that nobody can deny. Here's the proof:

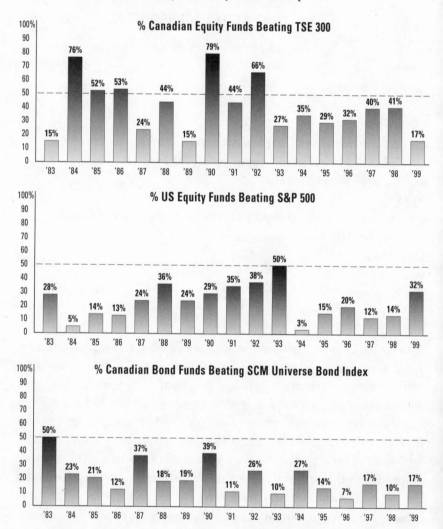

There are good reasons why the indexes outperform so many active managers. Index funds charge lower fees and have lower trading costs. And active managers are hard-pressed to beat the markets anyway, because they are competing with so many other managers, analysts, and investors around the world who are trying to do the exact same thing.

"So what?" you may think. "If I stick with the winning funds that *are* able to consistently beat the index, then my portfolio returns will be superior. Successful investors don't invest in the majority of funds that underperform the indexes. They invest in the minority of funds that beat the indexes."

## Picking the "Winning" Funds

Well, it's not quite that easy. The minority of funds that do beat the indexes are not the same from year to year. It's very difficult to predict exactly which funds will beat the market index in any given year. It's easy to pick out the funds that have done well in the past. Unfortunately, the previously winning funds are rarely the winners of the future. Life would be easier if there were funds that were consistent winners. But there are not.

That's another fact that nobody can deny. Here's the proof:

**Percentage of Canadian Equity Funds Remaining in 1st and 4th Quartiles**

| Comparing past ('90–'94) 5-year returns to subsequent ('95–'99) 5-year returns | |
| --- | --- |
| 1st-quartile funds that dropped to 3rd or 4th quartile: | 71% |
| 4th-quartile funds that rose to 1st or 2nd quartile: | 58% |

What this means is that the vast majority of "winners" over the five-year period — 71 percent of them — became "losers" in the following five years.

No less surprising is that the majority of "losers" — 58 percent — became "winners." I purposefully used five-year periods, since most people would say that a fund with a great five-year track record must be a winning fund. The numbers are remarkably consistent over different periods of time. The simple and undeniable fact is that there is very little performance consistency among funds.

In natural systems, there is a tendency toward equilibrium, so that extremes are smoothed out over time. This "balancing process" is one of the most powerful and pervasive phenomena in nature; statisticians refer to it as "reversion to the mean." Investment management expertise seems to follow the same principle. Over time, extreme performance — measured by unusual mutual fund returns — reverts to the industry average. Even brilliant managers with outstanding track records tend to generate performance that is closer to, and often lower than, the average returns of the market.

Look how hard it is for above-average funds to remain superior:

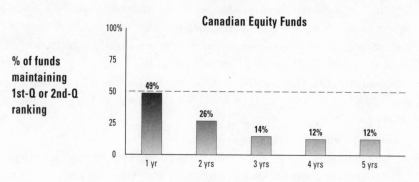

These charts track the percentage of funds, over the five years ending December 31, 1999, that were able to sustain above-average performance, year after year. For example, 49 percent of Canadian equity funds that were in the top half over one year (1994) managed to sustain top-half performance in the following year (1995). But that group drops to only 26 percent of the original top-half performers when the track record is stretched to two years (to 1996), and by the time you get to a four-year history, only 12 percent managed to stay "winners."

The US equity funds suffer from the same drop-off effect — "winners" just don't seem to be able to maintain their "winning streak":

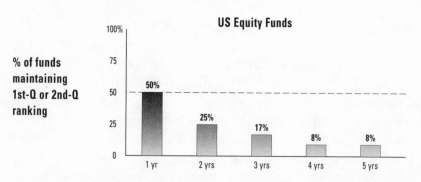

Over a five-year period, only 8 percent of the original top-half "winners" maintained their status.

I made it easy since all a fund had to do in this case was stay in the top half of its category. If I showed you what percent of Canadian equity funds were able to stay in the top quartile only (top 25 percent of their category), you might be surprised to discover that only 18 percent remained there in the subsequent year, only 5 percent remained in the subsequent two years, and none remained for four years running. US equity funds drop off even faster, to only one active fund with top-quartile performance in the subsequent year, and none in the top quartile in the following two years.

You may think that this phenomenon — of "winners" becoming "losers" and vice versa — is dependent upon the specific time periods I analyzed. But this is a consistent pattern no matter which time periods you assess. The majority of "winners" slip and most "losers" rise in just about every period you can think of.

Moral of the story? Looking at the past performance of a fund is not *in any way* a reliable indicator of its future performance.

Do you still think you can ferret out the winners? If you can, then presumably the gurus, who write the mutual fund books each year and spend their lives researching these things, would have the best shot at picking the winners.

In February 2000, the *Globe and Mail* published its annual mutual fund picks, made by a "blue-ribbon" panel of mutual fund gurus and analysts. Alongside their recommendations, the *Globe* published the results of their picks the previous year: Of the six experts, the best track record, achieved by only two of the experts, was 50 percent! If you followed the recommendations of these two, half of your funds would have done better than average, the other half of their picks would have done worse. The recommendations of three of the experts turned out to be 33 percent right — if you followed the advice of these three, one-third of your funds would have beaten the average. The other two-thirds were not just bad, but really bad — all of their recommended funds ended up being fourth-quartile performers. The sixth expert had one fund, of the six he recommended, that beat the average.

The results of this *Globe* survey are not surprising if you really appreciate the randomness of most mutual funds' returns — how often "winners" become "losers" and "losers" become "winners." Just as revealing as the track record of the experts is the complete lack of agreement between them. If "winners" were predictable to some extent, you'd expect that there'd be some agreement on which funds were winners, wouldn't you?

Have you lined up all the mutual fund recommendation books in a row and compared their recommendations? Here's what jumps out at you right away if you do: The experts don't agree. For example, there were seven "top mutual fund" books in 1998 which all purported to recommend the best funds for 1999. In the category of Canadian equity funds, there was only one fund that they agreed on — in fact they didn't unanimously choose this fund, but six of the seven did. The one and only one Canadian equity fund that six of the seven books agreed on was the Bissett Canadian Equity Fund. A great fund, run by great managers who are highly respected in the industry. The year following the publication of these books' recommendations, the Bissett fund generated a 7 percent return while the TSE 300 was up 32 percent and the average Canadian equity fund was up 20 percent.

*Among the seven fund experts, there were 40 top Canadian equity picks and only one fund made it to six of the seven lists. And it was a fourth-quartile performer in the year after it was recommended!*

To be fair, the Bissett fund may well produce future long-term returns that are above average. It was still on five of the books' recommended lists in the following year.

How about the 1999 crop of mutual fund recommendation books? That year there were six books published. In the Canadian equity category, only one fund was picked by five of the six books (Bissett once again . . . so keep an eye on it. I'll bet it doesn't show up much longer if reversion to the mean exerts its influence, as it can be counted on to do). A few funds were picked by three. In the bond category, only one fund was picked by five of the six books; one balanced fund was picked by five; and two US equity funds were picked by four experts.

*If you add up all the chosen Canadian equity funds, only one fund was picked by five of the six books. One other fund was chosen by four. That's not much of a consensus!*

If the experts don't agree on what makes a winning fund, how likely is it that anyone can predict which funds will win? Not that you need more evidence to convince you, but let's take a quick look at what happens to managers who win the "Fund Manager of the Year Award."

Every year the mutual fund industry convenes to celebrate a number of achievements and top the night off by acknowledging the "Manager of the Year" with an award. The winner in 1996 racked up a 50 percent return on his fund in the year that he won, with some brilliant picks of small companies and resource stocks. The year after winning — 1997 — his fund returned negative 9.4 percent, and the year after that — 1998 — he generated negative 33 percent (you read that right, I'm afraid). The manager was dropped by the company and a new manager appointed to the fund.

Let's go to the 1997 winner. His fund earned 43 percent in the year he won, loaded up as it was on financial services companies. It returned only 6 percent in 1998, but that still made it a first-quartile fund. But in 1999, the fund was one of the worst performers of all Canadian equity funds, returning negative 13.4 percent (you read that right again), which brought its track record since winning the award tumbling down to the fourth quartile.

On to 1998. The manager was celebrated for a 5.7 percent return when most managers had negative returns, and the TSE was down almost 2 percent. But that's because he happened to have a lot of cash in his fund (which is great if the market is down). But a lot of cash is exactly what you didn't want to have in 1999 when the TSE was up over 30 percent. His fund generated an embarrassing fourth-quartile return of 3 percent in 1999.

In 1999 the manager who won had turned around a large Canadian equity fund. As 2000 unfolded, the return of this fund was still top half. Maybe he'll break the uncanny streak of disappointment that former honorees racked up after winning. But I wouldn't count on it.

There are four important points to note:

1. *A majority of "winning" funds become "losers."*
2. *A majority of "losing" funds become "winners."*
3. *The experts don't have good track records at picking future "winners."*
4. *The experts don't agree on what the "winners" are.*

What's the problem here? Are "winners" even pickable?

## Skill Versus Luck

The problem with predicting winners is that it's very difficult to distinguish luck from skill. Winning funds are only winners if their performance is the result of skill. There's no point in investing in a fund that derives its performance record from nothing more than chance. If luck is all that lies behind the numbers, then the likelihood of the funds with good histories continuing to outperform is just 50 percent — same as tossing a coin.

If 1,000 people flip a coin 10 times, the odds are reasonable that at least one of the coin flippers will flip 10 heads in a row. Was that coin flipper skilled, or lucky? Obviously it was luck. But take 1,000 fund managers, and all of a sudden we start to overinterpret by assuming there's a lot of skill involved in beating the market 10 years in a row.

We can be even more specific. In a sample of 1,000 funds, how many funds would we expect to beat the market in eight years out of 10, just by chance? Statistics inform us that the answer is 4.4 percent — 44 funds. That is equivalent to the odds of getting eight heads in a 10-flip coin toss. The managers of those 44 funds *could* be skilled. But how do you know? It's an important question to ask before you invest your money. *If a fund outperformed in eight of the last 10 years on the basis of luck alone, then it has a 50-50 chance of repeating that success in the following year — not very enticing.* How do you differentiate skill from luck? If it were easy, there'd be more agreement among the experts on what the winning funds are, and their recommendations would have proven to be more useful than they have been.

There are a few mathematical ways to assess how many years of excellent performance it takes to be able to confidently say that a manager is skilled, and likely to outperform in the future. The greater the size of a manager's outperformance each year, the less time you need to identify skill; in other words, the detection of skill is a function of both the *amount* by which a manager beats the market, and *for how long* she does it.

There's one other consideration in analyzing a manager's skill, and that is the size of the sample you're comparing her with. If there are a lot of managers in a category, then there will be more "outliers," or managers that achieve superior performance just by chance, in the same way that in a large group of 1,000 coin tossers, you'd expect to witness more tossers flipping a run of many tails than you would in a smaller group. The size of the sample determines the certainty you'll require: In a very large group of managers, where there are more chances for lucky performance to appear, you'll need a 99 percent probability that outperformance is attributable to skill; in a smaller sample, a 95 percent probability is good enough.

So how can we quantify the two factors that indicate a high probability of skill — *the amount* by which, and *the duration* over which, the manager outperformed? If we're comparing a star manager's track record to the average of all similar funds, how do we capture what we need to see before we're confident that skill — not luck — was the driver of the outperformance? We do it by understanding the statistics:

Chance alone allows 2.3 percent of all Canadian equity managers (one in 44) to outperform the average annual return by 4.5 percent over a five-year period. For an even higher degree of certainty, chance alone allows 0.135 percent of all managers (one in 741) to beat the average by 4.5 percent over 11 years.

There are about 250 Canadian equity managers in Canada, so if our star manager beat the average by 4.5 percent over five years, there's a reasonable probability that she is skilled, since fewer than six managers (2.3 percent of 250) would be expected to achieve this feat by luck alone. Still, she might just be one of the lucky six whom we'd expect would beat the average by random chance. But if our star manager was able to pull off that track record for eleven years, then the probability is much higher that she is skilled, since chance would indicate that *fewer* than one person out of 250 would be expected to do that (0.135 percent of 250, or one in 741 managers). I'm not making this up, by the way. There is a mathematical formula that relates all these variables; if you're interested, it's in the upcoming math break.

This type of analysis reveals how few managers have track records that can really be considered demonstrative of skill — far fewer than most investors are inclined to think. The two skill-seeking requirements of outperformance — by how much, and for how long — are inversely related, so as one goes up, the other can go down. That means we can loosen the criteria for the required size of the outperformance, but only by extending the time period over which the manager must beat the average:

Where we would expect chance to allow 2.3 percent of managers to outperform by 4.5 percent over five years, the same number of Canadian equity managers would be expected to beat the average by only 2 percent over 25 years.

We can also analyze the requirements for skill by fixing the time period, and then determining by how much a manager must outperform:

If a manager has a seven-year track record, then we'll require her to outperform by 3.8 percent on average each year, since only 2.3 percent of managers would achieve this by luck alone. If we want to be even more sure — achieve a 99.7 percent probability of skill —

then we'll need outperformance of 5.7 percent over the seven years, which only 0.135 percent of managers would be expected to do by chance.

All we're doing is trying to eliminate luck as an explanation of good returns. Unfortunately, luck is not eliminated simply by choosing a fund whose return is much better than average, because chance will produce funds with great returns. We need to narrow the candidates down to the few funds that have a high probability of skill behind them. Only skill-driven performance is likely to persist in the future, and there are not many funds in Canada that demonstrate a high probability of skill, as this math break shows.

---

## MATH BREAK

Here's a little math that demonstrates how high a hurdle a manager must overcome before you can ascribe skill to him with confidence.

The trick is to know how many good performance records we'd expect from chance alone. A manager's performance might be stellar, but if the laws of chance suggest that it's not unexpected for some managers to have that track record, then we don't have convincing evidence of skill. How good does a manager's performance have to be to convince us? Say we're assessing a Canadian equity fund run by Mr. Skill-or-Luck (SorL for short). In a year where the average return of all Canadian equity funds is 10 percent, and the standard deviation of the returns is 12 percent, Mr. SorL's fund returned 35 percent, which suggests he really knows what he's doing, doesn't it? Let's see.

His fund's return of 35 percent is marginally better than two standard deviations from the average return of all managers (which is [12% x 2] + 10%). But we expect 2.3 percent of all the managers to have returns that are two standard deviations above the average, just by luck. This is true because two standard deviations represent 95.4 percent of all managers, which leaves the remainder, or 4.6 percent of managers, outside of that range. Half of the managers outside of two standard deviations will be above the average and the other half will be below the average. So we'd expect 2.3 percent of the 250 managers — or just under six — to beat the average by two standard deviations, just by chance alone. His impressive return of 35

---

percent could be as attributable to luck as it is to skill. That doesn't mean that he's *not* skilled; it means we can't be very confident that his numbers are generated from skill, since we can't discount luck as a reason for his return.

If the number of managers in the sample is large, then the criteria need to be more stringent, since more managers are likely to beat the average by higher amounts. In larger samples we require performance that is better than three standard deviations above average, since only one manager in 741 will pull this off by luck alone. If you want an even higher degree of confidence, you could insist on returns that are four standard deviations above the average — only one in about 30,000 managers could pull that off! But for smaller samples, two standard deviations above average is a good indicator, since one in 44 will achieve that by luck.

The equation that relates the *size* of the outperformance to its *duration* is straightforward: To demonstrate a high likelihood of skill in a large sample, we're looking for returns that are better than three standard deviations above the average. For any given number of years, the required outperformance (OP) simply equals three standard deviations (SD) divided by the square root of the number of years (YRS). So, OP = $[3 \times SD] \div \sqrt{YRS}$. For example, let's say Mr. SorL manages a fund with a five-year track record in a large category where the standard deviation of funds is 5 percent. A manager with a five-year track record, whose skill can be identified with some confidence, will need to beat the average return by at least 6.7 percent annually ($[3 \times 5\%] \div \sqrt{5}$).

Rather than starting with the number of years, we can start with the outperformance, and then determine how many years are required to demonstrate skill — we just rearrange the equation: YRS = $[3 \times SD]^2 \div OP^2$. So if Mr. SorL outperforms the average by 4 percent each year, then the number of years required for him to do this is 14: $[3 \times 5\%]^2 \div 4\%^2$.

Let's look at the Canadian mutual fund market so we can draw some reasonable conclusions about what kind of outperformance is needed to demonstrate skill. Only about 100 Canadian equity funds have five-year track records. The average five-year return is 14 percent, and the five-year standard deviation is 5 percent. Three standard deviations represent a return of 29 percent, which only one in 741 managers would beat by luck. Because our sample size is small, we could accept two standard deviations above the average — a return better than 24 percent. This hurdle is a reasonable indicator of potential skill since we'd expect only two managers to beat this by luck alone (2.3 percent of 100).

So how many managers generated returns that were better than two standard deviations above the average? Four — not a large selection of possibly skilled managers to choose from, especially when you consider that 54 funds generated returns that were better than the average of 14 percent. Many investors would consider the majority of the above-average performers as "winners," even though there are only four that exhibit the characteristics of potential skill. Since we'd expect two managers to meet the criteria just by chance, we need a second test of skill to narrow down the candidates further, so later in this chapter, we'll explore how to make a *qualitative* assessment of managers' skill, so we can further reduce the likelihood of chance being the driver of returns.

Remember — the purpose of this exercise is to differentiate luck from skill, because only skill gives us sufficient reason to think a manager can outperform in the future and is therefore a good candidate for managing our money. But even if we've uncovered a manager whose outperformance suggests skill, we can't be assured that the skill will persist. Great athletes have slumps. Great actors appear in bad movies. And the type of analysis I've shown here is not entirely foolproof because performance returns are rarely distributed normally, so a straightforward application of standard deviation isn't entirely reliable. However, the fact remains that most investors are too easily enamoured with high short-term returns, which rarely demonstrate any convincing evidence of skill. So in spite of the caveats, using a little math to differentiate luck from skill will give you superior odds in choosing managers who are likely to outperform in the future — much better odds than choosing a fund because it has a good write-up in the paper, or because it appears to have stellar (but not two standard deviation) returns. Just as important, the math goes a long way in demonstrating how difficult it is to confidently identify skill in a crowd of returns that might be just lucky.

## The Problem of Manager Style

If differentiating skill wasn't hard enough, there's another problem. The market simply may not favour a particular manager's type of skill over a lengthy period of time. For example, there are some brilliant value managers who specialize in buying stocks whose prices appear relatively low. But their funds performed miserably for the last years of the twentieth century because "value investing" was not a rewarding style to be in, while investing in growth stocks was extremely profitable.

Warren Buffett is a good example of this problem. You can say with a reasonable degree of confidence, but not certainty, that the celebrated stock picker is skilled. But his stock, Berkshire Hathaway, which trades on the New York Stock Exchange (BRK-NYSE), was down 50 percent in 1999 because his style was not in vogue. That's a hard pill to swallow when the US market was up over 20 percent in US dollars. That's why a lot of people in the investment industry are talking about "style diversification," a strategy whereby investors are encouraged to make sure that they are invested across a broad range of styles such as value, growth, momentum, and small companies. By picking the best managers in each style, and combining them in your portfolio, you are protected against any one style going out of favour. New "style-focused" funds have been created to capitalize on this trend; most of them have high all-in fees, or MERs, of around 2.50 percent or more.

It's true that different investment styles perform better at different times. In the decade of the 1990s, there were five years when value outperformed in the TSE 300 (1990, 1993, 1994, 1996, and 1997) and growth outperformed in the other five. But besides the higher fees involved with style-focused funds, there are two additional problems with the strategy of mixing styles.

First, most stocks are not purely value or purely growth. Managers use various tests to classify stocks into distinct styles, such as the ratio of a stock's price to the company's earnings. But the classification is difficult in markets such as Canada. Whereas two-thirds of US stocks can be classified as either growth or value, leaving only one-third of US stocks as a hybrid of both, only about 25 percent of Canadian stocks are purely growth or value, and 75 percent are a mix of both. But even in the US, the 1999 returns of three large-cap value indexes are completely unaligned, suggesting that there is no agreed-upon method of defining a style such as "value":

### US Large-Cap Indexes — 1999 Returns

S&P/Barra Value: 13%
Russell 1000 Value: 7%
R&T Large Value: −12%

The second problem is that the traditional styles of growth and value are not necessarily the best categories to use in differentiating stock characteristics for diversification purposes. A more consistent and effective way to classify stocks, current research suggests, is stock-price variability; in other words, stocks whose prices trade within a narrow range can be compared with stocks whose prices are more volatile.

There is an easy way to get around all of this confusion about style diversification: If you index your portfolio, you have exposure to all the stocks, no matter what style is in vogue. And you can do it for a small fraction of the fees.

Whether you combine specific style managers, or just shoot for the best overall managers, we've seen that "winners" rarely stay "winners," so it is very difficult to predict which ones *will* end up beating the index. So why don't people get this?

## The Behavioural Explanation

- *Illusion of Control*
- *Confirmation Bias*
- *Fear of and Feelings of Regret*
- *Innumeracy*

It's fundamentally contrary to human nature to want to relinquish control. In fact, our natural tendency is to live under what psychologists call an "illusion of control"; in other words, we perceive ourselves as having more control over the world than we really do. That's why we so often feel disappointment and intense frustration when we are subverted, when the world doesn't co-operate with our ambitions. This "illusion" is more pronounced in the Western hemisphere. In the Eastern world, especially where Buddhism is practised, the predominant belief is that we are ultimately not separate from the world at all. Suffering is only a result of living as if we are agents, acting in and against an external world, instead of seeing ourselves as part of, and the same as, the world we live in.

Spiritual enlightenment aside, the "illusion of control" permeates many aspects of our lives, including the realm of investing. We saw a good example in Mistake #2 when we examined how we tend to overinterpret random events such as short-term market moves. We read more meaning into randomness than really exists, because that gives us increased control (we think) over understanding and acting on such random things as market moves. Active management is based in part on our need to have control. It's comforting to invest your money knowing that someone somewhere is watching over it for you, picking the best stocks and bonds, and raising cash when the markets become choppy to protect your money.

Anyway, choosing winners — whether stocks or funds — is fun. Why would you want to own an index fund, when you could own a fund that generated 156 percent last year? Our illusion of control tends to feed the thinking that we have unique skills in picking funds or stocks and this overconfidence is nurtured with a little "confirmation bias." For instance, when asked, the vast majority of people — usually around 75 percent — consider themselves above-average drivers. Since only half can be truly above average, at least 25 percent of them are overestimating their own abilities. Same with stock and fund pickers. There are a lot of investors who consider themselves shrewd stock or fund pickers, but also take the blame for low returns as well, rather than attributing their returns to the luck of being in a bull or bear market, or the luck of being in the right fund at the right time. That's why trading volume has been shown to be very high in bull markets and substantially lower after market corrections. Overconfident investors overtrade in good markets because they feel empowered by their success. The reverse occurs in bad markets, when investors often feel that they've lost their touch. You can see the "confirmation bias" at work here — investors seek out confirming evidence that supports their view that their returns are largely determined by their own skills in choosing investments.

On the flip side, but having an equal psychological impact, is the stress of watching high-flying sector funds generate returns that make the index returns look miserable. We are susceptible to feeling intense regret over what we could have earned, when we see ads in the paper for funds with fancy names like "biotech–super octane–global discovery fund" and 156 percent returns last year. Many investors make decisions in order to avoid the potential feelings of regret they might suffer if they don't have some of the current hot funds in their portfolio. Or, even worse, they may dump their current holdings so they can invest in last year's stars because they are feeling intense regret at having already missed out.

It gets worse. On top of our "need to take control" personalities, our "I can pick winners" overconfidence, and our "got to avoid regret" tendencies, we are vulnerable to innumeracy. Most people simply aren't aware of just how random the returns of most mutual funds are and how difficult it is to distinguish a lucky manager from a skilled one. When we explored market timing in Mistake #2, we saw that we tend to struggle with probabilities. The randomness of multiple coin tosses makes predicting the odds of 10 heads in a row very difficult for most people. The same lack of intuition about randomness makes it difficult for many investors to appreciate how many managers with great track records have just been randomly lucky. And because math is not intuitive for most of us, we tend to give too much credit to numbers — ascribing a power or authority to them that they often don't deserve. It's intellectually tempting to take a great track record at its face value, rather than try to understand the intricacies of randomness, standard deviations, etc. But distinguishing lucky numbers from skilled numbers is absolutely crucial: Luck doesn't repeat itself in the future nearly as reliably as skill does.

## The Solution

### Is There a Place for Active Management?

Yes, there is a role for active management. Active funds that are run by truly skilled managers earn their higher fees.

If an active manager is going to beat the index of the market she is investing in, she is going to have to

- rely on information that is not commonly known by every other investor, which would otherwise already be reflected in the price of the security;
- rely on synthesizing all available information in a unique and creative way that allows her to generate conclusions about a security that are not commonly shared and therefore not already reflected in its price; or
- be lucky.

Obviously, only the first two methods give her the ability to consistently beat the index. The possibility of securing less readily known information, or having new uncommon insights, is higher in some markets than in others. The value of active management therefore proves itself in markets that are less scrutinized by other investors seeking out unique information:

- Southeast Asian markets such as Singapore, South Korea, Malaysia, and Taiwan;
- emerging or developing markets such as Latin America and Eastern Europe;
- the markets of small-capitalization stocks — smaller company stocks in Canada, the US, and Europe.

These markets are not subject to the same degree of examination by analysts and institutional and retail investors. It's easier for a fund manager to uncover new information about a lesser-known company than it is to have unique knowledge about Microsoft, Nortel, or British Airways.

Active management is also useful in market sectors that are either difficult to index, or where it's easier for skilled managers to gain special knowledge. Sectors such as technology, health care, and natural resources are good examples where active managers can play an important role. Having said that, I'll quickly add that it's perfectly legitimate to avoid sector investments altogether in favour of investing in broad geographic market indexes.

## How Do You Find Skilled Active Managers?

So how do you find a skilled active manager who's not just lucky? The numbers are a good place to start. There are two quantitative assessments to make: returns and risk. You need to assess the performance of a manager over a number of different time periods. You also need to confirm that the manager did not take excessive risk to get high performance. High risk can easily turn a star into a dog. Taking risk into account is no simple feat. As we've already seen, there are many ways to define risk. Perhaps the greatest value offered by some of the annual mutual fund books is their comprehensive analysis of each fund's risk. The good books assess funds using a number of criteria such as the number of years the fund underperformed a GIC, and the number of years the fund had a negative return. If a fund manager generates returns far above the index, but takes on a lot of extra risk to do it, then that does not necessarily represent skill. But if she generates superior returns with the same or less risk than the market, then there was some value added in the process. Since adjusting for risk is not a cut-and-dried formula, however, it's not easy to measure the value added by a manager.

## MATH BREAK

A common term used in the investment industry to assess the value added by a manager is the "information ratio," or the manager's average excess returns above the index divided by the degree to which his excess returns deviate from the index most of the time. It's called the "information ratio" because it is intended to measure the quality of the manager's information — is it really good, in the sense that it helps the manager beat the index? In order to properly assess the quality of the manager's information, we need to compare his outperformance in a given year with the extent to which his outperformance varies from year to year. If he outperforms by 2 percent each year *on average*, but his performance ranges from beating the index by 5 percent one year to underperforming it by 10 percent the next year, and then outperforming by 20 percent the next, the quality of his information is suspect.

Let's say a manager beats the index by 2 percent each year on average. And 68 percent of the time (i.e., one standard deviation), his excess return deviates from the index returns by about 1.5 percent. The information ratio of the manager is 2 percent divided by 1.5 percent, or 1.3.

Generally, an information ratio of 0.5 is considered good, 0.75 is very good, and 1.0 is exceptional. Only 10 percent of all information ratios are above 1. So you can see that the example I used demonstrates a manager with an exceptional information ratio.

I will outline specific ways to compare a fund's return with a suitable benchmark in the "Solutions" section of Mistake #7, which specifically addresses the issue of effective benchmarking. Comparing a fund's performance and risk against the wrong benchmark is a common and very costly error, which I cover in that chapter.

But the point here is that an investor must not rely exclusively on past performance. Even Morningstar — the biggest fund ranking company in the world, which started a Canadian operation in 2000 — is careful to point out that their star rating system is purely quantitative and as such does not reflect an opinion of the future potential of any fund. They go out of their way in their marketing materials to point out that their assessments give a quick summary only of how a fund has performed *historically*, not how it's expected to perform *in the future*.

We've seen that in general, the longer the time period, the more reliable the performance numbers become. But do you have to wait for a manager to rack up 20 years of performance before you have confidence in her ability? The good news is that you do not. You can increase your confidence in a manager's skill over shorter time periods by going beyond the numbers. You need to confirm that there are sound reasons for thinking that the short-term numbers are meaningful. For example, if you are watching a blackjack player and she wins five hands in a row, you really don't know if she's lucky or is employing a sound methodology. You wouldn't be sure if she was a truly skilled blackjack player. If you ask her how she won so many hands, and she mumbles something inaudible about instinct and picking the right table, you are probably going to conclude she was lucky. If, however, she impresses you with a detailed explanation of the basic blackjack strategy that she's been using for a number of years, then there's probably some skill involved.

Blackjack is a good analogy for investment management because in blackjack, luck dominates for most people, giving the casino the edge. But there is a small minority of players who are skilled card counters, able to significantly increase their odds of beating the casino — just as there is a minority of skilled managers who can consistently beat the index.

A skilled manager should be able to articulate a specific strategy for picking securities. And he should be able to demonstrate that he has used this strategy consistently over a period of time, with great results. The four most common stock-picking strategies are these:

- *Value* — buying stocks that are priced below their calculated intrinsic value;
- *Growth* — buying stocks of companies that are poised for significant growth;
- *Momentum* — buying stocks of companies whose sales, earnings, and stock price are increasing faster than the rest of the market, and usually faster than expected;
- *Combination* — two or three of these strategies combined, such as growth at a reasonable price, or "GARP," as it's called.

Look for a great performance track record over a minimum of five years, but preferably over 10 years, and preferably by the same individual. A change in managers on a fund is also an important event; it usually obviates all previous performance records, since the historical numbers are no longer related to the new manager, unless he is part of a team that employs a consistent strategy. A good track record alone suggests the *possibility* of skill — it means the manager has passed the first test and is at least eligible to be considered skilled. But what you need is a high *probability* of skill. If a good track record is underpinned by a well-articulated strategy that has been used consistently for a number of years, then the *probability* of skill, while never 100 percent, is that much higher. The *qualitative* test for skill complements the *quantitative* test by determining if there's substance behind the numbers — a disciplined and rigorous approach to picking securities.

Here's a summary of the two approaches to ferreting out skill. We want to have high confidence — 95 percent — that the track record of a manager we're thinking of investing with was generated by skill, not luck. Only skill has a better-than-even chance of repeating itself in the future. Let's assume the average fund and the market both generated a return of 10 percent over a 10-year period, with an average volatility of 6 percent over that time. We are assessing a fund that has beat the market and average fund by 3 percent on average each year.

**10-year track record of outperforming the market by 3 percent each year**

↓

**How do we know if manager is skilled or lucky?**

↓                    ↓

**Wait another six years**        **Assess coherence of manager's strategy**

You don't need to worry about how I got six years. I used the same methodology I explained in the math break earlier in the chapter. We need 16 years to indicate a 95 percent chance that the manager is skilled, so we need another six on top of the 10 we've already got.

You have your pick of ways to get to a high enough confidence level that the manager is likely to continue outperforming. Three percent outperformance in a market with 6 percent volatility must persist for 16 years before we can reasonably say the manager is skilled. That's because only one in 44 managers would be capable of doing that by chance alone. If you want to be more certain — 99.7 percent certain — then you'll need a track record of 36 years, which only one in 741 managers would be expected to generate from chance alone.

The solution to overestimating active management expertise lies in being aware of how few truly skilled active managers there are, and how difficult it is to distinguish them from the lucky ones. Even the skilled ones will have difficulty consistently beating the market over extended periods of time, which is why there is such a strong argument for indexing the core holding of your portfolio, and using active management selectively to add to the core.

## Indexing
Why index?

1. *Recognition that the inherent unpredictability of the markets makes it very difficult for all but the most skilled managers to beat the indexes.*
2. *Appreciation of just how difficult it is to distinguish these few skilled managers from the others. Only the skilled ones have a shot at persistent outperformance.*
3. *Acknowledgement of how well the indexes do against most active managers in most markets, over most time periods.*

There are fundamental reasons why index products have done so well, as you saw at the beginning of this chapter. The fees on indexed products — the MERs — are much lower than those on actively managed products, so that puts the active managers at a disadvantage — often a 2 to 3 percent disadvantage. The active manager has to make up the difference in fees even before she has a shot at beating the index. On top of the fee difference, there is the cost of buying and selling securities, which is much higher for the active manager because she does a lot more trading; the index manager simply buys and holds the securities that are in the index with a minimal amount of trading. This can add up to a difference in extra costs of over one percent each year. Then you add in the costs of paying more frequent capital gains tax on active funds because of the extra trading, as well as what's called cash drag, which is how much holding cash in active funds drags down its performance. You add it all up and the difference in all-in costs between active funds and index products is typically 4 percent, often more. Four percent is a hefty disadvantage for an active manager to have to overcome to compete with an index product, *each and every year*. It's not impossible. But it's not easy. It takes a good manager — one with a high "information ratio," to compete with the index.

It's worth noting that many academics consider stock markets to be "inefficient" to an extent, meaning that stock prices do not always exactly reflect their fair values. We've already explored how prices can deviate from their rational values over a period of time because investors' emotions can exaggerate market movements in the short term. But this "inefficiency" does not mean that a shrewd active manager can easily beat the index, which is a common misconception. It is the fundamental unpredictability of the markets — their random, chaotic, and often "inefficient" movements — that makes beating the index so challenging, precisely because you can't reliably predict when and how prices will deviate from their rational values, and when they will return to them.

You can index either with index funds, or with exchange-traded funds (also known as index participation units). Index funds can be purchased from most Canadian banks, whereas the ETFs, as they're called, can be bought through a broker or discount broker, and they cover the Canadian, American, and some international markets. The funds have no buy or sell commissions, which the ETFs do. But the ETFs have lower annual fees. I tend to favour index funds in most cases, even though the fees are slightly higher — between 0.1 percent and 0.8 percent higher in most cases. For instance, SPDRs, which track the S&P 500, have MERs of just 0.12 percent, compared with 0.9 percent for the average US index fund. But with the funds, you don't have to pay commissions and your dividends are reinvested automatically for you (whereas with the ETFs, you have to accumulate the cash dividends and then pay more commissions to buy more ETFs). With the funds you don't have some of your capital returned to you (whereas the ETFs do this every year when large institutional accounts exchange their units for actual shares; this usually generates a capital distribution to unitholders). And, most important, the funds track broader market indexes, which is the whole point of passive management. Canadian index funds typically track the TSE 300, which covers about 97 percent of the Canadian market, whereas the i60s tracks 60 stocks covering about 70 percent. You can get a US index fund that tracks the Wilshire 5000 — the broadest US index covering 99 percent of the US market. But SPDRs cover only about 70 percent. Diamonds, which track the 30 stocks of the Dow Jones Industrial Average, cover only about 25 percent, and QQQs, which track the Nasdaq 100 index, cover close to 40 percent. If you're going to index, why would you want to own only part of the market, instead of the whole market? What if the part you're missing does the best? This was exactly the case in 1999, when the S&P 500 had less technology exposure than the Wilshire and underperformed it by 3 percent.

## How Much to Index?

Active management is best used as a complement to your indexed holdings, when you have confidence in a manager's ability to use specific strategies to beat the market. Here's a suggestion for how you might want to consider combining indexing with active management. I'm showing the range of each asset class within which you would index. For example, it makes sense to index between 50 and 100 percent of Canadian stocks.

| Market | Index Range |
|--------|-------------|
| Bonds | 80–100% |
| Canadian Stocks | 50–100% |
| US Stocks | 80–100% |
| European Stocks | 80–100% |
| Japanese Stocks | 50–100% |
| Asian Stocks | 0–100% |
| Emerging Markets Stocks | 0–100% |
| Specialty Sector Stocks | 0–100% |

There's nothing wrong with indexing all parts of your portfolio where you can. This is the better approach if you don't have a lot of confidence in finding a skilled active manager. But if you do complement a core holding in indexed product with active management, you have to pick a skilled active manager. This is not easy since most investors don't have the opportunity to personally interview fund managers and ask them about their strategies. Therefore, a good investment advisor is necessary to help you choose an active fund that has a high probability of skill behind its performance. Just like in *The Wizard of Oz*, you have to pull back the curtain to see if there's anything of substance behind what might initially appear as very impressive numbers. The annual crop of mutual fund books can play a role as well, not so much for their recommendations, but for the information they offer on the major funds.

The beauty of indexing is that it protects you against severe underperformance in any market. That's why I refer to it as "performance insurance": It protects you against underperforming the market. You might not have the best fund in each asset class, but you'll almost certainly never have the worst. And over time, you're likely to have first-quartile performance with much greater consistency than if you constantly chase after last year's winning funds.

# Recap of Mistake #4: Overestimating Active Management

1. Asset allocation contributes significantly to a portfolio's ultimate return; however, the right asset mix, with the wrong securities, can easily lead to sub-par returns.

2. But the problem with security selection is that it's not easy — not for individual investors, and not for professional money managers. Even if the market is not perfectly efficient in the short term, it's still unpredictable. In fact, it is precisely its irrational randomness that makes beating the index such a challenge; there are too many short-term surprises to make it easy to outsmart the market.

3. As if picking stocks wasn't hard enough, picking fund managers that are skilled in picking stocks is no easier! Winning funds rarely stay winners. And many losing funds become winners.

4. Multiply the two low probabilities together — how hard it is for stock pickers to "outpick" and how hard it is to pick skilled stock pickers — and you can see how much trouble investors get into if they overrely on active management.

5. Investors overestimate active management, because of a natural tendency to harbour the "illusion of control"; a fear of regret about having not invested in the "winners"; and a failure to see randomness in the track records of fund managers.

6. There's only one way to protect against severe underperformance from poor security selection. That's to index the core part of your portfolio while using active management to complement the core. The extent to which you use active management depends on the particular market and the confidence you have that the manager is truly skilled.

7. Indexing is performance insurance — it protects you from under-performing the market. Even better than that, the odds of actually generating top-quartile performance with an index strategy are quite high.

# MISTAKE #5

## Succumbing to Home Bias

*Eye Opener:*

Q: *Which are there more of — words starting with the letter "k," such as "kite" or "kitten," or words whose third letter is "k"?*

A: ***There are about three times as many words where "k" is the third letter, as in "cake." Almost everyone gets this wrong, because it's easier to think of words that start with "k": The availability of these words biases us in favour of the wrong answer.***

There is a sentiment shared by investors all over the world: There's no place like home. Swiss investors have about 60 percent of their equity investments in Swiss stocks, despite the Swiss stock market making up less than 3 percent of the value of all the world's stocks. Crazy, eh? Look in the mirror — Canadian stocks make up even less than Swiss stocks!

American investors overweight their portfolios in US stocks. It's not such a big problem for our neighbours to the south because the US market is so large anyway — it represents over half of all the stocks in the world. But home bias is not as easily justified in Switzerland, where the stock market represents only 2.6 percent of all world stocks. Nor is it justified in Canada, where the stock market is just as small.

# The Problem

This is one of the simplest and most common mistakes — the tendency for Canadians to overweight their portfolios in Canadian stocks.

Here's a breakdown of what the average Canadian investor holds in stocks:

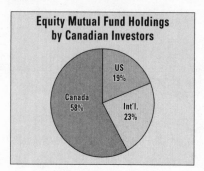

We're overinvested in the stocks of our own country, just like everyone else in the world. Here are the figures for the average US investor:

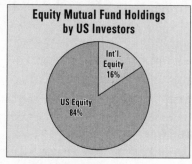

So what exactly is the problem? When you look at the long-term returns of the Canadian, US, and European markets in local currency (meaning what local investors would earn in their own currency), you can see that Americans and Europeans — who invest more heavily in their own countries — are getting richer than we are!

|  | 5-Year Return | 10-Year Return |
|---|---|---|
|  | Ending December 31, 1999 | |
| TSE 300 | 13% | 9% |
| S&P 500 | 28% | 18% |
| MSCI Europe | 26% | 16% |

As any mutual fund investor knows from being told over and over again, past performance is not necessarily indicative of future performance. In fact, the Canadian market enjoyed stellar gains in 1999 and into 2000. Maybe our market could end up being the best performer of all world markets in the future. That's possible, but unlikely. As you might imagine, many incredible investment opportunities lie beyond our borders. The Canadian market has only been among the top 10 performing country stock markets in three of the past 15 years.

More revealing than the actual stock market performance is the underlying structure of our economy; I want to reveal some of its more

surprising elements, then show you some equally enlightening characteristics of our stock market. I've chosen to compare both our economy and
stock market to those of the US, because of the size and diversity of our
American counterparts.

## Our Economy

The US economic engine is a good benchmark against which to compare
our own economy, especially since foreign investors are drawn to invest
in the US more than in any other country.

An economy is measured by Gross Domestic Product (GDP), which is
simply the market value of goods and services produced by a country. The
first thing to note is that our GDP is much smaller than that of the US —
about one-tenth the size. Our economy represents barely 2 percent of
worldwide economic production, whereas the US economy makes up
almost 30 percent. Not only is our economy that much smaller, but we're
much more dependent on exports, which means we're more reliant on
the economic health of other countries that import what we produce.
About 40 percent of our economy is export-based, compared to only 11
percent of the US economy. The combined economies in continental
Europe have exports that average about 14 percent of GDP. Japan has
about 10 percent, and the United Kingdom has about 19 percent.

Unlike the US, which has been successful in diversifying its export
business across the world, we're heavily dependent on the health of one
foreign economy in particular. Eighty-five percent of our exports go to
one place — the US market — while US exports are sent to many countries all over the world, none of which buys more than 25 percent of all
US exports on its own.

Not only is our smaller, export-dependent economy more reliant on
only one country — the US — for importing what we produce, but our
export business itself is focused on one particular industry — resources.
About 30 percent of our exports are commodity-based. By comparison,
only 15 percent of the US export business is commodity-based. Here's a
summary of the differences:

**Two Economies Compared**

|  | Canada | US |
| --- | --- | --- |
| **GDP** | $0.9 trillion | $9 trillion |
| **Percent of GDP that is export-driven** | 40% | 11% |
| **Export destinations** | 85% → US | 24% → Asia<br>23% → Canada<br>21% → Europe<br>16% → Latin America |
| **Percent commodity-based exports** | 30% | 15% |

Even though most of our exports go to the US, a good portion of our economy is driven by the strength of commodity prices, which are largely determined by Asian economic growth. Japan and the rest of Asia consume 35 percent of global commodities such as copper, iron ore, and oil. So when the Asian economies are not growing, the demand and therefore price of commodities is stagnant, and Canadian resource exporters don't make much money.

## Our Stock Market

Let's take a look at the stock markets that are based on these two different economies. We'll compare the TSE 300 with the S&P 500 since they are the two most commonly quoted stock indexes for each country. You can see how much more resource-dependent the TSE 300 is compared with the S&P 500.

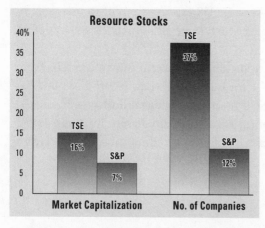

In many respects, our economy and our stock market are more geared toward mature and cyclical industries, whereas the US economy and stock market are geared toward high-growth, high-technology businesses. Make no mistake — we have our fair share of successful high-growth companies in Canada. But in comparison, we're more "trees and rocks" than most countries, and our industrial sector is less heavily weighted in the "businesses of tomorrow."

Sticking with the comparison of stock markets, the TSE 300 is dominated, to a far greater extent than the S&P 500, by only five companies.

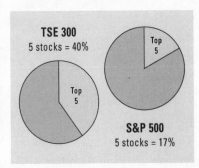

**TSE 300**
5 stocks = 40%

**S&P 500**
5 stocks = 17%

Five companies make up over 40 percent of the Canadian stock market. At the same time, five companies make up only 17 percent of the US market. While these weights change daily, it's clear that the rise and fall of our stock market is much more dependent on the success or failure of just a handful of companies. This was never more obvious than in 1999. The TSE 300 rose 32 percent, but that was because the two biggest stocks — Nortel and BCE — rose 281% and 129% respectively, while the rest of the index (nicknamed the TSE 298) rose only 9%. If you wanted to do well investing in Canada in 1999, you better have owned Nortel! Nortel currently makes up over one-third of the TSE 300; the US market is clearly more diversified.

The broader diversification of the US equity market is not surprising when you consider its size compared with the Canadian market.

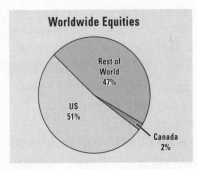

**Worldwide Equities**

Rest of World 47%

US 51%

Canada 2%

The market capitalization of Canadian stocks represents about 2 percent of the capitalization of roughly 35,000 stocks available in the world (2.3 percent to be exact). The US represents just over 50 percent. It's not just that our stock market is small in size; the stocks within our market are also small. Some analysts have commented that the Canadian market behaves more like a small-company stock market: the average market capitalization of a stock in Canada is under $2 billion (US), while it's around $25 billion for the average US stock. In fact, the small-cap index in the US — the Russell 2000 — has stocks whose average market caps are close to $3 billion, so you can see why those analysts liken Canada to a small-cap market.

So from a bird's-eye perspective, looking at the whole world of investing opportunities, the size and structure of our economy, and the size and structure of our stock market, why would anyone want to invest most of their money in the Canadian market?

## The Behavioural Explanation

- *Framing*
- *Availability Bias*
- *Lack of Knowledge*
- *Ambiguity Aversion*
- *Endowment Effect*

It's perfectly natural for us to invest heavily in Canada. After all, we live here, we read Canadian newspapers, listen to Canadian radio, and we're immersed in Canadian politics and culture. We are more familiar with Canadian companies since we hear about them in the news. For these reasons, we tend to see Canada as much bigger and more prominent, relative to the rest of the world, than it really is. This distortion is an issue of "framing," to an extent; we make our investment decisions within the frame of our experiences, which are largely immersed in the Canadian ethos.

"Availability bias" is also at work, since there is so much Canadian information available that the significance of our country is exaggerated in our minds. Foreign markets can seem mysterious to us, because of how "unavailable" they are. Our aversion to ambiguity feeds our tendency to oversimplify our perceptions of foreign countries that we haven't visited and don't know much about. There is certainly an endowment effect, which disinclines us to sell the Canadian investments we already have. And you could even argue that there's a degree of endowment effect operating in the sense that we "own" our country and are reluctant to be disloyal by investing more heavily in other countries.

Although it's natural for investors to favour domestic stocks, it's not logical. Don't forget the hallmark of a properly diversified portfolio: securities with contrasting characteristics that, when combined, reduce the overall volatility of the portfolio. Many investors simply don't know or understand that foreign investment opportunities can improve returns and portfolio diversification. They are unaware of certain facts:

- There are many foreign companies with distinct expertise that cannot be found in Canada. They are companies that are uniquely positioned in the global arena to benefit from emerging trends.
- There are countries at different stages of economic development than Canada, such as Latin America and Asia.
- There are countries that may be at similar stages of development, but

whose economies are at different stages of the economic cycle. When we are in recession, Europe may be thriving.

## The Solution

Here's a better approach:

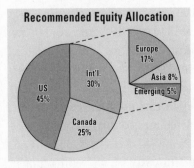

**Recommended Equity Allocation**

US 45%
Int'l. 30%
Canada 25%
Europe 17%
Asia 8%
Emerging 5%

This particular solution may not be perfectly suited to your individual circumstances and objectives. But it represents an important departure from the average Canadian's portfolio. In general terms, the solution to home bias lies in holding fewer Canadian than foreign stocks in the equity part of your portfolio.

Past returns have demonstrated that Canada has rarely been the top-performing market, but that's not the only reason to limit your Canadian holdings. After all, I would be the first to agree that you can't make big investment decisions based exclusively on past performance numbers. A more compelling reason to reduce your Canadian holdings is simply diversification. The likelihood of losing money over any period of time is dramatically reduced if you are diversified by combining Canadian and foreign stocks, since the timing of the ups and downs of the Canadian market will usually be very different from the timing of the ups and downs of the US, Japanese, or European markets.

The only time country stock markets tend to move closely together, thereby reducing the diversification benefit, is when global shocks affect all markets. The oil shortage of the early 1970s is an example of a time where market correlations increased between countries. Same with the 1987 stock market crash, the 1990 Gulf War, and the 1998 Asian markets crisis. For example, although correlations between international markets are normally about 50 percent (meaning that they track each other about half the time), the correlations between countries rose to 90 percent during the 1987 market crash — most markets around the world went down together. But shocks have been short-lived, and over time, different country economies and stock markets tend not to move in sync. It is more typical for one region — Europe for example — to be in recession while another, say North America, is booming, and yet another, say Asia, is just recovering.

## But Isn't Globalization Reducing the Diversification Benefit?

While no one can dispute that global economies are integrating, we're still a very long way from losing the diversification benefit of investing in different countries. Some industries are more similar across all countries; financial and consumer goods companies, for example, have been determined to be the most integrated of all global sectors. Stocks of these companies tend to be at least as influenced by how their sector is doing globally as they are by the country they are located in. Some academics have argued that a portfolio should be structured along industry sector, rather than national, lines; but the fact remains that the country effect on most stocks' returns is still larger than the industry effect, with a few exceptions. While industry-related factors can explain, on average, about 40 percent of a stock's returns, country-related and company-specific factors explain the larger portion.

There is no reason to think that the "industry effect" will replace the "country effect" too quickly. Just look at Europe: First there was the Maastricht Treaty of 1992, which introduced the harmonization of fiscal and monetary policies and culminated in the introduction of the euro. Not only does continental Europe now share a common currency, but there are virtually no trade barriers between the countries in Euroland. Still, the German market was up 51 percent in 1999, while the French market was up 39 percent. Country effects still have an enormous influence on the stocks of local markets, because different markets reflect different organizational structures and industry specializations, and each economy seems to respond to economic shocks in different ways.

So although at some point national economies may become so integrated that industry effects will become more important, for the time being asset classes are best thought of along country lines. Having said that, the weight of industries in your portfolio should not be completely ignored in the asset mix decision. If you are employing a predominantly indexed strategy, you will already have a reasonably diversified mix of industries, by virtue of diversifying by country. In fact, Morgan Stanley Capital International, which is the world's largest player in the construction of international equity indexes, ensures that each of their country indexes represents 60 percent of each industry within the country. So you're getting automatic industry diversification with most international index products. (Yet another reason to consider indexing the core part of your portfolio.)

There's only one obstacle to the recommendation to hold more foreign stocks than Canadian: the foreign content constraint in registered accounts. How do you hold a majority of foreign stocks in your RRSP or RRIF when the government only allows a maximum of 30 percent?

## How to Overcome Foreign Content Restrictions

There are two alternatives: clone funds and derivative-based index funds. They're both designed to give you full exposure to foreign markets, while not using up your foreign content limit. They do this by investing in Canadian-dollar T-bills, and entering into futures or forward contracts that replicate the returns of foreign stocks. Even though they sound a little complicated, they're perfectly safe and a very popular way of increasing foreign exposure in your registered account.

Clone funds track their active fund equivalents — meaning that many fund companies offer fully RRSP-eligible versions of their active foreign funds. This is different from an index fund, which simply tracks a foreign index. Both types of RRSP-eligible funds generate returns similar to what they are tracking: the underlying active fund (in the case of the clone) or the index (in the case of the index fund).

Which is better? Generally the index funds. They have much lower ongoing fees and tend to do quite well against active managers. Fees for index RSP funds range from 0.3 to one percent, while most clone funds have MERs that are about 2.1 percent plus a less conspicuous fee of 0.3 percent for the forward contract used to replicate the underlying fund, for a total cost close to 2.5 percent or higher. But in some markets and sectors where active funds have proven to be successful, the clone funds can be quite effective, especially where no index funds are available. For instance, emerging markets RSP clone funds are very useful, as are specialty sector funds such as global technology RSP clone funds.

If you understand the benefit of international diversification, you may well ask why I'd even suggest something as high as 25 percent in Canadian stocks, if Canada only represents 2 percent of all the stocks in the world. The answer is that we want to limit currency risk — the risk that the Canadian dollar appreciates against foreign currencies such as the US dollar, euro, and Japanese Yen.

## What Is Foreign Currency Risk and Does It Really Matter?

Most of us will spend much of our lives, including retirement, in Canada, so we have Canadian-dollar purchases ahead of us. For this reason, we don't want to be exposed to excessive currency risk — the chance that the Canadian dollar will increase in value against foreign currencies and cause our investments to fall in value. If you are invested in a European equity fund, then the manager of the fund has taken your Canadian dollars and converted them to euros in order to buy European stocks for the fund. But if the Canadian dollar rises in value while your money is invested, then your euro investments will fall in value, when converted back to Canadian dollars: The euros are worth less than when they were purchased.

Here's an easy way to look at it: When you buy a European fund, you're essentially buying two things — European stocks and the European currency. If the euro falls in value against the Canadian dollar, then your investment has lost value in the same way that falling European stocks will reduce your investment. The currency can easily offset some of the stock gains: The stocks in your European equity fund may have increased by 10 percent, but if the euro fell by 4 percent against the Canadian dollar, your investment will have increased by only 6 percent. This is opposite to what a lot of people intuitively think, since a rising Canadian dollar sounds like a good thing, but it's not when you're invested in foreign stocks denominated in foreign currencies. Of course exchange rate risk can work in your favour: If the Canadian dollar falls in value by 4 percent, your European equity fund will have returned 14 percent — 10 percent in stock appreciation, and 4 percent in euro currency appreciation.

If all of our investments were in Canadian stocks, and none in foreign stocks, currency risk wouldn't be an issue. But because it is prudent for us to invest aggressively outside Canada, we have this residual risk to deal with. Does it really matter? Yes, it does matter. But not that much in the long run. The best way to manage foreign currency risk is to overweight Canadian equities, relative to what you would hold in Canadian stocks if you weren't a Canadian; hence the 25 percent Canadian stock recommendation.

When you invest in foreign securities, you have two elements at work, and ideally they both go up — the security itself, and the currency in which the security is denominated. In 1998 that's exactly how it worked for Canadian investors. But in 1999 the opposite occurred.

Let's look at the impact of exchange rate from a Canadian perspective in 1998 and 1999 — two very different years for the Canadian dollar. We'll look at the US stock market returns, as well as the stock markets of Britain (FTSE 100) and Japan (Nikkei 225). By "local market," I mean the market in which the stock exchange resides, so S&P 500 local market returns are what a US resident would earn (i.e., US-dollar returns).

| | 1998 | | 1999 | |
|---|---|---|---|---|
| | Local Market Return | Canadian-Dollar Return | Local Market Return | Canadian-Dollar Return |
| **S&P 500** | 28% | 38% | 21% | 14% |
| **FTSE 100** | 18% | 28% | 21% | 10% |
| **Nikkei 225** | −8% | 12% | 38% | 45% |

See what a difference the exchange rate made to our returns. In 1998, the falling Canadian dollar boosted our international investment returns significantly. It even turned a loss on the Japanese Nikkei into a two-digit gain! In 1999, the Canadian dollar rose 6 percent against the US dollar, which cut our returns. In the same year, though, the Japanese Yen appreciated against the Canadian dollar, which boosted Japanese investment returns. The difference that the exchange rate exerted on US and Japanese returns raises an important point: The most commonly referred-to rate in Canada is the Canadian–US dollar rate. But the Canadian dollar can rise against the US dollar at the same time as it falls against another currency, as it did against the Yen in 1999.

Let's look at longer time periods of five and 10 years — both ending on December 31, 1999. We'll expand the research to include Morgan Stanley's EAFE index, which covers Europe, Asia, and Australia, as well as Morgan Stanley's Emerging Markets index.

| | 5 Years | | 10 Years | |
|---|---|---|---|---|
| | Local Market Return | Canadian-Dollar Return | Local Market Return | Canadian-Dollar Return |
| **S&P 500** | 28% | 29% | 18% | 21% |
| **FTSE 100** | 22% | 23% | 11% | 14% |
| **Nikkei 225** | 0% | 0% | −7% | −1.5% |
| **MSCI EAFE** | 16% | 14% | 7% | 10% |
| **MSCI Emerging Markets** | 10% | 2% | 24% | 8% |

You can see that currency has an impact on our returns. Sometimes it works in our favour, as it did for the 10-year Japanese and EAFE returns. Sometimes it works against us, as it did for the five- and 10-year emerging market returns. The Canadian dollar *depreciated* against the Yen over the past 10 years, which added to our Japanese returns. The Canadian dollar *appreciated* against Latin American and other emerging market currencies, which subtracted from those returns.

What can we expect the currency effect to be in the future? We know that stocks — whether Canadian or foreign — offer an extremely high probability of rising over the long run. And stocks tend to adhere to the golden risk–reward rule, where the more risk you take, the more return you can expect to earn. Currency risk is different, though: There's no investment law that says that exchange rate risk will be rewarded. Also, unlike stocks or bonds, currency does not offer a long-term gain. If you buy a bond and hold onto it until it matures, you will have earned its yield. If you buy a stock and hold onto it for a number of years, you will have earned its dividends and capital gains. But if you use your Canadian cash to buy Yen, euros, or US dollars, you are not assured of any gains at all; in fact, you could easily end up with a loss.

To make matters more complicated, currency fluctuations have dramatically increased over the past few decades. It used to be the case that worldwide currency trading was driven by the flow of trade between countries. In the late 1970s, 25 percent of all currency trading originated from trade, whereas today less than one percent of currency trading is related to trade — over 99 percent is a function of financial asset trading. The good news is that currency volatility generally reduces the risk of your portfolio, because it often offsets other securities' volatilities. So the ups and downs of the Canadian dollar–Yen exchange rate, and the Canadian dollar–euro rate, can offset each other to an extent, and offset other price fluctuations within your portfolio.

And in the long run, currency fluctuations are not likely to have too significant an effect on your portfolio. But to play it safe, I've suggested limiting your foreign currency exposure to 75 percent of the equity portion of your portfolio. The 25 percent equity weighting in Canadian stocks, in addition to holding Canadian-dollar bonds and cash, limits the foreign currency risk to a reasonable level, for most investors. This exposure is reduced further for the Canadian homeowner, whose dwelling is a Canadian-dollar asset.

We could hedge some of this exposure so that we reduce the foreign currency risk even further, while maintaining our equity weightings, but this is an expensive and usually cumbersome process. Appendix 3 includes more detail on currency risk and the more technical ways in which it can be reduced, without reducing foreign stock investments.

Life may not be quite so easy for Canadians planning to retire in the US or abroad. A falling Canadian dollar will boost foreign equity investments; however, it will reduce purchasing power outside of Canada, which can be very costly. If you are planning to spend a lot of time outside of Canada, then the benefit your investments get from a falling Canadian dollar will be offset by the higher cost of purchasing items outside of Canada. If you are planning to spend considerable time abroad, you will want to consider reducing your foreign exchange risk with one of the strategies outlined in Appendix 3. Foreign exchange is a separate asset class and should be managed as such. It can be reasonably ignored by most Canadians, but not necessarily by snowbirds or other extensive travellers. Ultimately, currency risk should not deter you from investing in foreign equities.

The bottom line of home bias is that Canada is a great place to spend most, if not all, of your life. But that doesn't mean you should invest most of your savings in our market. Maximizing your returns in the long run means making sure you don't have any heavy bets on a single investment — and that includes the Canadian stock market. Our economy is small and export- and resource-dependent. And our stock market is tiny on the world stage, so it offers significantly fewer investing opportunities than are available beyond the Canadian borders. You can likely increase your returns, and definitely reduce your portfolio risk, by avoiding this common mistake.

## Recap of Mistake #5: Succumbing to Home Bias

1. Investors around the world are psychologically inclined to favour their home markets. This is a function of not understanding the importance of international diversification, and of distorted thinking that results from attachment to one's own country.

2. That's not a big problem for an American investor whose stock market makes up over half of the entire world's stock market capitalization. But it is a problem for Canadian investors whose economy and stock market are very small by world standards.

3. Our economy is quite export-dependent, with a heavy weighting toward resource exports. And we're largely dependent on the US for our export business, whereas the US has a smaller export business, which sells to buyers in countries all over the world.

4. Our stock market is much more concentrated — five stocks make up over 40 percent of our total market. The US market reflects its more diversified economy since it is not as captive to the success or failure of a few companies.

5. A better approach to investing is to have less in Canadian stocks and more in US and other international securities. Depending on the individual, the *stock* portion of a portfolio can be effectively allocated by a 25/45/30 split between Canada, US, and international stocks.

6. The foreign content constraint in registered accounts can be overcome with the use of derivative-based index and clone funds.

7. The currency risk of overweighting foreign investments is mitigated by holding about 25 percent Canadian content in the stock portion of your portfolio (which is high, relative to the size of the world market), in addition to holding Canadian-dollar bonds and a home in Canada. Although there is no reward for taking on currency risk, foreign currency has a good diversification benefit, and is unlikely to have a severely detrimental effect in the long term. Currency risk should only be a serious consideration for investors planning on retiring outside of Canada, in which case a hedging strategy can make sense.

# MISTAKE #6

## Not Knowing
## What You Own

*Eye Opener:*
*Fund managers have different objectives than you do! Their objectives*
*are not wrong, since they're entirely consistent with how managers are*
*judged. But the difference in your goals and theirs can seriously reduce*
*your portfolio returns.*

You walk through a beautiful home that appeals to you. Would you buy
it without a building inspector giving it the once-over first? A sharp-
looking car whizzes by you and really catches your eye. Even though it
looks great, would you purchase it without investigating its features and
maintenance history?

These may sound like facetious questions. But most investors do not
honestly know what they're buying when they invest in a mutual fund.
They don't know exactly what's in it. Does that matter?

It's *at least* as important to know what you're investing in as it is to
check how many calories are in a carton of premium ice cream before
you throw it in your shopping cart!

## The Problem

Most actively managed funds are not pure. They hold a lot of goodies in
addition to what they are supposed to hold. The average Canadian equity

fund holds US equities, other international stocks, perhaps a bond or two, and always some cash — sometimes as much as 30 percent of its assets can be in cash.

Is this cheating? Not really. In fact it could be argued that because of the restrictions on foreign content holdings within a registered account, it's reasonable for Canadian equity managers to hold some US and international stocks in order to boost foreign exposure. It can also be argued that managers who consider themselves "value" oriented — meaning they restrict their investments to stocks that are priced less than their long-term worth would suggest — should be able to hold cash, if they cannot find stocks that meet their criteria.

Two distinct problems can arise: funds that corrupt your macro-level asset mix, and funds that hold securities that you didn't anticipate owning.

## Asset Mix Surprises

Here are the asset mixes of some of the biggest and most popular funds sold in Canada.

- A very heavily advertised "income plus" fund holds 72 percent Canadian equities. You can't rely on a fund name to help you determine what asset class you're investing in. This fund would have been better named "income-plus-a-huge-helping-of-equities" fund.
- There are a few large dividend funds that hold 25 percent or more in bonds and cash. The managers of these funds presumably think that bonds will outperform stocks for the time being — a perfectly legitimate call on the market . . . *for a balanced fund*! If you invested in this fund because you wanted the preferred tax treatment of dividends, then you're in the wrong fund.
- Another very popular dividend fund holds 46 percent common stock, 16 percent foreign stocks, and 10 percent in bonds, among other securities. Aside from this interesting mix of assets, the high weighting in common stocks — most, but not all, of which are dividend-paying stocks such as banks — will be more volatile than the preferred shares which are traditionally considered the best way to access dividend income. If the market suffers a correction, the common stocks will suffer more than the preferred shares.
- A very popular "global government bond" fund holds 26 percent Canadian bonds and 10 percent cash. (It also carries a hefty 2 percent

fee, by the way, presumably to pay for all the difficult research required to find the good global bonds that make up less than two-thirds of the fund.)

- The most popular Canadian equity fund in 1998 held 20 percent in foreign equities — mostly US stocks. Not surprising that it did very well in that year when the US market beat the Canadian market by 40 percent! The investors in this fund would have been quite over-weighted in US stocks if they had also had a US equity fund. That worked nicely in 1998, but not in 1999, when Canada outperformed and this fund suffered.

Every mutual fund has to define its investment objective in its prospectus. You'd think that would be the place where you could ascertain what securities the fund will hold. Here are the investment objectives of two of the most highly rated Canadian equity funds:

*"To provide long-term capital growth."* Well, that's broad enough to encompass just about anything you want it to. You wouldn't even know that it's a Canadian equity fund. It would be nice if there were a little more detail to help investors decide what the fund is all about, wouldn't it? There's a reason that the fund has such a broad mandate, I suppose: it has 28 percent of its assets in foreign equities, and another 27 percent in cash. (I don't know how cash is supposed to generate long-term capital growth!)

Here's the mandate for the second fund: *"This fund is designed to achieve long-term capital appreciation while continuing to emphasize the preservation of capital. Its portfolio will consist mainly of Canadian equity securities in areas of the Canadian economy where superior rates of growth are expected but will, at all times, be fully diversified and may have a fixed income component."* Funny how this statement uses 10 times the number of words as that for the previous fund, but doesn't tell you anything more helpful. This is an equity fund, but it sounds like it could be a balanced fund if the manager had a change of heart. It also sounds like a growth fund that preserves capital — a feat that most magicians wouldn't even attempt.

The good news is that regulators are tightening up the requirements for the wording of fund objectives. Since asset allocation is the base upon which your entire investment plan is built, it's important that the fund implement it properly. The following chart compares a suggested target asset allocation with an actual asset allocation. The target allocation is an example — let's say it's what you have determined to be the right asset mix to meet your objectives. The actual asset allocation is what you would really get if you bought the most popular mutual funds in each category to fill each asset class. The reason the target doesn't match the actual is because the actual mix consists of active funds that are not pure, but rather "dirtied" up with all sorts of other asset classes.

| | Target Asset Allocation | Actual Asset Mix |
| --- | --- | --- |
| Cash | 0% | 7% |
| Bonds | 25% | 23% |
| Canadian Stocks | 15% | 11% |
| US Stocks | 35% | 45% |
| European and Asian Stocks | 25% | 14% |

The popular Canadian fund has some US stocks and some cash in it. The international fund that is supposed to cover European and Asian markets holds a lot of US stocks as well. So you end up with an asset mix that strays markedly from what you wanted. If European and Asian markets do very well, and US stocks underperform, you may wonder why your portfolio didn't show the kind of returns you would have expected, based on your target asset mix.

This example is not exaggerated. The average Canadian equity fund holds 5 percent in cash, 7 percent in US equities, and another 5 percent in other foreign stocks. The average global equity fund holds as much as 35 percent in US stocks, and another 8 percent in Canadian stocks.

## Security Surprises

In addition to asset mix corruption, there's a less conspicuous problem with the impurity of most active funds. It relates to the types of stocks you hold. Because the holdings of the funds can often deviate from their primary mandate, you could end up investing in securities you didn't want. The key word is "primary" because the securities regulators allow a fund to hold securities that do not fit its name or mandate, as long as the majority of its holdings do. Here's what I mean:

- In one of the most highly ranked Canadian small-companies funds, one-third of the top 15 holdings are from among the TSE's *largest* 100 companies. Oops! Looks like you own a good helping of large-company stocks in your "small-cap" fund. Is that a problem? Only if you specifically wanted to own small-company stocks, either because you thought they were going to outperform stocks of large companies, or because you were diversifying your portfolio with a predetermined mix of large- and small-cap stocks. If you went to the trouble of separating out a small-cap and a large-cap mandate for your portfolio, your rationale will not be served by this popular fund.

- Three of the top-ranked US equity funds all hold Nokia as their single largest holding. One has as much as 9.9 percent invested in Nokia. You may know Nokia as the cell-phone manufacturer — the biggest company on the Finnish stock exchange! To be fair, it does trade as an "American depository receipt" on the New York Stock Exchange, which is a way for foreign companies to have their shares traded in the US. But I would still question whether a US equity fund should have a foreign company as its largest holding, especially 10 percent of the whole fund!
- One of the most highly ranked Canadian small-companies funds, whose investment objective specifies *"investing primarily in the stocks of smaller or lesser-known companies,"* has half of its largest 10 holdings in very large companies: Rogers, Mackenzie Financial, CanWest Global, Power Corp., and Shaw Communications. Yeah . . . never heard of those "small" companies before.

## Impurity Often Means Paying Too Much

Aside from the problem of unknowingly altering your asset mix, and unknowingly holding securities that are not what you intended, the other problem is that you are paying for, and expecting, the expertise of managing a certain asset class. Most small-cap funds charge higher fees because they require more research; smaller companies are harder to investigate since they issue less public information and they have less developed investor relation functions. The small-cap fund used in the last example has a management expense ratio of 2.6 percent, which is much higher than the average large-cap Canadian fund of 2.1 percent. So you're paying a higher fee, even though less than 60 percent of the fund is invested in small companies. In fact, part of the high fee is going to the management of cash and bonds! You're obviously not getting your money's worth, since a money market and a bond fund would have fees of between only one and 1.5 percent.

Not only are you paying an unjustified premium on some of the assets in the fund, but the manager of the fund is probably not the best person to be managing the other asset classes. For instance, here's the breakdown of one of the most popular global equity funds in Canada:

| | |
|---|---|
| Cash | 17% |
| Canadian Stocks | 11% |
| US Stocks | 32% |
| European Stocks | 35% |
| Hong Kong | 5% |

Now if you are using this large fund to fulfill the international equity part of your portfolio, you have a few problems. As we've already identified, your asset mix will badly overweight US equities if you're already holding a US equity fund, and you will be underweighted in Asian equities, especially Japan.

You're also paying an all-in fee of 2.7 percent. Understandably, international funds have higher fees, because it's easier to fly to New York to visit a company than it is to visit a firm in Geneva. And it's even more expensive to open an office in Geneva from which to manage all the European equities. But with this fund, you're overpaying for the management of the part invested in US and Canadian stocks, not to mention the 17 percent that's simply sitting in cash! If you separated out the asset classes and invested in them individually, your all-in fee would be about 2.1 percent. You're losing 0.6 percent each year, which is what the manager has to overcome before he adds any value. How likely is it that he can easily add value by mixing all those asset classes? We looked at this question in Mistake #3 when we considered tactical asset allocation, and determined that it's not easy to add value this way. In fact, it's easier to subtract value.

An important question is this: Is the manager's skill really that broad that he can pick the best US stocks, as well as the best European and Canadian stocks? You would only be getting proven expertise on each component of this fund if a different manager were responsible for each part. Even then, it's unlikely that the same fund company will have access to the best US, European, and Canadian stock pickers (not to mention Hong Kong). It so happens that the US portion of this "global" fund did underperform the S&P 500 index. *So you're paying a premium fee for a mixed bag of underperforming securities and cash!*

## Assessing Active Funds — Bad Ones Can Look Good (and Vice Versa)

The whole point of buying a mutual fund is to get access to expertise. You want the best Canadian equity manager, the best Canadian bond manager, the best US equity manager, and the best manager for your European, Asian, and emerging markets stocks. Otherwise you might as well index the whole portfolio, since only the best will consistently have a chance of beating the index anyway.

As I described in the last example of a global fund holding lots of poorly performing US stocks, this is a common problem that is overlooked by virtually all mutual fund investors and most mutual fund analysts. Let's take a hypothetical Canadian equity fund that is highly regarded and very popular. It holds 23 percent US equities, which many advisors will tell you is a good thing, because then you can increase your overall foreign content in your registered account. The performance of the fund is above average for most periods over the last 10 years.

But this fund is holding much more in US equities than the average Canadian equity fund. Because US equities have outperformed Canadian equities over the past 10 years, this fund had a big advantage over its competitors. In fact, although the fund's performance is better than most of its competitors', the US portion actually underperformed the S&P 500, and the Canadian stock picks were only mediocre. You could, I suppose, credit the manager for having the foresight to include a lot of US stocks. But is that what you really want from a Canadian equity fund? A manager deciding to hold a large amount of US stocks because he's not enthusiastic about the Canadian market?

The fund's performance can fool you into thinking you've got a winner, even though it's basically a loser. It's a loser because the stock picks were not good in either country, but the heavy weighting in US stocks masks the problem. Even worse, your asset mix is not aligned with what you intended since you'll be overweighted in US stocks. You've lost control over the two factors that you should have the most control over — your asset mix and the risk of your portfolio, which is a function of this mix.

This problem is even more pronounced with international and global equity funds. You may think you have a great fund based on performance, but it could easily be that the fund has very poor security selection, and benefited from a lucky overweighting in US stocks. Even so, your overall portfolio returns (which is all that ultimately matters) could have been much better, since Latin America may have been the strongest market, and your wonderful international fund didn't hold any Latin American stocks. You lost out because (i) your asset mix is not allocated properly to each asset class, and (ii) within the portfolio, the performance of your foreign assets is sub-par because of poor stock selection. But you *think* you've got a good international fund because it generated above-average returns. You probably won't be making any changes because the problem is invisible, as long as you don't know what you own.

Do you know how much cash your mutual funds hold? Or how much they deviate from their core mandates, such as a Canadian equity fund holding European stocks, or an international equity fund holding some Canadian and US equities? If you don't know, there's nothing to be embarrassed about. You're in the same position as 99 percent of all mutual fund investors.

## The Behavioural Explanation

- *Lack of Knowledge*
- *Overinterpretation*

This one's easy: Most investors in the popular equity funds simply don't understand how their asset mixes can end up being altered. They may not understand either the importance of a properly implemented asset mix, or how implementing the right mix is made difficult with the use of active funds, or both.

This "unawareness" is aggravated by the fact that we are all tempted to chase after the winners. Last year's hot funds are often the ones we want to invest in. And we inevitably overinterpret performance numbers. The overinterpretation is based on assuming that above-average performance is attributable to great stock-picking ability. Not knowing what you own can lure you into thinking great numbers are likely to persist in the future because you ascribe too much skill to the manager, when elements of performance are often the result of circumstances, rather than explicit managerial decisions. When value stocks are hot, value managers look brilliant. When Europe is hot, a manager will look like a genius if she has a heavy weighting in Europe, even if it's just because she has no experience investing in Asia, so avoids that region. What if last year's hottest Canadian equity fund did so well because it had large holdings in two US technology companies that both quintupled in price, even though the rest of the fund had returns below the TSE 300? Not knowing what your fund holds can encourage you to pick bad funds that look good.

It's not that anyone is trying to cheat you — the mutual fund managers are simply trying to generate the best performance they can. If they were managing all of your money, then they could ensure your asset mix had integrity. But because they are only managing the piece they've been assigned — for example, the Canadian equity piece — their investment strategy might not dovetail nicely with the rest of the pieces in your portfolio. They're trying to maximize returns on their fund, since they're judged against their peers. So if throwing some US stocks into a Canadian fund helps separate a manager from the pack, there's an incentive for her to do that. Or if the manager has no knowledge of Asian markets so doesn't invest there, you don't get any Asian stocks. It's important to understand the behavioural motivation of managers, because their objectives often differ from yours.

The fancy term for this behavioural finance problem is "agency conflict." This is the conflict that arises when you hire an agent (a fund manager) to manage your money: The agent is often motivated by different goals than yours. The fund manager is trying to maximize the returns of his fund, while you are trying to maximize your *portfolio's overall* returns. Or he may aspire to winning the "Manager of the Year" award, which entices him to take more risk than you would be comfortable with, or hold securities that aren't aligned with his mandate.

The impurity of active management can be very damaging when it goes unnoticed by investors. This lack of knowledge extends all the way to not realizing your portfolio returns might be substantially less than they could have been, if your asset mix hadn't been "spoiled." It's entirely possible, for example, to be invested in the best Canadian, US, and international funds, but when they are combined in your portfolio, your returns are sub-par: The combination of the three funds left you underweighted in European equities and overweighted in US equities at a time when European stocks were top performers and US stocks were the worst.

## The Solution

Easy fix: either find out exactly what the funds actually hold, or increase your investment in index products.

By investigating what a fund actually holds, you can decide to either compensate for the areas where it strays from its mandate, or reject the fund altogether. If a strong-performing Canadian fund holds 20 percent in US stocks, then you'll want to lighten up your holding in US stock funds a little so your asset mix is kept intact. Just make sure the fund is not above average just because it holds more US equity than other funds, at a time when US equities are outperforming Canadian stocks.

Even by reducing your US equities to compensate, the manager can change the fund's holdings anytime without informing you. So while you may have had 20 percent US equities in your Canadian fund when you bought it, that may no longer be the case if the manager later decided to sell a portion of, or all, the US stocks. But as long as you check your funds twice a year, you should be able to keep track of their makeup. Read the annual and semi-annual reports that the fund companies send you, as well as the prospectus you receive when you purchase the fund. Or call the fund company and ask their customer service department to tell you what percentage is invested in countries outside of the fund's main mandate.

A good advisor will analyze the holdings of your funds very carefully to avoid the problems associated with the impurity of active funds. The following list outlines potential problems that you want to be particularly careful to avoid.

## Red Flags

1. *Equity Funds:* They hold a small amount of cash to fund unitholder redemptions. Make sure the cash holdings are not too high — below 10 percent of the fund's total assets most of the time. Throughout January and February, the cash levels may increase slightly as investors make RRSP deposits that the manager has to invest. There are two possible reasons for a fund to hold more than 10 percent in cash for a period longer than a month. First, you may have specifically chosen a fund because you want the manager to attempt to time the market, in which case she will hold more cash when she's bearish. This is what some "tactical asset allocation" funds do. Be cautious about these funds, given how hard it is to add value with tactical asset mix calls, as we saw in Mistake #3. Second, value fund managers, who choose stocks based on an analysis of their fair market value, may hold a fair amount of cash if the manager feels that there aren't many stocks that represent good buys. There are two potential pitfalls to this strategy. It is difficult to determine the exact "fair" value of a stock; many stocks are trading at low prices precisely because they are not good long-term

investments. And it is even harder to determine how long it will take for an "underpriced" stock to rise to its "fair" value, if it ever does, and if it's truly priced below its fair value in the first place. Value investing can be very lucrative, but sitting in cash for long periods of time is dangerous. If you're committed to maintaining integrity in your asset mix, the best value managers are the ones that limit their cash to 10 percent.

2. *Small-cap Equity Funds:* They often hold some large-cap stocks, which can mask the manager's ability to pick good small companies. The bigger the small-cap fund, the greater the risk that they hold large-cap stocks. If a small-cap fund has total assets that substantially exceed $100 million, the manager will be inclined to invest in larger-company stocks, because he'll have too much money to be able to restrict the fund to small stocks only. The "market breadth" — or availability — of small stocks is much less than that of large stocks, so bigger funds are harder to restrict to small stocks. Because small-cap funds charge a higher fee than large-cap funds, you want to make sure you're getting what you pay for.

3. *International and Global Equity Funds:* These can be tricky because they have the ability to invest in many different countries. You could end up owning a fund that has a major weighting in Europe and only a small holding in Asia. This is not a problem per se — it should reflect the manager's preference for European stocks. But if your asset mix is supposed to give you exposure to Asian equities, you should make sure that you are holding a second fund that balances out your low Asian exposure. And keep track of any changes the fund makes: If the manager changes course and loads up on Asian stocks, you want to make sure you don't end up overweighting your portfolio in Asia. Global equity funds are even more problematic. Unlike international equity funds, which are traditionally not supposed to invest in North America, global funds can invest anywhere in the world. So the biggest risk of global equity funds is being overweighted in US stocks. If you're using a global equity fund as part of your international asset class, make sure that you determine the US stock holdings of the fund. If the fund owns a lot of US stocks, you'll want to reduce your holdings in the US equity class. Even then, you should satisfy yourself that the global manager is adept at picking US stocks, as well as European, Asian, and Latin American stocks. And keep watch to see if the manager maintains or changes the US weight. Global funds are not ideal for maintaining rigorous asset mixes. Are you starting to see why I love

the purity of index funds? Speaking of which, they have their traps as well . . .

4. *Index Funds:* The catch to indexing is knowing which index your fund is tracking. A Canadian index fund will track either the S&P/TSE 60 index, or the TSE 300. As discussed in Mistake #4 ("Overestimating Active Management"), I prefer the index that covers the largest part of the market (TSE 300 in Canada, Wilshire 5000 in the US). The other wrinkle in index funds is currency exposure. Most index funds are denominated in the currencies of the underlying assets. European index funds are denominated in euros; Japanese index funds in Yen. The problem lies in derivative-based RSP index funds, which are invested in T-bills and futures contracts on the foreign indexes that they track. These funds can either be denominated in Canadian dollars or foreign currencies. For instance, a US RSP index fund might have no foreign currency exposure — only exposure to the S&P 500 in Canadian dollars, since it is invested in Canadian-dollar T-bills and futures contracts. Or it might track the S&P 500 in US dollars, by being invested in US-dollar-denominated T-bills and futures contracts. Which is better? As we explored near the end of Mistake #5 ("Succumbing to Home Bias"), it is very difficult (some would say impossible) to predict currency movements. As we concluded in that chapter, most investors are better off to invest in funds that give you full exposure to the currency of the underlying asset. A US RSP index fund that has full US-dollar exposure is preferred for most investors.

## Indexing (Again)

The easiest way to manage asset allocation, as we explored in Mistake #4, is with index product. Indexing is pure — you know what you get. If you don't have the time or interest in keeping track of your funds to make sure you're getting what you think you're buying, then decrease the amount you hold in active funds, and increase your index holdings.

Whatever you do, you don't want to make the mistake of investing in a fund just because it appears to be a top performer. It might be a superior-performing Canadian equity fund for reasons other than good Canadian stock picking. If you don't know what you own, you will spoil your asset mix, and you may end up owning securities you don't want. By not knowing what you own, you may also end up with another problem, which is explored in the next chapter — you may have great difficulty making an appropriate assessment of your investment performance.

# Recap of Mistake #6: Not Knowing What You Own

1. Effective asset allocation relies on the right mix of different asset classes.

2. But many active funds are not pure — they hold countries and securities that are not consistent with their principal mandates.

3. Not knowing what you own is problematic because (i) your asset mix gets skewed; (ii) you end up owning securities you didn't expect; (iii) you can pay premium fees that aren't warranted; (iv) you can't properly judge the performance of your investments. The result of any or all of these problems is that your portfolio returns are penalized.

4. Fund managers have objectives that are not necessarily aligned with investors'. In most cases, the managers are trying to beat the other funds in their category. But investors are trying to maximize their portfolio's overall return. This gap can work to the disadvantage of the investor, even though managers are just doing what they are paid to do in most cases.

5. Unfortunately, most investors don't know exactly what they own — especially if they are invested heavily in actively managed mutual funds. This is just a simple matter of "unawareness" and a tendency to chase after winners, based on an overinterpretation of returns which often attributes skill to managers that is not warranted.

6. Make an effort to investigate what your funds hold so you can accommodate their holdings in your asset mix decisions. And if you don't have the time or inclination to properly research the active funds you own, consider increasing your investment in index products — their purity will assist you in maintaining integrity in your asset allocation — the most important decision in the investment process.

# MISTAKE #7

## Not Knowing
## How You're Doing

*Eye Opener:*

Q: *Can you compare the speed of two swimmers if one is allowed to use only the breast stroke, while the other has to use the breast stroke 70 percent of the time, but can use any stroke at all for the other 30 percent?*

A: *Obviously not. They're playing by different rules, and the first swimmer is at a disadvantage.*

What if you don't even know what each swimmer is allowed to do? You are given the speed of both, but don't know what limitations there were on each. Who would you bet your money on for the next race? Presumably you wouldn't be willing to bet much money.

Remember getting a mark in school that was lower than you were expecting, but that you weren't sure was really bad until you checked to see what others got? What looked like a bad mark was often pretty good compared to other students' marks. Unfortunately the reverse case also applied: good marks sometimes became less spectacular when you discovered that everyone had aced the test.

How do you know if your investments are doing well? It's important to know; otherwise, you can't make the necessary changes to fix the problem. I speak to a lot of investors on an ongoing basis and without doubt the most common expression of dissatisfaction I hear is that they feel their returns fall short. Their investments don't stack up against the hottest mutual fund or stock. This refrain is not uncommon: "My advisor blew it last year. I only earned 14 percent on my money, but I've seen some technology funds that went up over 100 percent."

# The Problem

You may laugh at the above example. But I take it very seriously after hearing it over and over again. Be honest: Do you not cringe and start to question your investment acumen, or that of your advisor, when your neighbour boasts that he doubled his money with some incredible Internet company that he discovered on his favourite website? Do you not start second-guessing your entire investment plan when you see that your returns pale in comparison to a mutual fund ad that trumpets a 125 percent return?

Maybe you invested in a high-quality international equity fund recommended by your advisor. But after you invested in it, the fund returned only 12 percent while another global equity fund written up in the paper generated a 25 percent return in the same year. Many investors in this circumstance are motivated to switch funds and go for the higher performer so they don't get "stiffed" again the following year.

There are two challenging aspects to determining the performance of your investments. The first is assessing the components of your portfolio, such as a particular mutual fund. The second is assessing the returns of your overall portfolio. How do you know when there's a problem with part or all of your portfolio?

## Benchmark Problem #1: Assessing a Fund Manager's Performance
As with school grades, you can only judge a fund's performance by comparing it to something. If your Canadian equity fund went up 16 percent in 1999, would you have considered that spectacular? If so, does it matter that the average fund earned 20 percent over that year? And how important is it that the TSE 300 index went up 32 percent in 1999? Do you still think your 16 percent gain was extraordinary? Probably not.

What about a Canadian equity fund that returned negative one percent in 1998? Dismal? Not compared to the average Canadian equity fund, which returned negative 4 percent in the same year, or the TSE 300 index, which returned negative 2 percent over the same period.

That's how important benchmarks are. Benchmarks are the comparisons you use to know how well you're doing. They let you determine how your investments are performing. The absolute numbers by themselves are only useful for looking at how much your portfolio value has changed and whether it's closer to, or further from, your ultimate financial objective. But the numbers by themselves don't help you determine if your investments are performing well *compared with alternative investments that you could have made.*

Benchmark problem #1 can be examined on three dimensions: the fund's holdings, its inherent risk, and the time periods over which you assess the fund's performance.

*Specific Holdings:* While it's a step in the right direction, benchmarking is not as simple as just comparing your return to the average fund in each category, or to a market index. You need to examine what the fund holds. Here's an example that shows the returns of two Canadian small-cap equity funds:

| | 1998 Returns | 1999 Returns |
|---|---|---|
| **Canadian Small-Company Fund #1** | 5% | 45% |
| **Canadian Small-Company Fund #2** | −4% | 22% |
| *Avg. Cdn. Small-Company Fund* | *−13%* | *18%* |
| *TSE 200* | *−7%* | *24%* |

Fund #1 appears to have done well, when we consider how the average fund and the index did (I'm using the TSE 200, which tracks the smaller companies of the TSE 300 index). No contest. Probably better to dump Fund #2 and buy Fund #1.

The problem is that our analysis and decision are dependent upon one key assumption, which happens to be invalid: that both funds should be compared to the same benchmark.

As we saw in the previous chapter, just because they're both called "small-company fund" doesn't mean they're managed the same way. And if they're not managed the same way, they shouldn't be judged the same way.

The first fund happens to have about 30 percent of its assets devoted to larger companies, while the second fund holds exclusively small companies. Large companies generated much better returns in 1998 (one percent on average) than smaller companies (negative 22 percent). So the more large companies a fund manager had in her "small company" fund, the more likely she was to beat her small-cap competitors, as well as the small-cap index.

Even though both funds in this example are from the same category, and appear to have the same mandate, the first one is allowed to hold a more significant portion in stocks of larger companies. So the two funds must be judged differently. You can't compare the speed of two swimmers if one is limited to using the breast stroke, while the other can also use any other stroke for 30 percent of the time. The two swimmers need to be judged against different standards.

From the last chapter, we know that it's important to examine exactly what a fund is holding, so we can determine if and where it belongs in our asset mix. But it's crucial to know what it holds for a second reason: So we can assess whether or not it's performing well. Only by knowing what the fund holds can we determine the most appropriate benchmark to use in judging the fund.

But, you may ask, what if both fund managers are on equal footing, and the first manager adroitly chose to put more large-company stocks into her portfolio because her analysis indicated that large-company stocks would do better than small-company stocks? Shouldn't both managers be judged against the same benchmark and the first manager be credited with having more skill?

If both managers have precisely the same mandates and are both allowed to mix small- and large-cap stocks, then the first manager does deserve credit for more skill — although credit for having more luck is probably more appropriate over such a short time period. Whether or not you want a fund that can invest in both large- and small-cap stocks is another question — one that we addressed in the previous chapter. Managers are not usually endowed with the extraordinary ability and extra time they would need to master all there is to know about small-cap stocks, while maintaining expertise on the larger companies as well.

We also saw in Mistake #4 how well managers do after they've won the "Fund Manager of the Year Award." We considered one well-regarded fund manager who won the award in a year when the market went down. He managed to preserve a positive return from some good stock picking, and by having nearly 40 percent of the fund invested in cash. Was he cheating? No. The fund's mandate allowed him to hold cash. Did he think the market was going down so he wanted to hold a lot of cash? Not really: His stated reason for holding so much cash was that he couldn't find any stocks that were trading at reasonable values. Rather than just buying a stock for the sake of buying it, he decided to wait and sit in cash, until he felt the prices of some stocks were more reasonable. That strategy worked well in a year when the whole market went down — the year he won the award. Was he really skilled enough to deserve the award, or just lucky? Hard to say. But the following year his fund was one of the worst performers; his heavy cash holdings were not helpful in a market that went up 32 percent. In assessing his performance, you need an appropriate benchmark; otherwise, you can't properly ascertain a manager's skill. Maybe he should be celebrated — in both years — for maintaining a very low risk level in his fund. Maybe an appropriate benchmark to compare his returns would be one that was made of 30 percent cash and 70 percent TSE 300. By this standard, his returns were pretty good in 1998 and not very good in 1999. With this benchmark, he was neither a superstar, nor a big loser. But unfortunately he was perceived by most investors to be both over two subsequent years, even though nothing about his strategy changed!

*Risk:* One of the most important elements of benchmarking is how much risk the manager took to generate her returns. If your purpose is to assess the skill of a particular Canadian equity fund manager, it would be senseless to compare her fund's returns to a money market fund. That's obvious. But it's equally problematic to compare a very risky fund with one that does not take on much risk. The risky fund should have higher returns over time; otherwise, why would you want to accept the higher risk? Excessive risk is an easy way to look like a hero — if the risk pays off.

*Time Horizon:* The last problem relating to benchmarking a fund's return is the time period used. Many investors think the longer the period the better. But that's only partially true. A long period is required to properly distinguish skill, but that doesn't mean a 10-year track record suffices. Relying exclusively on a 10-year record is just as dangerous as judging a fund's return over a one-year period only.

Here's an example. One of the largest Canadian equity funds had a 12 percent average annual return over three years ending December 1999. A fair bit better than the average Canadian equity fund, which had a 10 percent average return. Sound like a buy? Some investors might think so; after all, a three-year track record of good performance is impressive.

In addition to the three-year return, let's look at the three calendar years. I've put the quartile ranking beside the return of each period:

| | 3-Year Return | 1999 Return | 1998 Return | 1997 Return |
|---|---|---|---|---|
| **Popular Fund** | 12% [2nd Q] | 48% [1st Q] | −9% [4th Q] | 4% [4th Q] |
| **Average Fund** | 10% | 21% | −2% | 14% |

You can see that the fund benefited from a very strong 1999, which pulled its three-year return out of its dismal fourth-quartile performance in the prior two years. Longer track records can bury years that are distinctly unimpressive. If you had no other information about this fund, you'd probably be best to wait at least another year or two to confirm that the manager is not vulnerable to underperforming as badly as he did in 1997 and 1998.

A fund with nine years of average performance, but a tenth year of outstanding performance, can easily rack up an above-average one-, three-, five-, and 10-year track record. Using the right benchmarks, or the right combination of benchmarks, is crucial in order to judge a fund manager. And the right benchmarks must reflect the appropriate securities, level of risk, and time horizon.

But there's an even more potentially damaging benchmark problem.

## Benchmark Problem #2: Assessing Your Portfolio's Performance

What happens to many investors is that they see the incredible returns of a few hot asset classes, and they change their asset mixes to take advantage of the hot trends. Has it happened to you? You miss the big run-up in Asian equities because you had "too much" invested in US stocks. So you make some changes and your portfolio ends up getting badly abused. You keep kicking it around because it's "under-performing." And the more you tweak, fine-tune, and fuss, the more frustrated you get that you keep missing the big opportunities when everyone else seems to be getting rich! All the tweaking and fussing is eroding your returns because the changes you keep making are overweighting you in the wrong asset classes. And you keep paying capital gains tax on the funds you sell. So while your focus is on what you could have made, you are completely oblivious to the returns you gave up by not staying with your initial asset mix.

Let's look at an example with some real figures. Say you were a fairly aggressive investor with an initial asset mix at the beginning of 1998 that is described in the box on the next page. Also in the box are the actual market returns of each asset class in 1998:

| Asset Class | 1998 Starting Mix | 1998 Returns |
|---|---|---|
| Canadian Bonds | 20% | 9% |
| International Bonds | 5% | 24% |
| Canadian Stocks | 20% | −2% |
| US Stocks | 35% | 38% |
| European Stocks | 10% | 38% |
| Asian/Emerging Markets Stocks | 10% | 8% |
| *Total Portfolio* | *100%* | *21%* |

To simplify the example, we'll ignore fees and commissions, so your total portfolio returns in 1998 reflect the weighting you had in each asset class. At the end of 1998, you calculate that you earned 21 percent. Not bad, but you look at what you could have got if you had put more into the European market and less in those disappointing Asian and emerging markets. And how about those global bond funds — unbelievable. Who would have thought you could make over 20 percent in a bond fund?

You decide to make some adjustments so that you won't miss out in 1999. After all, Europe is unifying under one currency which everyone says will make it a new world powerhouse of prosperity. As for the Asian markets, the consensus is that the Y2K bug will have disastrous consequences for Asian and less developed countries, which are way behind North America in addressing the computer problem. Might as well pull out of Asia and Latin America for now, and see how they cope with Y2K. And you should probably have a more balanced bond portfolio, right? You can't afford to miss any more of those international bond returns. Finally, everyone is saying that the Canadian economy is stuck in the old mature industries, whereas the US economy has so many more high-growth companies. That's why the US market had an almost 40 percent return and the Canadian market was down. No way are you going to get stuck again with minus 2 percent returns on Canadian equities.

Here's your 1999 starting mix, based on the changes you make to take advantage of international bonds and Europe, and the subsequent 12-month returns on each asset class, as they actually were.

| Asset Class | 1999 Starting Mix | 1999 Returns |
|---|---|---|
| Canadian Bonds | 10% | −1% |
| International Bonds | 15% | −11% |
| Canadian Stocks | 10% | 31% |
| US Stocks | 40% | 14% |
| European Stocks | 25% | 10% |
| Asian/Emerging Markets Stocks | 0% | 50% |
| *Total Portfolio* | *100%* | *9%* |

For crying out loud! Who would have thought little Canada would have done so well. And you live right here, for Pete's sake. And what's with Asia and the emerging markets? You thought everyone agreed Japan was going nowhere — its whole banking system faltering, a recession, and a paralyzed government. The infamous Y2K bug was supposed to wipe out the emerging markets for a long time. So much for listening to the pundits. And what happened to international bonds? Better make some changes.

You get the picture.

Or do you? If you had stayed the course, and simply rebalanced annually back to the initial mix, you would have earned an average annual compound return of 18 percent on your money. But the adjustments every year yielded an average annual compound return of 14.8 percent over the two years. So you lost over 3 percent average annual return over the two years, which equates to $7,450 on a portfolio of $100,000.

| | Rebalance to original asset mix | Adjust to new asset mix |
|---|---|---|
| Avg. annual compound return | 18.0% | 14.8% |
| Cumulative return | 39.2% | 31.8% |
| *Ending value of $100,000 portfolio* | *$139,240* | *$131,790* |

Never mind the high-flying technology sector or Asian stocks that you wished you would have invested more heavily in. You lost over $7,000 by needlessly jumping around.

That loss was attributable to not having an appropriate benchmark against which to compare your returns. Even if you understand that jumping from one asset class to another is fruitless, it will always be tempting if you don't have a way of discerning whether or not your portfolio is generating good performance. As long as your portfolio generates returns that are less than the best-performing asset class, you'll always feel you could have done better. Clearly, the best-performing asset class each year is not what you should be using as a benchmark, because it will cost you money!

## The Behavioural Explanation

- *Lack of Knowledge*
- *Overconfidence*
- *Confirmation Bias*
- *Pain of Regret*

### Benchmark Problem #1: Behavioural Basis for Assessing a Fund Manager's Performance

Nothing too complicated here. Unless you've worked in the investment management business — and the mutual fund business in particular — you wouldn't know some of the "tricks of the trade," or things to look at when you're assessing a fund's performance. The biggest challenge in assessing fund performance is determining if a manager is truly skilled, or just lucky — not an easy task, as we discovered in Mistake #4. What we didn't explore in detail in that chapter is exactly what you should be comparing a fund to when you assess it. Using inappropriate benchmarks is a common problem that arises from lack of understanding. The consequences can be very damaging as you jump from one fund to a "better" one, without understanding why the two may not be comparable, or interchangeable. Very often, the lesser-performing fund is the better one to have because it is more effective in complementing the other parts of your portfolio, and therefore your overall asset mix is better served by it.

Overconfidence in its many forms has a role here too. Rather than modestly assuming that we may not have sufficient information to properly assess the skill of last year's hot fund manager and therefore the *future* merits of his fund, we're eager to get a piece of the action — and leave it to suckers to sit cautiously on the sidelines.

The lack of knowledge of how to effectively judge performance and the overconfidence many have in predicting next year's winners can combine to severely handicap your portfolio returns. Without the ability to properly benchmark your fund returns, you'll be inclined to make a lot of expensive switches that cannot only put you in underperforming funds, but also inadvertently mess up your asset allocations.

## Benchmark Problem #2: Behavioural Basis for Assessing Your Portfolio's Performance

It's human nature to suffer intense regret when we compare the returns we earned with the returns we could have earned, if we had had the benefit of magical predictive powers. We hate losing money — it hurts. Regret doesn't originate just from money we had, but lost. Regret can also stem from money we *could have earned*, but didn't. Psychologists have measured the regret we experience from lost opportunities and compared it to the regret of actually losing money. Although an actual loss is more painful than a lost opportunity, or "paper loss," reflecting on what we could have had can still make us feel pretty miserable. Combine the powerful feeling of regretting lost opportunities with an overconfidence in our ability to pick winning asset classes, and you have a costly mistake. The problem arises from an attempt to avoid future regret by ensuring we always own some of the "winning" funds. If an investor is unaware of how damaging it can be to constantly change an asset mix each year in the hope of avoiding regret, the mistake can become quite serious over time.

We've seen how dangerous overconfidence can be. Our brains gravitate toward simple solutions, filtering out all the complexities that can't be quickly understood or integrated into the conclusions we start to draw. So it's easy for us to decide that it's time to invest in the Asian markets, since they posted great returns last year and most analysts and columnists are forecasting another good year. If we missed out on last year's incredible returns, there is a powerful psychological incentive — confirmation bias — to believe any commentary that suggests Asian markets will continue to outperform, because the fear of regret is driving us toward investing more in Asia anyway. If we were a little more humble, we might hesitate before confidently jumping to conclusions about the Asian economies based on a few newspaper articles and the returns we regret having missed last year. But many of us tend to think that it's better to avoid kicking ourselves two years in a row than to sit tight with our predetermined asset mix.

See how an investor can end up increasing risk — overweighting certain asset classes — in order to reduce future regret? And overconfidence is regret's partner in crime, making an asset mix vulnerable to abuse. We'll be in trouble as long as we keep making the wrong comparisons — using the wrong benchmarks to judge our investments' performance. We'll be locked in a vicious cycle of changing asset mixes that reduces our returns over the long run (and often in the short run, as we saw in the two-year example above). It's amazing how our psychology can work so hard to undermine our own objectives.

## The Solution

The concern of this chapter is to learn how to assess whether your investments are doing the job they should be, or underperforming. But the question is, "underperforming what?" Should you be comparing your Canadian equity fund to the best-performing one available? Should you be comparing your portfolio returns to the rip-roaring technology sector? If not, what should you compare it to? The real question is this: How exactly do you know if you're doing well or not? There are two solutions for two related but distinct problems.

### Solution to Benchmark Problem #1: Assessing a Fund Manager's Performance

At this point, you may have learned a bit more than you previously understood about how impure active funds are and how you have to be conscientious about knowing what you own. Only by knowing what you own can you determine the suitable benchmarks against which to assess a fund's performance. Only then do you have a fighting chance at judging the skill of a particular fund manager.

I say "fighting chance" because the process of assessing a fund manager's skill is neither purely scientific nor foolproof. As we saw in Mistake #4 ("Overestimating Active Management"), it can take quite a few years before luck can be reasonably ruled out as an explanation of a fund manager's good track record. The smaller the amount by which she outperforms the index each year, the more years you need to be able to have high confidence that her outperformance is attributable to skill rather than luck. As we saw, it could take a track record of 36 years to be able to say with 99 percent confidence that a manager who outperforms by 3 percent a year is skilled and likely to continue outperforming. But the good news, as we explored in that chapter, is that there is a way to speed up your assessment. We can increase our confidence in a manager's skill by introducing some *qualitative* assessments of the fund — by going beyond just the straight track record to look at how the manager picks securities, and what exactly is in the fund.

The assessment of a fund's performance can be broken down into these steps, all of which rely on comparing the fund to an appropriate benchmark.

1. *Time*: Compare the fund's return over a number of time periods, against the median or average fund in the same category, as well as the index that best represents that category. Time periods should consist of calendar years, as well as the typical one-, three-, five-, and 10-year periods. Both are important for different reasons: The calendar years avoid end-date bias, while the longer time periods are reflective of a manager's long-term ability. If the fund was able to beat the index and the average fund manager over most time periods, that's a good start. The national newspapers provide monthly mutual fund reports that offer this information.

2. *Risk*: Compare the risk of the fund to the average fund and the index — is the fund's volatility or risk ranking, as listed in the newspaper, much higher than that of the average fund and market index? Although volatility is not an ideal measure of risk when assessing different mutual funds, it's the only one that's widely available, so it will have to do. Getting good performance by taking extra risk is not a reliable indicator of skill, since you'd expect riskier funds to generate higher performance; at least they should. Additionally, the extra risk may simply generate substandard performance in the future.

3. *Specific Holdings*: One of the most important steps is often overlooked by most investors, and even by many mutual fund "gurus." Check out what the fund holds! As you know from the previous chapter, many funds hold surprising things. If a Canadian equity fund was the best in its class, and it had a higher-than-average holding of US stocks while the US market generated twice the returns of Canadian stocks, you can probably guess why it did so well. Maybe the manager was a genius and deliberately held a lot of US stocks to take advantage of the outperforming US market. But is that what you want in a Canadian equity fund? How is a good Canadian equity manager going to be able to consistently outperform his peers when his claim to fame was avoiding Canadian stocks? If you're perfectly happy that he's doing this, then at least judge him against the right benchmark — a mix of Canadian and US stocks. If he held 20 percent in US stocks, how did he do against the following benchmark: [TSE 300 returns x 80%] + [S&P 500 returns x 20%]. A small-cap manager who holds 30 percent of his fund in large-cap stocks should probably be compared to both

the average small-cap manager and the average large-cap manager, ideally by blending 30 percent of the average large-cap fund with 70 percent of the average small-cap fund. Naturally, this customized benchmark is only appropriate if the manager held the 30 percent in large caps for most of the year.

The best funds for asset allocation purposes, and for the purpose of judging performance, are the most faithful to simple mandates: for example, Canadian equity funds investing exclusively in Canadian stocks; and small-cap funds investing only in small companies.

4. *Strategic Discipline*: If the fund has passed the previous three tests, it may be a winner. There's a definite *possibility*. But you have to convert the possibility into a *probability* if you're going to give the manager credit for skill. As described in Mistake #4, the only way to increase your confidence in the probability of skill is to evaluate her strategy and how consistently she has applied it. If she is a value manager, how closely and consistently does her strategy mirror a value index? The myriad mutual fund review books that come out every year serve a useful purpose in this regard since many of them describe in some detail the strategies of each manager. Many of the authors have access to the managers themselves so they can ask important questions and assess them against suitable benchmarks such as the Russell value and growth indexes. Individual investors are generally not able to make this assessment. The books are also useful for their risk comparisons — many of them go beyond volatility to use a broader range of risk measures to assess funds. So use the books, or rely on a financial advisor who has met with the manager either personally, or through their head office, which may have a mutual fund assessment group that meets with fund managers regularly.

## Solution to Benchmark Problem #2: Assessing Your Portfolio's Performance

This is the potentially more serious problem, because your portfolio's return matters much more than the component parts within it. The problem is that it's not always easy to determine portfolio returns in the first place. You should ask your financial advisor to calculate them for you, if you are not already receiving them. It's crucial to know what kind of returns your portfolio is generating, so you can make the appropriate comparisons. How would you otherwise know whether you are getting good advice or making the right decisions? You can also make your own estimates of returns, as I outline in the following math break.

## MATH BREAK

At the beginning of the year, usually in late January, you can calculate your portfolio's return over the previous year. This is a simple calculation since it's just the percentage change of your portfolio from December 31 in the previous year to December 31 of the current year. The value of your portfolio at each date will be on your year-end investment statements sent to you by your advisor, bank, or discount broker:

$$\frac{(\text{December 31 portfolio value}) - (\text{December 31 portfolio value last year})}{(\text{December 31 portfolio value last year})} \times 100$$

Life gets more complicated if you've put additional money in, or taken it out over the course of the year, as is usually the case. You can make some adjustments to reflect these changes. Or if you want to get a general feel for your portfolio's returns, you can create a simple spreadsheet. The sheet has the percentage holding of each fund at the beginning of the year, multiplied by the returns of that fund over the year, which you get from the monthly mutual fund section of a national newspaper, in January. Just add up the weights to arrive at your portfolio's overall return for the year. Here's a simplified version, in which the goal is to calculate the 12-month return of a simple portfolio. The portfolio return is the sum of the individual weights multiplied by their 12-month returns.

| | Portfolio Weight | 12-Month Return | Weight x Return |
|---|---|---|---|
| Canadian Bond Fund | 20% | 8% | 1.6% |
| Canadian Equity Fund | 30% | 10% | 3.0% |
| US Equity Fund | 30% | 12% | 3.6% |
| International Equity Fund | 20% | 11% | 2.2% |
| *Total Portfolio* | *100%* | *?→* | *10.4%* |

The only catch to this method of calculating portfolio return is that it does not account for any changes in the weights over the course of the year, nor does it account for any money you put in or take out during the year. These problems can be corrected by doing two six-month versions — one in July based on returns from January to June, and the other in January on returns from August to December. In July, you use the portfolio weights as at the end of June, which you get from your July account statements. The calculations are not perfectly accurate, and the more money you put in, take out, or move from one fund to another, the less accurate they'll be. But they give you a reasonably good sense of how your portfolio is doing overall.

Once you know how your portfolio did, there are a number of potential benchmarks to gauge your overall returns.

- If your portfolio is close to being evenly balanced between stocks and bonds, then compare it to the average balanced fund, which generally has an even split between bonds and stocks.
- Many of the banks list the returns of their asset allocation programs in the monthly mutual fund reports of the major newspapers. You can see how your portfolio compared to one of their programs. Just make sure that if you have an aggressive portfolio, you compare it to a growth-oriented asset allocation program; an income-oriented safe portfolio should be compared to a conservative program.
- The *National Post* prints returns for its three "FPX" indexes, which were designed by Eric Kirzner and Richard Croft. The three indexes are very good general benchmarks for three types of investors ranging from conservative to aggressive.
- You can customize a benchmark that reflects the exact asset class weights of your portfolio. Using the returns listed in the paper of indexes or index funds for each asset class, calculate what your weighted-average return would have been if you had invested only in the relevant indexes. Compare the all-indexed portfolio to the returns of your actual portfolio. An even easier method is to check out the returns of the few banks that offer index asset allocation programs. These returns are listed in the monthly mutual fund reports as well.

Ultimately you want to know two things:

1. Are there any underperforming funds that you have good reason to believe will continue to underperform?
2. Is your asset mix working, compared with your portfolio benchmarks?

*Fund Assessment:* If a fund is not performing well, but you think it's too early to abandon it, that decision should be made in the context of its weight in the portfolio. If it has a heavy weight, then the risk of it continuing to underperform is high, and you might want to make a switch. But don't switch just because of poor numbers. Satisfy yourself that the manager's skill is not as assured as you thought when you purchased the fund. *If you are rethinking an active fund that you own, there was presumably good reason to invest in it initially, when the alternative would have been to index: Has anything substantially changed in your assessment?* A few bad months, or one bad year, will not turn a good fund into a bad one.

*Asset Mix Assessment:* How do you judge your overall asset mix — especially since you don't want to be making many changes (if any) to a good long-term asset mix that suits your objectives? As we discovered in the "The Rules of Successful Investing," success has as much to do with staying the course, as it does with setting up the right plan in the first place. Every asset mix you use as a comparison for your portfolio is going to be slightly different. That's exactly why I use a number of comparative benchmarks, including the bank rebalancing programs and other mutual fund company asset allocation programs listed in the newspapers. No single comparison gives you the right answer, but using a number of relevant benchmarks will give you a reliable indication.

The only time I would recommend considering a change to your asset mix is if all of your funds are performing at least as well as the average in their category, but your portfolio is clearly underperforming compared with the majority of benchmark portfolios. In this case, you'll want to explore how your mix differs from others. If you're much more heavily invested or significantly underweighted in one asset class, you may want to consider making an adjustment. This would constitute a strategic asset mix change because, as we examined in the chapter on tactical asset allocation, the change is not driven by a call on which markets will do better than others. It's an adjustment that is made to reflect a long-term change in one of two things: your circumstances, or worldwide economic fundamentals.

The most important part of proper benchmarking is to avoid making comparisons against the hottest funds or sectors. The fundamental premise of this book is that successful investing is about putting the odds in our favour. The odds are against you if you move from asset class to asset class. But the odds are in your favour if you:

- have exposure to all major asset classes;
- hold the asset classes in the right proportions to suit your objectives and practical risk tolerance; and
- do not deviate from that predetermined mix, except for the reasons I've listed above.

The hottest funds and stocks are not suitable benchmarks. Don't let the pull of human psychology, especially the pull of regret, motivate you to make unnecessary changes. Compare your returns with what you could have earned in a similarly diversified portfolio, not a portfolio that was designed by someone who was able to predict the future a year ago.

## Recap of Mistake #7: Not Knowing How You're Doing

1. One of the most common reasons for changing asset mixes is to take advantage of the hot markets that you're missing out on. Your portfolio will always appear to be underperforming in comparison with the returns you could have got if you had had heavier weightings in the strongest-performing markets of last year.

2. The particular mutual funds you own are subject to the same sorts of comparison. There are always funds with better returns that will tempt you to switch.

3. The problem in both scenarios is the comparisons themselves, which are not only unproductive, but usually quite destructive. Comparing your funds' returns and your portfolio returns against the wrong benchmarks will lead you to make changes that undermine the integrity of your asset mix.

4. It's human nature to want to avoid the regret that comes when we contemplate what we could have earned last year, if only we'd been more heavily invested in such-and-such a market, or with such-and-such a hot fund manager. It's also human nature to be overconfident in our ability to increase returns by switching to the hot markets and the hot managers. Not knowing what a fund owns and why it performed a certain way makes these switching decisions very costly.

5. Effective benchmarking solves these mistakes; it allows you to productively assess your asset mix and the funds within each asset class. There are two benchmark solutions for two distinct problems. First, to assess a particular fund (that is, the skill of its manager) you need to judge the manager over a series of different time periods, against similar funds and an appropriate market index. Otherwise, you're vulnerable to investing with a lucky manager, whose prospects for future outperformance are remote. The second challenge is to judge your whole portfolio against some useful public benchmarks, all of which are printed in the monthly mutual fund sections of the national newspapers.

# MISTAKE #8

## Underestimating the Power of Compounding

*Eye Opener:*
*Einstein has been attributed with the comment that compound interest is the greatest mathematical discovery of all time. The problem is that, just like E=mc², everyone's heard of it, but most really don't understand its awesome power.*

## The Problem

While most people have been exposed to the concept of compounding, at minimum as part of a math lesson at school, Einstein's alleged remark may seem surprising. If it does seem like an odd or overly dramatic thing to say, maybe the following two scenarios will give you pause. The examples depict the investment strategies of two different couples, each representing two distinct errors related to underestimating the power of compounding. Ms. Late and Mr. Early each started investing at different times. Ms. Diversified and Mr. Cautious each used different investments to take advantage of compounding.

### Compounding Mistake #1: Timing
Ms. Late had a lot of fun in her early years. She didn't give any consideration to saving money until she was 33, when she met and married Mr. Early. They agreed to manage their financial affairs independently, as they

decided not to have children. Upon marriage, Ms. Late began putting aside $500 each month into a balanced mutual fund. She continued this good habit until she retired at age 65. The fund generated an average annual return of 10 percent (which I've assumed compounded at 0.83 percent each month).

Mr. Early was the opposite. He was initially very conscientious, starting his savings program right after university. He saved $500 each month from age 22, in a balanced fund, which also returned 10 percent on average each year. But at age 32, after a near-death experience in a bad car accident, he stopped saving, choosing instead to live day by day.

Here's what they each saved, and the size of their portfolios at age 65.

| | Ms. Late | Mr. Early |
|---|---|---|
| Monthly Savings | $500/month | $500/month |
| Duration of Savings Plan | age 33–65: 32 years | age 22–32: 10 years |
| Total Savings | $192,000 | $60,000 |
| Average Annual Return | 10% | 10% |
| *Retirement Portfolio Value* | *$1,392,563* | *$2,739,230* |

Ms. Late put away *more than three times as much as Mr. Early*, but she ended up with almost half as much at retirement!

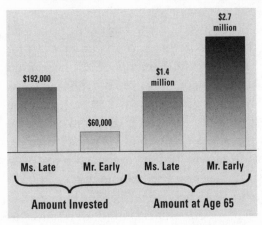

Understanding the concept of compounding is one thing. Really appreciating its power is another. You can see why Einstein was so impressed.

Many investors don't realize how significant the effect of compounding is, since they focus most of their attention — if not all of it — on choosing the best investments. But *timing* your investments is just as important — not timing as in "market timing," but timing as in "getting in early." It is common to wait to invest until "the market settles" or "I can see where the market is heading" or "I have more money to invest" or "after I buy a new car." The longer you wait, the less you are able to maximize the effect of compounding because *the magic is based on the accelerated impact that occurs in later years*. But you never get to those "later" years if you don't start early.

For instance, $10,000 will be worth just over $16,000 five years from now if invested at 10 percent per year. But that $16,000 will be worth almost $26,000 five years later, and almost $42,000 five years after that. As the underlying value grows, there's more money to compound! So the investment grows exponentially. This is the key to compounding that is not intuitive for most people: Most of the benefit accrues in the latter part of an investment's life, so the longer the life, the bigger the impact.

This characteristic cuts both ways, however. For instance, inflation is compounding in reverse. If you put your money under your mattress, it will lose value if there is inflation in the economy. And it loses more and more value the longer it sits there (and the higher the inflation rate). A manageable amount of inflation in an economy is a good thing since it provides governments and central banks with some flexibility in managing the economy and "oiling" the system. But inflation preys on money under a mattress. Remember, money is only useful as a means to an end — to purchase things with. But if the purchasing power of money declines, then its value falls. Invested money does not lose its purchasing power as long as it earns returns that are the same as, or higher than, the inflation rate. But mattress money gets ravaged as the compounding effect of inflation reduces its value year after year.

Here's another example showing how compounding can be as harmful as it can be beneficial. Compounding can be especially problematic for highly volatile funds. When you assess the returns of a volatile fund without considering the impact of compounding, you can miss out on its subtle but powerful effect. How about a fund that loses 59 percent in one year, and gains 80 percent in the next year? You might think you're up overall, since the second-year gain was quite a bit higher than the first-year loss. But your real return, if you held the fund over the two years, is a loss of 26 percent! Volatility can drag down compound returns. It takes larger gains to make up for losses — compounding working in reverse — since big losses reduce the base of your investment, on which you need to compound to make up the loss. For instance, a 10 percent loss in one year requires an 11 percent gain the following year to break even. A 25 percent loss requires a 33 percent gain, and a 50 percent loss requires that you double your money to get back to where you were before the loss. Highly volatile funds have an extra burden: When they go down a lot, you have less money to compound on, so it takes even bigger returns to recoup.

## Compounding Mistake #2: Rates of Return

A second compounding-related mistake investors make is underestimating how much the end value of your investments can diverge when compounding at a higher rate compared to a lower rate. Here is a comparison of the investment history and ending portfolio values for Ms. Diversified and Mr. Cautious. The only difference between their investment strategies was what they chose to invest in. Ms. Diversified invested in a balanced fund, which returned 10 percent on average each year (compounded monthly at 0.8 percent). Her husband, however, was much more cautious and insisted on investing in GICs exclusively, which averaged 5 percent (compounded monthly at 0.4 percent). Ms. Diversified and Mr. Cautious both started saving when they met at age 20, although they only contributed $100 each month to their respective investments.

|  | Ms. Diversified | Mr. Cautious |
|---|---|---|
| Monthly Savings | $100/month | $100/month |
| Duration of Savings Plan | age 20–65: 45 years | age 20–65: 45 years |
| Total Savings | $54,000 | $54,000 |
| Average Annual Return | 10% | 5% |
| *Retirement Portfolio Value* | *$1,048,250* | *$202,644* |

Mr. Cautious really paid a heavy price for his conservatism. Even though they both saved the same dollar amount, Ms. Diversified ended up with over five times the portfolio value! Thankfully, Ms. Diversified will be able to ensure they retire comfortably.

We examined this difference in an earlier chapter when we discussed the risk of not investing aggressively enough for retirement. But we didn't explore just how much acceleration occurs in a diversified portfolio such as Ms. Diversified's. As in the case of starting early, the higher-returning investment accelerates the growth of Ms. Diversified's portfolio. The divergence between her 10 percent portfolio and her husband's 5 percent portfolio just keeps on growing. As the underlying value of her portfolio gets bigger, there's more to compound, and so it gets even bigger, which allows even more to compound, and so on. That's why her portfolio diverges so dramatically from her husband's as time goes on. The divergence grows with time.

# The Behavioural Explanation

- *Satisfycing*
- *Innumeracy*

Here's an interesting psychological experiment that is purported to test the self-control of an infant. The results, it is claimed, can suggest the future success of the individual, since the experiment tests for one of the key factors of "life success" — the willingness to forgo some current pleasure for greater future pleasure.

The experiment was developed in the 1960s and tracked the success of four-year-olds until they graduated from high school. The four-year-olds were given a simple test. They were offered a marshmallow, but told that if they were willing to forgo the marshmallow and wait until the experimenter ran an errand, they could have two marshmallows upon his return from the errand. Some children patiently waited for 15 minutes so they could enjoy the bigger rewards. Others took the marshmallow right away and passed up the opportunity for bigger but deferred rewards. Those who resisted temptation and were able to delay their gratification for greater pleasure were compared as adolescents with those who were more impulsive and ate the one marshmallow right away. Those who demonstrated an ability to defer pleasure were markedly more socially competent, assertive, confident, initiative-taking, and better able to cope with frustration. They ended up being superior students with much better scores on their university entry exams.

I can't comment on the legitimacy of the test or its meaningfulness. But it does reveal an important part of our psychology. There's no question that it is difficult for most of us to pass up pleasure today for pleasure tomorrow. Most of us don't even understand just how much we're truly passing up. The initial sacrifice is obvious because it's in front of our faces and there for the taking. But the postponed pleasure is hard to quantify intuitively — much harder than the prospect of an extra marshmallow. Unlike a computer, which can assess a number of options and then print out the pros and cons of each along with a recommendation, our brains are not quite as rigorous in assessing tradeoffs. We tend to consider options only until we reach the first satisfactory one. We look at the fewest number of options to get to an outcome that meets our minimum requirements. Behavioural economists call this quirk "satisfycing," as we discussed in "The Limits of Our Thinking."

Satisfycing is a good strategy for buying a car when you don't have the time or energy to test-drive every single model. But the same shortcut approach to decision making can be harmful when you are choosing an investment — especially if you're choosing whether to invest now and consume later, or consume now and invest later. How many people really know the tradeoff they're making when they decide to consume now? How many have knowledgeably and purposefully weighed all the options and decided that an Accord now is better than an Acura later? Or that a trip to Florida now is better than a trip to France later? Or that an elaborately decorated home now is better than a retirement cottage later?

Satisfycing is a genetically useful time-saving device. But it is not as productive for assessing your investment options. And satisfycing is even more tempting in investing than in other areas, because of innumeracy — most of us are not intuitive about numbers. It's hard for us to internalize the acceleration of growth that occurs in the life of an investment. The steep line that shows accelerating dollar returns, where $10,000 grows faster and faster, appears odd to most people — as if it were a trick or illusion. With a few Einstein-like exceptions, our brains have not evolved to internalize complex mathematical relationships intuitively. So a lack of understanding feeds the satisfycing technique that most of us employ to assess alternatives and make decisions. Our brains are busy multi-tasking machines with many priorities and incoming data to sort out and make meaning of; they prefer quick solutions that ignore complexity such as the tradeoffs that result from the accelerating nature of compounding.

## The Solution

The earlier you invest, the better. In fact, given the conclusions we drew from Mistake #2 ("Timing the Market") on how unpredictable the market is in the short term, there's no time like the *soonest possible time* to invest your money. We don't know if the market will be higher or lower next week, next month, or even next year. But we do know that compounding starts as soon as you invest, so it alone favours an immediate investment.

You may have heard of the "rule of 72," which calculates how long it takes to double your money. You take the expected annual return on your investment — say 10 percent — and divide it into 72. In this case it will take just over seven years to double your money. If you are lucky enough to average 12 percent a year, it will only take six years (72 divided by 12).

This little rule captures the essence of compounding in a very simple but compelling way.

The magic comes from the acceleration effect, which is important to understand, because it's neither intuitive nor obvious for most people. Here's a chart that depicts the acceleration of the compounding effect, based on two investments of $10,000. One investment generates 10 percent each year; the other generates 5 percent each year. You can see how the compounding effect accelerates as the portfolios grow over 40 years; the divergence between the two investments expands with time.

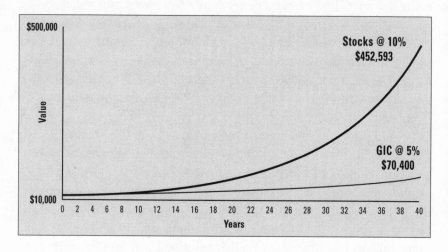

Compounding creates a virtuous cycle: *Compounding creates more money that benefits from additional compounding.* That's why the acceleration effect occurs if enough time elapses, and why it's important to get the cycle started as early as possible.

Don't underestimate the power of compounding. Maximize that power by (i) getting it working for you early; and (ii) investing in the highest-growth investments (and therefore the highest risk) that your practical risk tolerance will accommodate. Don't be a victim to "satisfycing": If you want to trade off some pleasure tomorrow for some consumption today, make sure you think through how much future pleasure you will be giving up and whether it's worth the future sacrifice. Psychology will pull you in the direction of quick intuitive decisions based on a tradeoff analysis that is superficial and usually not representative of the most profitable outcome.

## A Word About Dollar-Cost Averaging

Dollar-cost averaging is a widely promoted strategy in the investment industry. It is a technique that allows you to average down the cost of your investment by making purchases at regular intervals. The idea is to invest an amount, say $100, in a mutual fund at the same time every month. You'll end up buying fund units at a number of different prices, the average of which is likely to be lower than a lump-sum purchase, since you'll end up buying more units, when the price is down, with the same fixed purchase amount. This strategy is a hotly debated topic in academic circles because it doesn't support the idea of investing early to take advantage of compounding. Most academics agree that the major benefit of dollar-cost averaging is the psychological discipline that a regular savings plan enforces, not the possibility of buying at a low average price.

Regular savings plans — where you invest automatically a certain amount at regular intervals, such as monthly — are one of the best ways to enforce savings in a reasonably painless way. One of the advantages of a regular investment plan is the potential to benefit from dollar-cost averaging. But what if you have a large lump sum to invest — an inheritance, employment bonus, or gift? This is where the strategy of dollar-cost averaging is overused. Research on this topic generally favours investing lump sums immediately, in a mix of assets that reflect the objectives and risk tolerance of the investor.

Let's say you're quite risk-averse, and you inherit a large stock portfolio. Would you sell all the stocks and invest the money in T-bills as quickly as possible? Probably not. Why? Because you wouldn't want to be vulnerable to the intense regret you'd suffer if the stock market went up. Averaging into the market undermines the power of compounding and relies too heavily on short-term market volatility. Since the market goes up in the long run, and goes up in the short term more than it goes down, dollar-cost averaging a lump sum into the market is not prudent. Lump sums should be invested when they are received, in a manner that is consistent with the objectives for that money. The power of compounding outweighs the possible benefit of averaging down the cost of a lump-sum investment.

The best way to think about dollar-cost averaging, therefore, is as the secondary benefit of regular investment plans, whose purpose is to siphon off part of your monthly income, to be invested in a consistent way.

The bottom line is this: Get invested. The sooner the better, no matter what the amount. And get the best return your practical risk tolerance will allow. Time and compounding will work together to do the rest. Who are we to question the genius of Einstein?

## Recap of Mistake #8: Underestimating the Power of Compounding

1. Almost everyone has heard of compounding and how "magical" it is. But many investors don't really understand the acceleration effect of compounding. They therefore leave its power untapped.

2. There are two fundamental compounding errors: underestimating the impact of investing early, and underestimating the impact of investing in higher-returning investments.

3. This lack of true understanding is to be expected because most of us are innumerate; the math of compounding is not intuitive for us. Our overworked brains prefer to "satisfyce" when they can, choosing the first acceptable option that we contemplate, rather than analyzing the complexities and tradeoffs implicit in all possible choices. Additionally, many of us are reluctant to sacrifice a marshmallow right now for the prospect of having two at some point in the future.

4. Compounding is one of the most powerful tools you have to build wealth. Its magic lies in the acceleration effect that occurs in the latter part of an investment period. But you need a sufficiently long period to generate the magic. Compounding is free. It's easy. And it's taken advantage of by far too few investors.

# MISTAKE #9

## Underestimating
## the Impact of Tax

**Eye Opener:**

Q: *According to the monthly mutual fund report in the newspaper, Fund A had a better one-year return than Fund B. But Fund B actually made its investors richer. How can this be?*

A: *Tax. Returns are always reported before tax is paid by investors. But wealth is determined by the money you put in your pocket, not what you share with the government. The high portfolio turnover of Fund A imposed more frequent capital gains tax payments on its investors. Most of the investors in this fund will celebrate their great returns, and never know that they could have made more money in a fund with lower reported returns.*

If Einstein thought compounding was the greatest mathematical discovery of all time, I wouldn't be surprised if he also thought taxes were one of the most miserable inventions. Most investors are not fully aware of the enormous impact taxes can have on their returns and overall wealth. And this lack of awareness makes them helpless to do anything about it.

There are very few ways to avoid paying taxes, but there *are* some basic ways to minimize them. These opportunities are outlined by a number of good books that go into the fine detail of how you can manage your family's overall tax burden. In this chapter, I will focus on taxes only as they relate to three particular investing problems.

# The Problem

## Tax Problem #1: Misinterpreting Your Returns

Mr. Conservative and Ms. Aggressive decided they each wanted a new car in five years. They decided to each invest $20,000 in an equity fund of their choice, in a non-registered account. Mr. Conservative chose a popular large Canadian equity fund, while Ms. Aggressive chose a smaller Canadian equity fund that had a lot of technology stocks in it.

At the end of the fifth year, they both redeemed their money. Mr. Conservative, whose investment generated an average annual return of 12 percent according to the monthly mutual fund section of his newspaper, was initially quite pleased. But then he engaged Ms. Aggressive in a conversation, during which she proudly announced that she had earned an annual average return of 13 percent. He was disappointed and thought he should have taken a little more risk with his money. He could have ended up with $36,849 instead of $35,247. By his judgement, he missed out on $1,602, which would have paid for an alarm system for the new Jetta he was going to buy.

What neither realized was that Mr. Conservative actually made more money! But why?

If you guessed it has something to do with tax, you're right. Perhaps you guessed it's because Ms. Aggressive's fund held some bonds, so more of her returns came as interest income, which is taxed at a higher rate than capital gains. A reasonable guess, but not necessarily correct in this case. (I'd be very concerned about a small-cap technology fund holding a lot of bonds.)

Here's the answer. Mr. Conservative invested in an equity fund that had virtually no turnover over the five years he owned it. Turnover is a measure of how much buying and selling a fund manager does. The low-turnover fund was run by a manager whose philosophy was to buy stocks and just hold them, rather than always trying to switch the securities held in the fund.

The fund that Ms. Aggressive invested in was very actively managed. In fact it had an average annual turnover of 200 percent each year. This meant that there was so much buying and selling of stocks by the manager that it was as if all the stocks in the fund were sold and new ones bought — twice — within each year.

You may wonder why this matters. After all, Ms. Aggressive's fund earned the better return, so who cares that her fund manager bought and sold a lot? Her fund manager obviously made the right decisions since the fund's returns were superior. The reason it matters is that she was not able to defer any capital gains tax since capital gains were triggered every time the fund manager sold a stock at a higher price than he bought it at, and he did a lot of selling. Mr. Conservative, on the other hand, was not liable for any capital gains tax until he sold his fund at the end of five years. The manager of his fund did not sell any stocks.

Because Ms. Aggressive paid capital gains tax each year on the stocks that her manager had sold at a gain, Ms. Aggressive had to make an actual cash outlay each year. So some of her investment was taken out and paid to the government, while Mr. Conservative had all his money working for him throughout the five years. He was able to earn a return on *all* of his money over the five-year period, whereas Ms. Aggressive earned a return on *most* of her money, but not the part that went to the government at the end of each year.

The result of the different tax implications for each fund is that Mr. Conservative ended up with more in his pocket, even though his pre-tax performance was worse than Ms. Aggressive's. The capital gains benefit of his low-turnover fund more than offset her higher return.

The returns you see in the newspaper, or even on your account statement, are not the returns you get. The newspaper returns assume full reinvestment of all realized gains. While you may elect to have all distributions reinvested automatically, you still have to come up with the cash and pay the tax, so you're out-of-pocket one way or the other. The only returns that really matter are the cash flow returns, or the amount you pocket at the end of the day. Taxes can have as big an impact on your cash flow returns as mutual fund fees in some cases. But they're much less conspicuous and that's why many investors are oblivious to them. Recent research suggests that between 1 and 3 percent of returns are lost annually by investors not considering the tax impact of high portfolio turnover.

High turnover is not a problem if the fund is generating returns that are far in excess of the index or the average fund in the same category. You'll still be ahead with a very high-performing fund that does not allow you to defer capital gains tax. But as we saw in Mistake #4, on overestimating active management, not that many funds can consistently perform well above average, year after year.

Individual fund performance is also affected when a fund has very low turnover but high capital gains tax distributions. How can that happen?

Easy. Buy-and-hold fund managers can sit on stocks for a long time. So the stocks increase in value year after year, accruing a large capital gain. No problem there.

But two things can happen. One is that the manager decides at some point that the stock is no longer a good investment and decides to sell it. The large accumulated capital gain is crystallized and distributed to all unitholders, who have to pay tax on it. The other possibility is that the fund starts to suffer redemptions from investors. Perhaps its performance has been below average for a while. Or a number of investors happen to have decided to reclaim their money at the same time. The manager needs to pay out these investors so she has to raise cash in the fund, if there isn't enough cash already there to satisfy all the redemptions. To raise cash, the manager must sell some holdings, and she may choose to sell stocks with large accumulated gains if she thinks these are the least favourable ones in her fund. Again, the capital gains are crystallized and paid out to all unitholders at the end of the year.

So the opportunity to defer capital gains may be undermined even in a low-turnover buy-and-hold fund. *Almost all fund managers are judged against their peers on a before-tax basis, because that's what the newspapers report.* So they will naturally pay much more attention to maximizing the before-tax returns of their funds. This can cost investors money in the form of capital gains taxes that would otherwise be deferred. This is another case of "agency conflict," which we defined in Mistake #4. The manager, as an agent making investments on your behalf, has objectives (high before-tax performance) that aren't perfectly aligned with yours (high after-tax returns — money that you put in your pocket).

If you aren't aware of the tax you're paying on your returns, then you presumably aren't aware of how much money you're losing because of the lost opportunity to defer tax. Even worse, you are probably not structuring your portfolio in a way that minimizes tax.

## Tax Problem #2: Portfolio Construction

When we explored how to make a proper assessment of your returns in Mistake #7, we looked at both the fund returns and the portfolio returns. The same approach is required when we consider taxation. Allow me to demonstrate . . .

Mr. Unaware gives no consideration to tax in his investment strategy. But he's very diligent when it comes to asset allocation and has structured his RRSP and non-registered accounts very prudently to reflect his financial objectives. Ms. Accountant is all too aware of what taxes can do to her overall returns. She is equally conscientious about asset mix, and happens to have the same overall mix as Mr. Unaware, since her objectives and risk tolerance are very similar. But she structures her portfolios with a view to minimizing tax. They both have $100,000 in their RRSPs and $100,000 outside of their RRSPs. And they both have a mix of 10 percent cash, 30 percent bonds, and 60 percent stocks. Here are their respective portfolios:

| | Mr. Unaware's Portfolio | | Mix of Both Portfolios | Ms. Accountant's Portfolio | |
| | RRSP | Non-Reg. | | RRSP | Non-Reg. |
|---|---|---|---|---|---|
| Cash | $10,000 | $10,000 | 10% | $15,000 | $5,000 |
| Bonds | $30,000 | $30,000 | 30% | $50,000 | $10,000 |
| Stocks | $60,000 | $60,000 | 60% | $35,000 | $85,000 |
| Total | $100,000 | $100,000 | 100% | $100,000 | $100,000 |
| Annual Tax Bill | $0 | $1,200 | | $0 | $432 |

I've ignored dividends and assumed that capital gains accrue within the equity funds because the managers' buy-and-hold strategies result in no capital gains distributions. I've also assumed that both investors have a marginal tax rate of 48 percent on interest income, and that cash earns 4 percent and bonds earn 7 percent. The main difference between their portfolios is that Mr. Unaware is holding $40,000 in interest-earning securities, outside his RRSP, while Ms. Accountant only holds $15,000 in this way. The interest income Mr. Unaware has to pay tax on is considerably higher.

Ms. Accountant is saving a lot of money each year, since much of the income thrown off by her cash and bond portfolios will be reinvested to grow *tax-free* within her RRSP. Outside of her RRSP, her equity capital gains will accrue and taxes paid on them will be deferred until she sells her fund (as long as she's not invested in a fund with high turnover). Even a high-turnover fund will be subjected to lower tax than interest income since capital gains are taxed at 67 percent of the rate of interest income.

When Mr. Unaware and Ms. Accountant liquidate their non-registered portfolios at some point in the future, Mr. Unaware will have much lower capital gains tax to pay, by virtue of his smaller stock ownership outside of his RRSP. But year after year of paying three times as much in tax on interest income will put him far behind Ms. Accountant. In fact, the gap in the net worth of each individual will increase as time goes by. The longer the time frame, the richer Ms. Accountant will be, compared with Mr. Unaware. In the year we're looking at, she has almost $800 more money that will compound for her the following year. Let's assume that extra $800 compounds in her equity fund at 10 percent for 20 years until she retires. That's an extra $5,382 in her non-registered account that Mr. Unaware doesn't have. She'll have to pay tax on it eventually, but even after tax, she's over $3,500 richer. And that's just one year of tax savings compounding away! Imagine 20 years of tax savings each year, compounding. Now we're approaching a pre-tax bonus of $46,000, just for being aware of the impact of tax on a non-registered portfolio.

Poor Mr. Unaware. He could have taken an extravagant safari-type trip upon retirement, paid for with nothing other than the tax savings on a better-structured portfolio.

### Tax Problem #3: Principal Versus Income

Upon retirement, Ms. Accountant suffered from a different problem altogether. The interest and dividends from her portfolio were insufficient to cover the cost of her living expenses. She had no family to bequeath her estate to, and was therefore planning on using her portfolio to fund some luxury in her retirement. She complained to her advisor that she needed more regular income to pay for her expenses. When he suggested that she maintain her existing asset mix and simply sell some of her stock holdings to generate the income she needed, she recoiled in shock. Why in the world would she want to reduce her principal? That would be a slippery slope to starvation. If the interest income generated from her portfolio didn't cover her expenses, she would simply have to cut back some of the luxuries she was planning on. Since she didn't want to make the sacrifice, she decided to increase her holdings in bonds in order to generate more interest income.

Even though Ms. Accountant knew that interest income would be taxed at a higher rate outside of her registered account, she was not convinced by the logic of her advisor. She preferred paying the penalty of higher tax to the unappealing alternative of drawing down her principal.

## The Behavioural Explanation

- *Lack of Knowledge*
- *Mental Accounting*

Many investors don't know what they don't know. You never see your after-tax returns, unless you're really conscientious and figure it all out on your own. It would be nice if what you didn't know or see wouldn't hurt you. But it doesn't work that conveniently.

After-tax return reporting is very hard to come by. You won't get it on your investment account statement. In fact many fund companies, banks, brokers, and planning companies are just starting to invest in the technology to put personal rates of return on your statement, never mind after-tax personal rates of return. Even the monthly mutual fund sections in the national newspapers show only the absolute returns, without any attempt to approximate after-tax returns. This gap in reporting in the industry is understandable, since there are many different marginal tax rates, depending on which province you live in, and how much income you earn. It would be potentially misleading to assume one marginal tax rate for all investors.

Most mutual fund software programs show a statistic related to the tax efficiency of a fund, based on an estimate of how big the taxable distributions are to unitholders. A very tax-efficient fund, such as an index fund, will have a tax efficiency of 99 percent, meaning that an investor will pocket 99 percent of the total return. An active fund with a high turnover will be more like 70 percent, meaning that an investor will only keep 70 percent of the total return, with 30 percent going to taxes. I expect (and hope) that the newspapers will start to report a similar statistic eventually.

If you think of your RRSP or RRIF as completely separate from your non-registered accounts, which many of us do out of a tendency toward mental accounting, you will not be minimizing your tax liabilities. In the "Solution" section of this chapter we'll explore the scenario where it can make sense to treat them distinctly; however, effective tax planning requires for the most part that they be considered in combination.

Mental accounting is also the motivation behind the desire for many people to be inflexible around the old golden rule "don't dip into capital." By putting interest and dividend income into a separate mental account from capital gains, investors are reluctant to make homemade dividends by selling their shares. Selling shares is often a much more tax-effective way of creating income, but only if you get past the mental accounting problem. There's nothing fundamentally wrong with selling shares to free up money to spend. Pulling out $1,000 in capital represents the same economic activity as not reinvesting $1,000 of dividends or interest back into shares. Whether you withdraw $1,000 in capital, or you use your income instead of reinvesting it, you're still subtracting from the possible future returns of your portfolio. So why not take the more tax-effective approach?

On top of being invisible, tax information is a little intimidating for many people, because it can appear so complicated. It's the kind of issue that many investors are happy to ignore. But only at their peril.

## The Solution

The best defensive strategy against taxes is to defer them. *It's just another example of compounding!* The idea is to keep as much of your money working for you — compounding, that is — for as long as possible. As soon as you dispense your money — to someone else, including the government — it stops compounding. If you can postpone paying out cash, you can keep it compounding so you enjoy the incremental returns that are generated from the money that would otherwise be working for someone else.

If you could pay the government $100 today or in 10 years, you would be far better off to pay in 10 years. You can invest the $100 for 10 years at 10 percent, and keep the extra $159 you earn from compounding returns over the decade. The more you delay paying the government, the longer you have to earn money on your money. And of course a $100,000 portfolio offers a much bigger tax-deferral opportunity than $100.

The most common and obvious way to defer taxes (but one that is still underused by too many people) is the RRSP. The money you invest in an RRSP compounds until you take it out. As a bonus, the government allows you to deduct your contribution from your current income, thereby reducing the taxes you owe in the year you contribute. You'll eventually pay tax — on the withdrawals from your registered plan, since you've deferred the taxes until that time. But for most people that time is far enough in the future that they can get their money compounding in the most aggressive way possible — without paying tax on the returns as they compound.

In addition to registered accounts, there are other ways to defer paying tax. As we saw in the examples, you can effectively defer tax by taking advantage of buy-and-hold strategies that postpone the realization of capital gains. Mutual funds with low turnovers — index funds are good examples — accomplish exactly this. You do have some control over the tax you pay — more than many investors realize. And tax needs to be minimized like any other cost.

## Marginal Tax Rates

It's crucial to know your *marginal tax rate* because that's the rate you'll pay on your last dollar of income, dividends, or capital gains. Your marginal tax rate is your combined federal and provincial tax, and it is determined by your level of income and which province you live in.

Each province determines the level of income at which the highest marginal rate kicks in. For example, in New Brunswick the highest rate doesn't apply until you reach almost $100,000. In most other provinces, you only have to earn $75,600 to be subject to the highest marginal tax rate. Only British Columbia, at $82,500, and Nova Scotia, at $82,100, have higher thresholds.

But the top marginal tax rates also differ by province. The highest rate is 51.7 percent in Quebec, followed by B.C. at 51.3 percent. The lowest is 43.5 percent in the Northwest Territories and Nunavut, followed by 43.7 percent in Alberta. Ontario is in the middle at 47.9 percent; most of the other provinces are in the high forties. The highest rates apply to salary income and investment interest. A lower rate applies to investment dividends and capital gains because these types of investment income are given favourable tax treatment to encourage Canadians to invest in Canadian companies. Only 67 percent of capital gains are taxable, which brings down the top marginal tax rate on gains to around 32 percent (depending on the province). The dividend tax credit brings the top tax payable on dividends to 33 percent (again, depending on the province).

## Solution to Tax Problem #1: Misinterpreting Your Returns

There are at least two types of accrued capital gains you want to be cognizant of, although neither matters at all within your RRSP or RRIF, within which all investments are sheltered from tax. The first are the capital gains that the fund has *realized* by selling some stocks or bonds during the year. The second are the capital gains that are *unrealized* because the stocks in the fund have appreciated, but have not been sold. There's actually a third type, which is obvious: the capital gains that arise when you sell the fund yourself at a gain.

The first type — realized gains — are capital gains from appreciated securities that the manager has sold. These accrued gains are usually paid out once a year, typically in December. Even if you buy a fund in November or early December, you are likely to receive a capital gains distribution from securities that were sold during the year. And you will have to pay tax on this distribution, even though you didn't get the benefit of the rise in security prices. This is not quite as awful as it sounds since the adjusted cost base of your investment is increased as the capital gains distributions are reinvested in the fund. So your tax liability will be less when you eventually sell your fund units. However, it does mean that you are paying for capital gains up front, before you've earned them. This is the opposite of tax deferral and works to your disadvantage.

The easy way around this problem is to avoid making large equity mutual fund purchases near the end of the year. By purchasing in January, you are able to avoid having to pay tax right away on the previous year's realized capital gains. The problem of paying capital gains tax up front is not significant if the fund has accrued minimal realized capital gains, as is the case with many equity funds that employ a buy-and-hold strategy, and therefore have very low turnovers.

An alternative method of reducing your capital gains tax liability is to realize a capital loss in the same year as you realize a gain. If you sell a fund that triggers a capital gain, or are expecting a large capital gains distribution to be made by one of your funds, check to see if there is a fund you own that is currently valued at a price that is lower than its book value. If you sell the fund at a loss, you can use the capital loss to offset the gain on the first fund, thereby reducing or even avoiding capital gains tax on the first fund. The catch is that you can't reinvest in the fund that you've sold for at least 30 days, otherwise your capital loss may be disallowed by the tax authorities. Simply reinvest in a different fund within the same asset class. For instance, you can sell a European equity fund that is sitting with a loss, and invest in a different European fund.

The second type of gains are unrealized gains. These are stocks that have risen quite a bit but have not been sold by the fund. When the manager eventually sells them, a large capital gain will be realized, for which a distribution will be made; you will have to pay tax on the distribution, no matter how long you've been invested in the fund. So even if you wait until January to buy into a fund that has a large unrealized capital gain, you have to be aware of the eventual tax liability you could face if the fund manager sells those appreciated securities before you cash out of the fund. There's no way to avoid these unrealized gains on highly appreciated securities within the fund; however, you can minimize them by investing in funds run by managers who tend to hold on to the securities they purchase for a long time, no matter how high they rise in price.

It bears repeating that when capital gains are distributed from a fund, it's not that you're paying *more* tax. You're simply paying tax on the capital gains *earlier*, rather than waiting until you ultimately sell the fund. The problem with paying the tax early is that you lose the value of having that money compound for you as an investment.

## Where to Get the Capital Gains Information You Need

The best source of capital gains information is the annual and semi-annual reports that the mutual fund companies publish every year. Here's where to find the crucial numbers:

*Realized Capital Gains:* The "Statement of Operations" in both reports contains a table showing "net realized gain (loss) on sale of investments" for each fund. This is the amount of capital gains that were realized and will be distributed at year-end. This number isn't much use in the annual report since by the time you see it, it will already have been paid out. But in the semi-annual report, it gives you an indication of what's coming at the end of the year (although the manager may still offset any gains by selling some securities at a loss).

*Unrealized Capital Gains:* The "Statement of Investment Portfolio" contains this information. You have to subtract the average cost (or book value, as it's sometimes called) of the total portfolio from its current market value. The difference is what the fund is accruing in unrealized gains. The total unrealized gain will generate a tax liability for you if the manager sells the appreciated securities before you sell your fund. This value changes daily, since the market value will change as the security prices move. If it's a very large number, it's unlikely to come down significantly unless the market suffers a bad correction. On the other hand, it could be a high number, but the manager may be employing a buy-and-hold strategy, making it unlikely that the securities with large unrealized gains will be sold in the near term. A good way to determine the likelihood of selling and realizing some of the gains is to look at the portfolio's annual turnover.

*Turnover:* This is the best measure of buying and selling you can get for a fund. Listed in the fund's prospectus, it is simply the lesser of security purchases and sales, divided by the average assets of the fund. It is expressed as a percentage; for example, if a fund has a 100 percent turnover, this means that there was as much activity in the fund as if the fund manager had bought and sold all of the securities in the fund during the year — a high turnover of securities. It gives you an indication of how much trading occurs in the fund, which is what generates the taxable realized capital gains. A low turnover fund, such as an index fund at 5 to 15 percent, will not be selling many securities, so unrealized gains will continue to accrue without your having to pay tax on them (although the index fund, like any other fund, will have to sell some securities to fund investor redemptions). A high turnover fund, with a ratio of 100 percent or more, is likely to sell some securities, so the unrealized gains will be crystallized and you will have to pay tax. Turnover results from either the manager's active strategy, or from the buying and selling of fund units by investors — activity that forces the manager to buy and sell securities to accommodate cash inflows and outflows.

Aside from reading the prospectus yourself, you can ask your advisor to investigate the tax efficiency of your mutual funds. Or call the fund companies directly to ask for the funds' accrued capital gains — both realized and unrealized.

## Solution to Tax Problem #2: Portfolio Construction

Structure your portfolio with taxes in mind. Don't fall into the trap of thinking of your registered and non-registered accounts as completely unrelated. There's only one reason — albeit a very legitimate one — to consider your registered and non-registered portfolios separately. If your financial objectives are completely different for each portfolio, then they can be managed more independently. For instance, your RRSP portfolio may have a 20-year time horizon or longer. But you might be saving for a new home in four years with your non-registered savings. In this case, it wouldn't make sense to load up your RRSP with bonds and hold most of your equities outside of your RRSP.

But in most cases, you should view both accounts together as a whole, even if it's just to tilt your registered account toward more interest-bearing securities, so you can leave more equities in your taxable account. If you recall Ms. Accountant's portfolio, she didn't hold all her interest-bearing securities inside the RRSP and all her equities outside. Her mix, which you may want to take a second look at, reflected three fundamental constraints:

1. Most of her interest-bearing investments were inside her RRSP because they're taxed at a higher rate.
2. She tailored her RRSP mix and her non-registered mix to reflect slightly different objectives. She held some cash and bonds outside of

the RRSP since she needed some liquidity and some diversification in her non-registered portfolio, because she was planning to use some of this money within the next few years.

3. Her overall asset mix reflected her overall financial objective, which was generally long-term. She had to hold some equity in her RRSP to offset the holding of cash and bonds outside of it, so that her asset mix was in line with her goals.

Remember, your net worth is a function of the returns you get on your money *and* the tax efficiency of those returns, which will depend in part on how you've constructed your entire portfolio.

### Solution to Tax Problem #3: Principal Versus Income

Don't be intimidated by that old rule that dictates that you shouldn't touch your principal. The fact that the marginal tax rate on dividends is slightly higher than the tax on capital gains is a good reason for selling stock shares to raise cash for living expenses. The impact on your net worth is virtually identical: Since any dividends that are siphoned off to pay for expenses could have been invested in more shares anyway, the opportunity cost of taking dividends or selling shares is the same!

And it's much better to sell some shares than to overload your portfolio with bonds or cash that provide regular income, since you can end up losing a lot of that income to tax.

The money you have left in your pocket at the end of the day, to spend or bequeath, is the only money that matters. And that money is after-tax cash.

## Recap of Mistake #9: Underestimating the Impact of Tax

1. Many investors are unaware of their after-tax returns. These returns are not reported on account statements. To get an indication of how they're doing, many investors use the newspapers, which report pre-tax mutual fund returns.

2. Lack of appreciation for the effect of taxes can lead to some bad investment decisions — two in particular. First, investors are inclined to favour high-return funds, which can be low-return funds after tax is accounted for. Second, portfolio construction

that ignores the different tax effects of different asset classes can have a severely detrimental impact on ultimate returns.

3. Mutual fund financial statements contain important information that can help you take taxes into consideration. They track both the realized and the accumulated but unrealized capital gains of the underlying securities in the fund. Realized gains will involve a tax liability in the year the gain was crystallized, while accrued but unrealized gains involve a future potential tax liability when the manager sells the appreciated stocks. Armed with this knowledge, investors can time their mutual fund purchases wisely, and make offsetting transactions, such as selling another fund at a loss.

4. Structuring your RRSP and non-registered accounts with a view to minimizing tax requires that you consider them as two components of your overall portolio. This approach is contrary to what mental accounting would otherwise entice you to do.

5. Don't believe the adage that you "shouldn't touch your capital." Investors tend to separate capital gains from dividends and interest, placing them in different mental accounts. However, the best way to free up cash is often to sell shares, rather than to load up on interest-paying securities. Capital gains are taxed at only 67 percent of the rate that interest income is, and selling shares causes no more of an economic loss than does *not* reinvesting dividends or interest.

6. Taxes have an enormous impact on the only returns that matter — the cash you put in your pocket that you can make purchases with or bequeath.

# MISTAKE #10

## Overpaying
## for Guarantees

**Eye Opener:**

Q:  *How much money would you pay to eliminate a one-in-1,000 chance of dying within the next three hours? How much would you insist on being paid to accept a one-in-1,000 chance of dying within the next three hours?*

A:  *Most people would pay very little for the first offer, but require a large amount to take on the risk of the second. Studies have shown that many would pay around $200 to avoid the risk, while requiring $50,000 to take on the risk!*

Considering how quirky we can be when it comes to risk — and our willingness to pay to reduce it — guaranteed investment products might sound ideal. You get all the upside of the markets, with a guarantee on your original investment so there's no risk of losing money. What's the catch? You pay for that benefit, and it's like anything with bells and whistles: if you don't use them, you're paying for nothing. Would you buy a top-of-the-line audio system if you just wanted to listen to the radio once in a while? Why pay for something you don't need?

## The Problem

What's a guarantee worth? It's worth whatever benefit you as an individual derive from it. If you're 30 years old with a long investment horizon ahead of you, it's not worth that much. But if you're close to retiring on a modest investment portfolio, the ability to eliminate the risk of losing your principal has a lot of value. If you can't eat or sleep when the market gyrates in its usual way, then a guarantee has value to you as well. But guarantees are not free. They come with costs:

- higher fees — management expense ratios — on guaranteed mutual funds;
- lower long-term expected returns on GICs than on stocks, and higher taxes paid on GIC interest than on dividends and capital gains from stocks;
- lower market returns on index-linked GICs than on traditional equity funds.

There's no question that it's hard to quantify the value of a guarantee. Just how much should you pay in higher fees or lower market returns for peace of mind? Unfortunately, as it turns out, a guarantee is usually worth less than what most investors pay.

If we revisit the chapter on misunderstanding risk (Mistake #1), and look at the chart that estimates the risk of losing money, we can see that a 10-year guarantee doesn't have much value on its own. Over a 10-year period, the estimated chance of losing money is about 5 percent on stocks, and 2 percent on a diversified portfolio. Many studies suggest that the risk could even be lower than these estimates.

## Seg Fund Guarantees

Segregated funds — seg funds, for short — are guaranteed mutual funds that are sold by insurance-licensed advisors. They typically offer three benefits: a guarantee of principal (most guarantee 100 percent of your initial investment over a 10-year period, although some only guarantee 75 percent); bankruptcy protection (the seg fund assets are "segregated" from your other assets and have named beneficiaries, so that in the case of insolvency your creditors can make no claim on them); and a death-benefit guarantee (upon your death, your beneficiaries receive at least the principal you invested). Not surprisingly, there is a cost involved in offering these insurance guarantees; a seg fund's fees are generally 0.5 to one percent higher than those of a regular mutual fund.

Most investors are attracted to seg funds by the guarantee of principal, so I'll address this benefit first. Even if the chance of losing money on stocks is 5 percent over 10 years, you can see that a 75 percent guarantee is pretty much worthless. And when you take into account that $10,000 today is worth a lot less than $10,000 in 10 years, even the 100 percent guarantee is not worth as much as it might appear to be at first. If inflation averages 3 percent each year, $10,000 today will be worth $7,374 in 10 years. So the so-called "100 percent" guarantee of $10,000 is really only a guarantee of $7,374 in purchasing power, or 74 percent of your principal.

Here's another way to look at it. Let's assume Mr. Seg puts $25,000 into a seg fund with an annual fee of 2.7 percent. Ms. Reg puts $25,000 into a regular mutual fund with an annual fee of 2 percent. Both underlying funds, managed by the same person, generate a before-fee average annual return of 10 percent over a 10-year period. Mr. Seg earned 10 minus 2.7, or 7.3 percent on average each year. Ms. Reg earned 10 minus 2, or 8 percent. Doesn't seem like a big difference . . . at first.

They each ended up with a different amount:

|  | Mr. Seg | Ms. Reg |
| --- | --- | --- |
| Initial Investment | $25,000 | $25,000 |
| Annual Fee (MER) | 2.7% | 2.0% |
| Annual Average Returns | 10% | 10% |
| Net Annual Returns After Fees | 7.3% | 8.0% |
| Ending Value of Investment | $50,575 | $53,973 |
| Implicit Cost of Guarantee (sacrificed returns) | $3,398 | |

Mr. Seg gave up $3,398 for the comfort of knowing that his initial investment was guaranteed — 14 percent of his original investment, and 7 percent of his final portfolio. A reasonably high price to pay. Was it worth it? Depends on his situation and how disastrous it would have been for him to have less than $25,000 at the end of the 10-year period. Even though the risk of losing money over 10 years is low, the consequences of losing it may be very severe for Mr. Seg. Ms. Reg risks suffering a loss with no guarantee, but just how much money could she lose over 10 years, especially if her portfolio is diversified among different asset classes? The entire world would really have to be in an unprecedented global economic recession for her to lose more than a few thousand dollars.

Fees on seg funds are higher than "reg" funds, ranging from an average of 0.6 percent higher on Canadian equity funds to 0.9 percent higher on

US and international equity funds. This extra cost is seldom worth a 10-year guarantee. But what about the death-benefit guarantee that your beneficiaries will receive at least the original principal (or the market value if it is higher)? Now here's some value worth paying for, especially if you are elderly and not sure what the next few years will bring, or perhaps if you are in a particularly dangerous line of work. The value for the death-benefit guarantee is directly dependent upon the likelihood of your dying within the next 10 years — again, a value that derives from individual circumstance.

The insurance contract inherent in seg funds means they come with bankruptcy protection. The law generally does not allow creditors, who have money owing to them, to make a claim on seg funds. This feature can have particular value to business owners who want to protect some of their assets from the possibility of bankruptcy. The creditor proofing is also valuable to independent professionals such as lawyers and doctors who want to protect their investments from potential lawsuits. However, the laws around creditor protection are not black and white. There are circumstances where the courts will disallow the creditor protection feature of seg funds, most commonly when the investor owes taxes to the government. Ultimately, a judge can determine the extent to which the principal in a seg fund is protected from creditors, depending on the particular case.

Another valuable feature is that upon death, your investment in seg funds can be transferred to your beneficiaries directly, without their having to pay estate and probate fees. Probate fees are what the provincial governments charge for their role in verifying the will. Although the law does not require probate, financial institutions won't facilitate the transfer of the deceased's assets without proof that the will is valid. The fee varies by province, and generally runs around 1.5 percent of assets. Additionally, estate fees of about 2 to 4 percent will be levied by the executors of the will — often trust companies. The combined probate and estate fees can easily add up to over $8,000 for an estate of $250,000.

You don't have to use seg funds to accomplish the same goal of avoiding transfer fees. You can put your assets into joint custody with your beneficiaries, so they can take direct and immediate ownership of the assets upon your death. There is virtually no cost to this alternative. However, many people are not comfortable in forfeiting sole ownership of their assets, since it requires significant trust among all parties. The point, however, is that probate and estate fee avoidance can be accomplished in other ways.

The problem with seg funds is that they represent over $60 billion of Canadian investors' assets — they are very popular. But how many of these investors are retirees, near retirement, or entrepreneurs with a high risk of going bankrupt? These are really the only individuals for whom the cost of seg funds has meaningful value. The vast majority of seg fund investors are paying for something that has negligible value to them.

## Other Guarantees

There are other more obvious ways to guarantee your money. With a basic GIC, and GICs whose returns are linked to market indexes, the costs of the guarantee are more difficult to quantify. Whereas the seg funds have higher fees that can be compared to regular funds, the cost of GIC guarantees are embedded in the products themselves. The basic GIC has an obvious opportunity cost — the cost of not participating in market appreciation. This cost can be substantial over a long period of time; remember that the returns of stocks have historically been around 6 percent higher than GIC returns. On top of that, capital gains and dividends are taxed at a lower rate than the interest income from GICs.

In the following example, I've assumed a marginal tax rate of 48 percent on interest income, and 32 percent on capital gains. I've simplified the comparison by assuming that the gain in stocks is purely from market appreciation, and not from dividends. While dividends are taxed at a slightly higher marginal rate of 33 percent, the following chart does not overstate the after-tax gap between GICs and stocks — in fact, it understates it. That's because much of the capital gains tax is deferred until the fund is sold, whereas interest income from the GIC is taxed every year so you lose some compounding benefit on the GIC.

|  | GIC | Stocks |
| --- | --- | --- |
| **Average Long-term Return** | 6% | 12% |
| **Marginal Tax Rate** | 48% | 32% |
| **After-tax Long-term Return** | 3% | 8% |

After tax, the stock generates a return that is more than 2.5 times the GIC return, instead of just two times the pre-tax return. The gap is even higher if you give stocks the not-unreasonable benefit of tax deferral. Historically, the cost of having a guarantee on your money has been very high, especially after taxes.

The index-linked GIC has a less severe opportunity cost because it does allow some participation in the market. The cost of index-linked GICs is embedded in the returns you earn since the returns are either capped at a certain level, or limited to a "participation rate" that restricts the extent to which you receive the full market upside. For instance, an index-linked GIC with an 80 percent participation rate will yield a return that is 80 percent of the market return. In fact it's not even that straightforward because the calculation of the return is usually based on an average of the market's closing price at the end of each month or year. This averaging calculation protects investors from earning nothing if the market crashes just a month or two before the GIC comes due. If, however, the market goes up, as it does more often than it goes down, your returns are reduced by the averaging technique.

All returns on index-linked GICs are taxed as income, so you don't get the benefit of lower tax rates as you would with the dividends and capital gains generated by a mutual fund. Of course, the reduced tax benefit is only relevant outside of an RRSP. Unlike a fund, these products cannot be redeemed until they reach maturity — usually three or five years from purchase. This lack of liquidity is an additional implicit cost of the guarantee.

Both GICs, especially the plain vanilla ones, can have a place in the portfolio of a risk-averse investor. But like seg funds, they are used by too many investors who are unaware of what they are giving up.

## The Behavioural Explanation

- *Lack of Knowledge*
- *Framing*
- *Fear of Losing Money*

I could have included this mistake in the chapter focused on misunderstanding risk, but it is worthy of separate consideration because of the popularity of seg funds in particular. While many investors have a general appreciation for what they are giving up by investing exclusively in GICs, few really understand the cost of seg funds and index-linked GICs.

Fewer still understand just how low the risk is of losing money over a 10-year period, and how limited the worth of a guarantee that merely protects your initial investment, with no adjustment for inflation. The powerful fear that we all share of losing money doesn't help matters. The combination of these factors can be costly, because it leads many people to overinsure themselves against hazards that have a low risk of occurring and a downside that is not that severe. For instance, how much life insurance does a young, single, childless professional need? Probably none in most cases. Yet many who fit this description do have some. What's odd about human psychology is that the people who invest exclusively in GICs are often the same folks who drive their cars with no apparent indication that they are the slightest bit risk-averse! Go figure the contradictions of human nature.

As we saw in "The Limits of Our Thinking," the way a question is *framed* can have a large influence on your answer. Seg funds are sold on the basis of avoiding a loss, which anyone would find appealing. But if they were sold on the basis of forfeited returns, they wouldn't be nearly as popular! How many investors would be willing to give up almost one percent each year for a benefit that they could get for free simply by diversifying their portfolios?

## The Solution

There are two main considerations in paying for guarantees:

1. *What is the probability that the worst-case scenario will materialize?*
2. *Just how bad is the worst-case scenario, if it does occur?*

What many people fail to analyze when assessing insurance are these two relevant elements of risk: the probability of loss and the extent of the downside. If you have a family, the probability of suffering a disabling accident of some sort is not that high, but the downside is enormous if you were to lose your ability to earn income to support them as a result. Alternatively, most car accidents are not life-threatening, but the probability of their occurring is reasonably high. So both risks warrant insurance of some kind. But what about investing in the stock market over 10 years?

We saw in the chapter on risk that the likelihood of losing money over 10 years is not that high, especially in a diversified portfolio. And if you do lose money over 10 years, how bad will it be — how much will you lose? Recently, the worst stock market performance over a 10-year period has been the Japanese market, which lost about 3 percent for Canadian investors from 1989 to 1998, and about 1.5 percent from 1990 to 1999. North American markets have not suffered a negative return over any 10-year period, except over the Depression in the early 1930s, when the US market declined 5 percent over 10 years. Since its inception in 1956, the TSE 300 has had only three five-year-period losses, all in the early 1970s when the oil crisis hit. And the worst five-year loss was only minus 2.2 percent. Moreover, market crashes tend to bounce back pretty quickly. After the 1987 crash, the market took just over a year to get back to its pre-crash levels. The average of all market crashes is about a 25 percent decline, taking about eight months to occur, and 17 months to recover.

So if markets really do go down over 10 years, the worst case is probably not that bad. In fact, our global economies would have to be in extraordinarily bad shape for the stock markets to experience a significant loss over 10 years. If that kind of unprecedented loss really happened, you'd probably have a lot of other problems to deal with, like your job.

But more important, diversified portfolios have *never* suffered a negative 10-year return. *The risk of losing money is mitigated by diversifying your portfolio, not by giving up returns.* Rather than reducing your returns by paying higher fees, you can use asset diversification to reduce the risk of your overall portfolio very effectively. What's more, this method of risk reduction is costless! Your expected returns will not be penalized, but your risk will dramatically decline. With guaranteed investments, however, your expected returns are reduced by the cost of the guarantee.

Limit what you pay for guarantees. Seg fund guarantees are not worthless, but the greater value of their guarantee derives from the death benefit, rather than the 10-year guarantee of principal. And the death benefit has the most value to an investor with a shorter or uncertain life expectancy.

GICs can be a good part of your portfolio, but there is a high opportunity cost in overweighting them relative to equity funds, especially in after-tax terms in non-registered accounts. Only the most extremely conservative investors should hold a majority of their portfolio in GICs. Index-linked GICs are also more suitable for very conservative investors, especially those with short investment time frames. Because most index-linked GICs come in three- and five-year terms, they are a good substitute for seg funds if you think you'll need your money in that amount of time.

The expression "there's no free lunch" was never more appropriate than when applied to guaranteed products. With seg funds, most investors don't get what they pay for. There is a lot of inherent value in a seg fund for a 70-year-old cigarette smoker who is the owner and single operator of a high-rise window-washing company that has a lot of debt. But if you're paying a premium simply for the peace of mind of knowing that

10 years from now you can get your money back, be aware of the cost of this luxury. It doesn't come cheap.

## Recap of Mistake #10: Overpaying for Guarantees

1. Guarantees have costs. So the value of a guarantee has to be weighed against its cost. The cost varies with the type of guarantee, whether it be in the form of a seg fund, a GIC, or an index-linked GIC.

2. Mutual fund fees — in the form of management expense ratios — have a detrimental effect on returns. But there's value in the fees. They pay for investment management expertise, and they also pay for advice. The extra fees of seg funds also have value. But the extra fees — usually between 0.5 and one percent — are only worth paying if you can estimate a reasonable chance of actually losing money, which is what the guarantee protects you from.

3. Extra fees for a 10-year principal guarantee are rarely worth what many investors pay because the risk of losing money over 10 years is very low, and the downside is not that severe. Also, the guarantee applies to the original investment, which is worth much less after 10 years of inflation.

4. The greatest value to be found in seg funds is the death-benefit feature. The value of this benefit depends on the likelihood of the investor's dying within 10 years, which is unique to every individual's circumstance.

5. Diversification within a portfolio is a much cheaper way of mitigating the risk of losing money. Most investors do not understand the low probability of losing money in a diversified portfolio, and so they tend to overpay for a guarantee benefit that has more psychological than monetary value.

6. Segregated funds have other benefits that justify the fees, but these benefits have little value for most investors. These features have some value to those who want to protect themselves against bankruptcy or lawsuits arising from professional duties.

7. GICs and index-linked GICs have guarantees whose cost is embedded in the product because the upside of the market is reduced. Because of their shorter term of three to five years, index-linked GICs can play an important role in managing short-term risk, in circumstances where this is required.

# PART 3

## Bringing It All Together

# Recommended
# Asset Allocations

We determined at the outset that asset allocation is the first and most important decision in the investment process, followed by the "do nothing" second step. So the only question that remains is, *what exactly does an appropriate asset mix look like?* I offer the following recommendations as guidelines only.

You can see that what differentiates one suggested portfolio mix from another is the time horizon. As I outlined in "The Rules of Successful Investing," most investors have the same objective, which is to maximize their wealth. What differentiates their needs, and therefore their recommended asset allocations, are the practical risk constraints (not the emotional ones, remember), which can differ significantly from one investor to another. I can't account for every investor's unique risk constraints, which include income, net worth, job security, and financial obligations. That's why it's strongly advisable that you consult a qualified investment advisor in order to account for your personal circumstances.

But time horizon is an important risk constraint that can be standardized for all investors. The more time you have, the more risk you can accommodate. So each of the five portfolios outlined below is defined by the time horizon that you might have for investing. Implicit in this time horizon is a tradeoff between growing your money and avoiding a loss. For instance, if your time horizon is only three years, perhaps because you want to buy a new car in three years, the implicit tradeoff between growing your money and not losing it is tipped in favour of not losing it. That's because a three-year time period cannot accommodate an ambitious growth objective without incurring a significant risk of loss.

Alternatively, if you have a seven-year time frame to buy a new home, you can accept more risk and therefore your growth objective can have more influence on your asset mix. Similarly, if your time horizon is 20 years to save for retirement, your growth objective dominates your asset mix, since the probability of losing money over such a long period is low.

So I start with the assumption that everyone wants to maximize the growth of their money; the portfolios are differentiated by time horizon, and the tradeoff between growth and loss-avoidance that each time horizon requires.

| | Safe | Conservative | Balanced | Aggressive | Very Aggressive |
|---|---|---|---|---|---|
| Minimum Req'd. Time | 3 years | 5 years | 5 years | 7 years | 7 years |
| Implied Tradeoff | No Loss / Growth | No Loss / Growth | No Loss / Growth | No Loss / Growth | No Loss / Growth |
| Cash | 20% | 5% | 5% | | |
| Cdn. Bonds | 70% | 50% | 40% | 30% | 15% |
| Int'l. Bonds | 10% | 10% | 10% | 5% | 5% |
| Total Bonds | 80% | 60% | 50% | 35% | 20% |
| Canada | | 10% | 15% | 15% | 20% |
| US | | 15% | 20% | 30% | 33% |
| Europe | | 5% | 5% | 11% | 13% |
| Japan | | 3% | 3% | 3% | 4% |
| Asia | | 2% | 2% | 3% | 4% |
| Emerging Markets | | | | 3% | 6% |
| Total Stocks | | 35% | 45% | 65% | 80% |

There is no silver bullet to recommending asset mixes. That's because they are based on the long-term *expected* returns and *expected* risk of each asset class. All of the fanciest linear optimization computer programs in the world don't let us get away from the simple fact that inputs are required to generate outputs. In this case, the inputs are the expected characteristics of each asset class — that means predictions of the future.

And every investment professional will have a different set of expectations of future return and risk characteristics for each asset class. Don't forget also that historical return and risk characteristics are not necessarily the best predictors of the future. So what you see above are asset mix recommendations based on the reasonable consensus expectations, from many sources, of future returns and risks. While not carved in stone, they are solid enough that you'd want a good reason for deviating substantially from these allocations.

I've also kept currency risk in mind, as discussed in the chapter on home bias. For instance, you'll note that Canadian equities continue to play a major role in all portfolios, including the most aggressive, and Canadian bonds always have a much bigger role to play than international bonds do.

A question might arise: What about gold and real estate? The short answer is that both asset classes are already included to an extent in most mutual funds, especially gold and especially in index funds. The TSE 300, for example, has about a 3 to 4 percent holding in gold companies, which is plenty of exposure to allow you to benefit if the price of gold ever regains its former glory — $850 per ounce in January 1980. It has been a very volatile asset ever since Nixon ordered the US authorities to terminate the convertibility of US dollars for gold in 1971. There are some good reasons to include an exposure to gold in your portfolio, particularly as it is one of the best inflation hedges available. But to separate it out and hold more than you'd be exposed to through an index product is unnecessary. As for real estate, most Canadians are overexposed to real estate by virtue of being homeowners. Even if you don't own property, or aren't planning to eventually sell the family home or cottage, you will still get a modest exposure to real estate — about one percent — from the TSE 300.

One of the most important things I've learned in talking to people about investing is that many investors have a strong desire to personally influence their portfolios; this means they need flexibility. Despite all of the best arguments I can make to "stay the course," I've come to realize that human psychology needs to be accommodated (it will find a way, whether we plan for it or not!). So I've introduced an alternative set of recommended portfolios where there is a primary asset mix and room for playing. Playing can mean making your own tactical asset mix calls, if you just can't help yourself. Or playing can be putting money into some hot sectors or hot funds where you are prepared to take some losses.

Here are the same asset allocation recommendations, with some modest adjustments to allow for play money.

| | Safe | Conservative | Balanced | Aggressive | Very Aggressive |
|---|---|---|---|---|---|
| *Cash* | *20%* | 5% | 5% | | |
| Cdn. Bonds | 65% | 50% | 40% | 25% | 15% |
| Int'l. Bonds | 10% | 10% | 10% | 5% | 5% |
| *Total Bonds* | *75%* | *60%* | *50%* | *30%* | *20%* |
| Canada | | 8% | 13% | 15% | 18% |
| US | | 12% | 17% | 25% | 30% |
| Europe | | 5% | 5% | 11% | 10% |
| Japan | | 3% | 3% | 3% | 4% |
| Asia | | 2% | 2% | 3% | 4% |
| Emerging Markets | | | | 3% | 4% |
| *Total Stocks* | | *30%* | *40%* | *60%* | *70%* |
| Play Money | 5% | 5% | 5% | 10% | 10% |

"Play money" is not necessary to set aside for every investor. I offer it as an acknowledgement that for some investors, who thrive on playing the market, a little money — money that can be lost in the worst case scenario — is necessary to keep the "thrill of the game" alive. I figure it's kind of like designing a diet but allowing for a treat once in a while, which is probably the only realistic way you can diet for a long period of time. The key is to be disciplined so you don't lose a lot of returns while you're having fun. There's no point in watching what you eat during the week if you treat yourself to a whole chocolate cake every Friday. Most people go to a casino with a set amount that they're prepared to lose. The same prudent strategy applies to asset allocation — you should predetermine how much of your portfolio you're prepared to gamble with. The above allocations for play money are the maximum recommended amounts. And if you lose some or all of the original amount in a glamorous biotech fund, then I'd strongly urge you not to dip into the rest of your portfolio; use the same discipline that you would at the casino. Cut your losses and go home.

Many people have multiple goals that imply different time horizon constraints. You might be saving for your children's education in 15 years, while saving for retirement in 30 years and a vacation one year from now. To allow for this complexity, you could build a separate portfolio for each distinct goal. We explored the usefulness of this approach in Mistake #9, where we saw that a retirement portfolio could be managed independently from the non-registered portfolio. If your practical risk tolerance (notably your time horizon) is significantly different for your registered savings than it is for your non-registered savings, then two distinct portfolios should be established, each with a distinct asset mix. But keep taxes in mind so most interest-bearing securities are in the registered account, where possible. If you have multiple goals for your non-registered portfolio, you can simply establish an asset mix for each goal, them combine them into one portfolio that reflects the weighted average of each distinct goal. For instance, your portfolio might end up having a balanced asset mix overall, with a conservative portion for saving for a car, blended with a more aggressive portion for extra retirement savings.

## Recap of Recommended Asset Allocations

1. Asset mixes are defined by the practical risk tolerances (not the emotional ones) of each individual. This is based on the fact that the vast majority of investors want to maximize their wealth. The only things that constrain their ability to grow their money as aggressively as possible are their time horizons, level of income, job security, financial obligations, and other practical risk considerations.

2. The asset allocations recommended in this chapter reflect a balance between growth and preserving capital — the balance implied by a particular time horizon.

3. The asset allocations also reflect currency risk minimization, insofar as the portfolios are suitable for Canadian investors who have Canadian-dollar purchases ahead of them. (US investors, for example, will find these mixes are inappropriately overweighted in Canadian stocks and bonds.)

4. Recognizing that many investors have a strong psychological need to have influence over at least part of their money, I've allocated between 5 and 10 percent of the portfolios to "play money" for those who want to gamble — i.e., to play against the market odds

for fun (I can think of better ways to have fun that are less costly, but to each his own).

5. Many investors have multiple goals, such as retirement savings within a registered account and other types of savings in a non-registered account. Implementing a distinct asset mix for both the registered portfolio and the non-registered portfolio makes sense, but multiple goals within the non-registered account can be accommodated by one asset mix that reflects a balance of all goals at once.

# Final Recap

1. *The fact*: Successful investing, like other aspects of life, depends on putting probabilities in your favour. Investing probabilities are driven by the reality that markets are random and therefore very difficult to predict. So you need exposure to all the major asset classes. The only question remaining is how to allocate your money among the asset classes. Your practical risk tolerance, largely defined by your time horizon, determines the right mix. You want to maximize your returns? It's simple: Implement the right asset allocation, then stay the course.

2. *The problem*: Our minds. Obviously, they're great in many ways and are reasonably effective in facilitating our survival. But they often lead us astray. This is evident in the realm of human relationships, where we often say and do stupid things. Our cognitive limitations are equally significant in the realm of investing. We're emotional by nature, which can cause us to make bad decisions because feelings are often very misleading guides to action. We can also be illogical and irrational — we frequently solve problems in ways that reveal a simple lack of understanding as well as distorted thinking. To add insult to injury, we're immodest; in fact, we're perpetually overconfident about most of our beliefs and judgements, despite our tendency toward illogical and emotional thinking.

3. *The consequence*: The result of our emotional, illogical, and irrational thinking, combined with our blindness to these weaknesses, results in the 10 biggest investment mistakes that Canadians make — all various contraventions of the basic investment rules. These mistakes can all have a severely detrimental impact on investors' returns.

4. *The prescription*: The solution is to learn about your investor psychology, and then overcome the cognitive limitations that undermine successful investing in specific and consistent ways. Understanding and counteracting investor psychology is the secret to maximizing returns. Don't allow your natural human inclinations to deny you the benefits that a disciplined approach to asset allocation offers.

## Postscript

I mentioned in the Introduction that while I was in the process of writing it, the market was coincidentally tumbling and most analysts were predicting that things were going to get worse, especially for technology stocks, which were leading the charge down. Here are a few headlines that appeared the next day and the following week:

> **"Stock rally fizzles"**
> **"Investors warned of risk"**
> **"Danger lurks in battered stock markets"**

A few months later, now mid-summer, the TSE 300 has climbed 22 percent from its tumble in mid-April and the S&P 500 has risen 7 percent. You can imagine my disappointment! I was hoping the market would remain flat or even go down so I could continue to invest part of my paycheques at bargain prices. This would have worked out perfectly for my long-term investment strategy of maximizing my wealth upon retirement. Oh well; maybe there'll be a market dip before too long. One can only hope.

# APPENDIX 1

## Why Do Stock (and Bond) Prices Bounce Up and Down So Much?

Statisticians and economists refer to the movements of stock prices as "stochastic," which is a fancy way of saying random or chaotic. Their unpredictability is one of the reasons why equities offer what is known as an "equity risk premium" over bonds or cash. If stocks weren't so volatile, then they wouldn't offer the higher returns they do to compensate for this higher risk.

To understand price volatility, you have to understand what stock prices are. Essentially, they reflect the cash that a company's shareholders are entitled to.

### What Exactly Is a Stock Price?

Let's say you hire me to open and operate a new candy store for you. You invest $90,000 in the new venture: $40,000 goes to pay my salary, and $50,000 to buy supplies and operate the store. After the first year of operation, the store generates $150,000 of revenues (candy sales). Pre-tax profits are $60,000, which is the revenue of $150,000 less the expenses (salary and operating costs). Let's say you're left with $35,000 after paying tax. You have a choice: You can take out the money and close down the store, or you can leave enough money in the store's operations to keep it open for another year. It's your decision. But now you have a company that didn't exist before: a bona fide candy-selling business with a growing reputation and customer base, developing expertise in the burgeoning field of sweets, and the opportunity to reduce costs based on the growing volume of business. That combination of elements could be replicated by someone else who wanted to start from scratch, but there's value in the business you own today because someone would probably prefer to buy the up-and-running company for a fair price. After all, starting fresh would involve finding a location, decorating the store, hiring a manager, getting some customers, and so on.

Let's say I, as your humble store manager, approach you and offer to buy the store from you. What's the store worth? What price would you ask for?

The store's value is obviously related to its profits. If, after all the effort and expenses of running the place, the after-tax profits were only $5,000 — or 5.6 percent earned on your $90,000 investment — the store wouldn't be worth that much. But the store did quite nicely — $35,000 earned on an investment of $90,000, or a 39 percent return. If you are trying to set a price for the store, you will want to project the cash that the company is likely to produce in the future, based on its current earnings and its future prospects. If the nearby grocery store, which draws a lot of shoppers to the neighbourhood, is closing down, you might give your store a lesser value, since sales might suffer once pedestrian traffic starts to dwindle. Next year's profits don't look too promising in this case. If, however, a few new antique stores are opening up across the street, and word of mouth has it that your candies are great, the future looks bright and next year's profits are likely to be even higher.

So the price that we agree on is based on the future profits of the store, since the store is only worth what it will generate in after-tax cash returns for its owner. That's it. That's all a stock is really worth — the future cash flows that each share is entitled to. Cash flows are simply the revenues less the costs and investment expenditure that generate those revenues. A stock is only valuable insofar as it generates future cash flows for its investors.

Once a company's future cash flows are estimated (not an easy task, especially for companies whose earnings are unstable and therefore less predictable), the second step is putting a *value* on the future cash flows. You can't simply just add all the future cash flows up; $1 today is worth more than $1 in the future, because you can take today's dollar and invest it for extra returns. Future cash must therefore be "discounted" to determine its present value.

The rate at which future cash flows are discounted is determined by the risk-free rate (representing the rate at which you could invest today's money in a safe instrument, such as a government bond) plus a premium for the risk of the cash flows not materializing as predicted. One dollar paid a year from now, discounted by 10 percent (5 percent risk-free bond yield plus 5 percent risk premium), is 91 cents. So if I buy the store for 91 cents, and the store indeed generates $1 of after-tax profit in its first year, after which I close it permanently, I've earned 10 percent on my investment.

## How Does the Price Relate to Earnings?

What's a quick-and-dirty way of knowing how a particular company is being valued? For instance, if I tell you that a company stock is trading at $20, how do you know if that's high or low, relative to the cash flows that are expected to accrue to shareholders? You've no doubt heard of the price-earnings, or "P/E," ratio. This is a quick way of assessing a stock's price, since it calculates the gap between the stock's current market price and the earnings of the company, which are a good proxy for cash flows in most cases. The price of a share is divided by the earnings per share of the company (earnings divided by all outstanding common shares). The earnings are usually the anticipated earnings for the coming year, although they can also be "trailing" earnings, which are last year's or last quarter's earnings. A high P/E usually indicates that the market has ascribed a high price to future earnings, and therefore believes that the company will enjoy significant growth. The P/E ratio is also linked to the rate at which future cash flows are discounted to the present. A high P/E can indicate a high level of certainty associated with the estimate of future cash flows; low or falling interest rates; investor sentiment such as a general optimism about the company's prospects; or any combination of these three influences. All three factors are worth examining in more detail because they are reflected in the rate at which future cash flows are discounted to the present.

*Uncertainty of Projections:* The value of your projected future earnings will be lower if there is a great deal of risk associated with the projections. Using the candy store example, imagine you factored into your projections plans for a new local art gallery, which would attract many visitors. This would increase the long-term growth prospects of your business. But what if the gallery never gets built? Or worse, the street undergoes construction for sewer maintenance in the middle of the summer, which reduces your store's physical accessibility. Factors like these cast a shadow of unpredictability over your future cash flows, lowering their value and reducing the P/E.

*Interest Rates:* If interest rates are high, then the cost of borrowing is high, which makes growth harder to achieve for most businesses (including candy stores); that's because it becomes more expensive to borrow money to operate the business (to build a second candy counter, for example). High interest rates also dampen consumer demand (fewer people buying discretionary items such as gourmet candies). Finally, higher interest rates mean that cash flows in the future are worth much less today, since the alternative to investing in those uncertain cash flows is to invest in a bond that offers high-yielding and more predictable cash flows. Investing to earn money in candy profits three years from now is less attractive if I can invest in a bond yielding 10 percent. But the same candy profits look pretty good if a bond investment is only going to generate a 4 percent yield. The P/E ratio is largely affected by interest rates; in fact it has been estimated that up to 80 percent of all P/E ratio changes are driven by actual and anticipated interest rate changes.

For example, in the US, bond yields went from 4 percent in 1964 to 15 percent by 1981. That rise in rates caused the P/E ratio of the market as a whole to shrink from 18 to 7, which translated into stock returns of around 7 percent on average. Then, as inflation was crushed by the policies of the Federal Reserve Bank, long-term bond yields dropped back down to 5 percent by the late 1990s and the P/E ratio stretched from 7 to 25. Stock returns enjoyed an average return of 19 percent over that period.

*Emotions:* In the short term, emotions can have a large influence on the value that investors put on future cash flows: The market can go up by 15 percent in one day (October 6, 1931), and down by 21 percent another (October 19, 1987). An even more extreme example: the market can go down by 12 percent one day (October 29, 1929) and up 12 percent the very next day (October 30, 1929). Emotions — optimism and pessimism — tend to exaggerate price movements.

## Where Does the Volatility Come From?

Since a stock's price reflects the current value of future cash flows, any news at all can affect either the estimation of those cash flows, or the rate at which they are discounted back to the present.

Here's a simple summary; I've emphasized the four elements that contribute to stock-price volatility:

**Stock Price = future cash flows × the value placed on those cash flows**

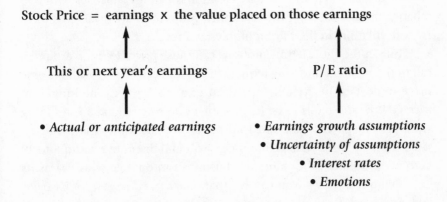

**Earnings growth**                **Discount rate**

- *Assumptions about economic and company growth*
- *Uncertainty of assumptions*
- *Interest rates*
- *Emotions*

Looked at from a different perspective, the price of a stock, or the market as a whole, is a function of earnings multiplied by the P/E ratio. The ratio simply reflects the growth prospects of the earnings, as well as the three drivers that underlie the discount rate — uncertainty, interest rates, and emotions. Here is a similar equation, which illustrates a different view of the same description of a stock's price:

**Stock Price = earnings × the value placed on those earnings**

**This or next year's earnings**        **P/ E ratio**

- *Actual or anticipated earnings*
- *Earnings growth assumptions*
- *Uncertainty of assumptions*
- *Interest rates*
- *Emotions*

The two different equations reflect the same phenomenon, using different variables. The factors that change — earnings or cash flow estimates, uncertainty, interest rates, and emotions — can all reinforce one another. All it takes is a little news to send the P/E bouncing around, as well as the earnings or cash projections estimates to change. For example, if there are rumours that a new candy store is opening up across the street to compete with your store, your projected earnings might have to be reduced, and the risk of those earnings being wrong increases since it's hard to estimate how your store might suffer lost sales. So you have both factors working against you — reduced earnings estimates and increased uncertainty. Or if interest rates appear to be on the verge of declining, your earnings might be expected to grow faster, and the value of those earnings might increase at the same time. When the factors are reinforcing, as they often are, short-term volatility in the market can be a bit extreme as new information is constantly being absorbed into both earnings projections and the worth of those future earnings.

Recently, the increasing number of individual investors in the market has aggravated volatility. It used to be that institutional investors such as pension funds or insurance companies dominated stock market trading. But with the advent of Internet trading, it is estimated that 60 percent of all trading volume on the Nasdaq is done by individuals. Stock ownership is nearing 50 percent of all households in both Canada and the US — either directly or through mutual funds. That's up from 40 percent in the mid-1990s. Individual investors tend to be a little less patient, and a little more reactive, than larger institutional investment managers. Adding further to the volatility is the growing dominance of high-growth companies in the market indexes. Much of the value of high-growth companies is derived from cash flows that are far off in the future; since it's harder to reliably estimate distant cash flows, their projections are riskier and there is more volatility in their P/E multiples as a result.

While in the short term, emotions can cause prices to jump around a lot, in the medium and long term, earnings and earnings growth become more important in the determination of a stock price. The long-term average P/E ratio tends to be less volatile, hovering around 15, meaning stock prices tend to be around 15 times anticipated earnings; this figure reflects general long-term economic growth and discount rates of 8 to 10 percent. Ultimately, the value of a business can only grow as fast as its underlying cash flows. You can see that *the factors driving a stock's short-term price are different from the drivers of its long-term price.* That is precisely why you shouldn't invest in the stock market if your time horizon is less than five years, but also why investing in the market over long periods of time is rewarding.

| Less Than 5 Years | Five to 10 Years | Greater Than 10 Years |
|:---:|:---:|:---:|
| ↓ | ↓ | ↓ |
| P/E dominates | P/E and cash flows dominate | Cash flows dominate |
| ↓ | ↓ | ↓ |
| Stock prices volatile, so avoid stock investments | Stock prices less volatile, so invest modestly in stocks | Stock prices reflect economic fundamentals, so invest more aggressively in stocks |

## Long-term Return Expectations

There are two basic ways in which a company converts its cash flows into something useful for its shareholders: paying dividends, or generating capital gains on its shares.

*Dividends:* Whereas dividends were once the primary method by which investors extracted cash from their shares, they are less relevant today in assessing a stock's value. Companies are using earnings less to pay out dividends, and more to generate capital gains. This is particularly true for start-up technology companies, which aggressively invest their earnings back into the growth of the company. In the early 1960s, 75 percent of the largest American stocks were considered value stocks; today 75 percent are considered growth stocks, many of which pay little or no dividends.

*Capital Gains:* To generate capital gains companies can reinvest earnings into existing or new projects to generate higher future cash flows. Or they can repurchase shares from investors willing to sell their stock, so that remaining shareholders are entitled to more of the company's cash — whether in the form of dividends or capital gains.

Over a long period of time, stock prices should reflect the dividends that investors receive, plus the growth of company earnings (which either produce higher dividends or capital gains), plus whatever change may occur in P/E multiples:

$$\textbf{Long-term returns} \; = \; \textit{initial dividend yield} \; + \; \textit{earnings growth} \; + \; \textit{change in P/E ratio}$$

To put numbers to this equation, dividend yields are low, at just over one percent, at the beginning of the twenty-first century. We can say that corporate earnings will likely continue to grow at around 5 to 8 percent. The P/E multiple may expand, contract, or stay the same. In the 1990s, the P/E ratio expanded to add an extra 7 to 8 percent on top of growth and dividends, driven by falling interest rates and robust economic growth. An argument can be made (and has been by many) that the P/E ratio will actually contract over the next decade, but if we're optimistic about the development of countries in Asia and Latin America, we can see a scenario where P/E ratios increase modestly, as technology increases productivity and millions of new productive consumers join the world economy. So a long-term expectation of at least 9 percent stock market returns is easy to justify:

**Initial dividend yield + earnings growth + change in P/E ratio**
= 1% + 6% + 2%
= 9%

The US stock market returns over the twentieth century averaged 11 percent, which was inflated by the last decade where the average return was closer to 20 percent. The Canadian market lagged a little throughout the century, especially in the last decade. It has a long-term average of just below 10 percent.

## Bonds

Bond values tend to be a little less "irrational" than stock prices in the short term for two reasons: First, since the bond market is dominated by government bonds, there is less credit risk involved with investing in a bond. Only about 20 percent of the bond index in Canada is made up of corporate bonds. A company can go bankrupt, and its shares can become devalued or worthless. But that's not likely to happen to a bond-issuing government in North America or Western Europe. Second, bonds have fixed terms, which means that if you hold them to their maturity, you're assured of earning the yield that the bond was offering when you bought it. That's not to say that bonds aren't volatile — their prices move around a fair amount from the date of their issue to the day they mature. And corporate bonds are even more volatile because they are subject to credit risk. But because they have a fixed maturity date, and because government bonds have minimal credit risk, bond prices are subject to fewer influences and are therefore generally less volatile.

A bond's price, like a stock's, is the current value of all future cash flows that will be paid to the bond holder. The bond's coupon and its maturity value are discounted from their future value to the present, at a rate demanded by investors for holding the bond. But this rate can and does vary. If interest rates go up, for example, the required return of bond investors increases, so bond prices fall (their fixed coupon and maturity payments are worth less than before interest rates increased). And bond prices will also change in *anticipation* of interest rate changes. For example, if analysts believe that the Bank of Canada will raise interest rates to slow down the Canadian economy after reports of low unemployment, bond prices will fall. That's because no one is going to buy your bond if it's yielding 10 percent while interest rates are expected to rise to 11 percent. You have to lower the offering price of your bond to make it attractive — the price has to drop so that the discounted price yields an 11 percent return on the future cash flows. You can see that an element of irrationality can creep into the bond market in the short term because investors' predictions of interest rates are not foolproof. The factors that cause interest rates to change are unpredictable, just as news about stocks is random.

The returns on bonds were about 10 percent over the 1990s, when bond holders enjoyed substantial gains in an environment of declining interest rates. While bonds have generated very strong returns with volatility that is about half that of stocks, the last two decades have been unusual because of the cycle of falling interest rates. It is more realistic to expect future bond returns of below 10 percent because the long-term bond returns usually reflect current bond yields (which are around 6 percent in Canada) as well as the long-term direction of interest rates (which cannot fall to the extent they did in the 1980s and 1990s).

# APPENDIX 2

## How Can You Lower Risk and Raise Returns at the Same Time?

It's worth exploring in some detail the "magic" of covariance. I'll use the stock of two companies: Coffee Café and Beans Corp. Coffee Café runs a chain of high-end coffee shops, and imports its coffee beans from Beans Corp., based in Brazil. When the price of coffee beans goes way up, for example, if heavy rainfall in Brazil spoils many of the bean crops, then Coffee Café's profits decline since heavy café competition prevents them from raising prices to offset the higher costs of the beans they import. Beans Corp. has a banner year in this circumstance, since it gets a lot more money for its crop of beans, even though some of its crops were wiped out by the rains. Other years, the reverse happens: Coffee beans are plentiful and many Brazilian exporters cut their prices to ensure they sell all their supply. Beans Corp. profits sink, but Coffee Café enjoys an extra boost from lower import costs.

Finally, let's assume a 10-year bond has no volatility (which is true if you hold it to maturity, even though over that period its value will bounce around) and an expected return of 6 percent. Here are the relevant statistics on both stocks, and the bond, over a 10-year period:

|  | Expected Return | Volatility |
|---|---|---|
| **Coffee Café** | 12% | 10% |
| **Beans Corp.** | 8% | 9% |
| **10-Year Bond** | 6% | 0% |

At first blush, many investors might think that Beans Corp. is a bad investment — its expected return is only 8 percent, but it's only a little less volatile than Coffee Café. So the best portfolio would be one of Coffee Café alone, or maybe a mix of Coffee Café and the zero-volatility 10-year bond.

By combining Coffee Café with the bond in a 50-50 ratio, we cut our portfolio volatility in half. The risk-free bond adds no volatility so we're left with the risk associated with the 50 percent weighting of Coffee Café, for a portfolio volatility of 5 percent. And we still end up with a good return of 9 percent, which is the average return of the bond and Coffee Café. What use is Beans Corp. in our portfolio?

Rather than combining Coffee Café with the risk-free bond, let's see what happens if we combine it with the stock of Beans Corp. The expected return is 10 percent — the average of the two stocks' returns — and better than combining Coffee Café with the bond. How about the volatility of the two stocks combined? That is the million-dollar question.

The combination of Coffee Café and Beans Corp. has a combined volatility of only 4 percent!

|  | Expected Return | Volatility |
|---|---|---|
| **Coffee Café & Bond** | 9% | 5% |
| **Coffee Café & Beans Corp.** | 10% | 4% |

Great magic trick, eh? The portfolio of the two companies combined offers a better expected return and a lower volatility than the portfolio of Coffee Café combined with the risk-free bond! How did that happen? Does a magician reveal his secrets? In this case, the secret lies in the math.

The volatility of the portfolio consisting of the two stocks together is a function of the addition of each stock's individual volatility *minus* the stocks' covariance. So the volatility of the portfolio is *reduced* by the extent to which the two stocks move in opposite directions from each other. While the long-term returns of each stock are expected to be positive, in the short term, one stock will likely do better while the other underperforms. They are negatively correlated and this reduces the volatility of the portfolio as a whole.

The key factor driving this reduction in volatility is the negative correlation between the two stocks. The mathematical formula for calculating the volatility of the portfolio as a whole is the square root of [portfolio weight of Coffee Café]$^2$[Coffee Café volatility]$^2$ + [portfolio weight of Beans Corp.]$^2$[Beans Corp. volatility]$^2$ + [2(weight of Coffee Café)(weight of Beans Corp.)(Coffee Café volatility)(Beans Corp. volatility)(correlation coefficient)] .

The correlation coefficient of the two stocks happens to be negative 0.6 (another formula that I won't bother sharing, because if I do, I'll have to introduce yet two other formulae. Suffice it to say that negative one (−1) indicates two stocks that move in exactly the opposite direction, while positive one (+1) indicates two stocks that move exactly together). The fact that the correlation coefficient is negative (−0.6) indicates that the stocks are negatively correlated — when one goes up, the other goes down. They offset each other to an extent, even though their expected returns are both positive.

One last look at the magic of covariance that diversification creates. Let's say we're combining two countries: Canada and Italy, which have traditionally not been strongly correlated. Our portfolio consists of 50 percent Canada and 50 percent Italy, and the correlation coefficient of the two countries is 0.17 (meaning that they move together, but not closely). Let's say the long-term standard deviation of the Canadian market is around 6 percent, and for Italy it's 8 percent. And the expected return of each market is 10 percent. What is the volatility of a portfolio that combines both?

It's the square root of [0.5]$^2$[0.06]$^2$ + [0.5]$^2$[0.08]$^2$ + [2(0.5)(0.5)(0.06)(0.08)(0.17)], which is 5 percent. So by combining the two countries, we've reduced the portfolio volatility to 5 percent from the two stocks which had volatilities of 6 and 8 percent respectively. Yet we haven't reduced our expected returns at all. Voilà: the magic of international diversification — security returns are averaged but volatility is less than the average of each country.

The important point is that the combining of two stocks (or two countries) can often reduce a portfolio's volatility to a greater extent than simply adding a risk-free bond to one stock. And the portfolio's expected return is not penalized as much as it would have been if a risk-free bond, or GIC, had been added. That's because a portfolio's volatility is a function of the correlation between all the assets within it. If the assets are negatively correlated, there will be a huge reduction in risk. If the assets are positively correlated, but not perfectly, then the risk of the portfolio will still be substantially less than the most volatile asset, and can even be less volatile than the least volatile asset. *Portfolio returns are not jeopardized by combining securities* since the returns represent the weighted average of all security returns. *Portfolio volatility, however, is reduced by combining securities* since the total portfolio volatility is less than the average of all securities.

# APPENDIX 3

## Currency Risk —
## What Should Be Done About It?

Research on currency management is unfortunately underdeveloped because the largest academic investment community in the world resides in the US, where currency risk is not a pressing issue. US investors are resident in the largest economy and stock market in the world, so their investments are going to be heavily weighted toward American securities, and appropriately so (just as a heavy weighting in US stocks makes sense for Canadian and European investors). Currency risk for an American investor, therefore, is not as problematic as it is for Canadians, whose proportion of international holdings will be larger.

Just because research on currency is light, compared with many other aspects of investment theory, doesn't mean it's not controversial. It's probably the most contentious element of investing. Some academics and money managers believe that currencies cannot be forecast; others believe they can. Some believe investors should fully hedge all currency exposure; others believe you shouldn't. What is clear is that currency must be treated as an asset class like any other, especially for Canadian investors with significant allocations to foreign markets.

Whether or not you believe currencies can be forecast, you can reduce the currency risk of your foreign stocks through "hedging" — reducing or eliminating the foreign currency exposure on a foreign investment, so you're left with exposure to the foreign security, but not the foreign currency. For instance, you can invest in derivatives-based index funds that give you exposure to foreign markets, but not foreign currencies. Some US, derivatives-based, index funds, which are usually identified by the "RSP" in their name, will invest in Canadian-dollar T-bills and enter into futures contracts that replicate the returns of foreign markets. What you earn, therefore, is the foreign return, but you are not exposed to any changes in the foreign currency.

Unfortunately, this strategy will only work within an RRSP, since the gains that are distributed by these special index funds are taxed at the higher rate of interest income, even if the gains are capital gains. So they are not suitable for non-registered accounts, from the point of view of minimizing tax. An alternative is to enter into the exciting world of currency options, which you can use to convert your US-dollar exposure back into Canadian dollars. However, this can be complicated and costly, and you won't be able to do it through a discount brokerage account. Most investment advisors, whether brokers or planners, will not be equipped to help you do this either, since it takes a very large amount of money to be able to effectively hedge currency exposure.

As luck would have it, a moderate amount of currency risk on its own can be quite helpful in reducing the overall volatility of a portfolio. Because foreign currencies have different return characteristics than many of the securities in a typical portfolio, the overall volatility of the portfolio will be reduced with the addition of foreign currencies.

Here are some of the advantages of two different options: leaving your currency exposure as it is — the unhedged residual of your underlying investment; or hedging the currency risk so it is reduced or eliminated.

| Pros of Not Hedging | Pros of Hedging |
| --- | --- |
| • Increased diversification<br>• Easy, convenient, no cost<br>• Don't have to decide how much to hedge — all or just part of foreign currency exposure?<br>• Canadian homeowners already own a big Canadian-dollar asset so foreign currency risk is small relative to total net worth<br>• Even if the Canadian dollar does appreciate (which is bad for foreign investments), this is partially offset by the cost of foreign imported goods falling for Canadian consumers | • Easy and cheap to hedge with Canadian-dollar foreign equity index funds. However, there are very few, and they are only effective within an RRSP<br>• Protects you against significant appreciation of the Canadian dollar against other currencies, which will reduce your foreign investment returns. Hedging can protect you from a double-whammy: At the same time that foreign returns get penalized by a rising Canadian dollar, some Canadian stocks may fall, since a higher dollar reduces the profits of Canadian exporters |

## To Hedge or Not to Hedge?

The pros of not hedging outweigh the pros of hedging for most investors. Leave your international investments unhedged. Most investors do not have to worry about foreign currency exposure, since a 25 percent allocation to Canadian stocks is high enough to protect you from excessive currency risk, while not so high as to forgo great investment opportunities abroad. Most portfolios hold some Canadian bonds and cash, which, combined with Canadian real estate, dramatically reduces foreign currency exposure to an acceptable level.

If you're planning to retire or spend considerable time in the US or abroad, a falling Canadian dollar will reduce your foreign purchasing power, since it will take more Canadian currency to buy the foreign currency you'll need to buy foreign goods. But this problem is offset by improved returns on foreign investments, which will enjoy the benefit of a falling domestic currency, but only if they are unhedged — yet another benefit to leaving your investments denominated in foreign currencies. A falling Canadian dollar will hurt hedged investors, especially those planning to spend a lot of money outside of Canada.

But here's the caveat: A *rising* Canadian dollar that is left unhedged means your investments will be penalized. If you're planning to move to the US or another continent to spend your retirement, your biggest risk is lost purchasing power if the Canadian dollar appreciates significantly and most of your money is invested in foreign currencies. In this case, your returns will be penalized — your foreign currency investments will be worth less when you redeem your money back into Canadian dollars. The remedy may be to have some of your investments hedged against the possibility of a higher Canadian dollar, depending on how much time you are planning to spend outside of Canada. Or you can invest in the few funds available that are fully denominated in foreign currencies. These funds are almost exclusively US-dollar funds: You buy in US dollars, and are given US dollars when you redeem; there is no exchange rate risk since your investment is made and returned in US dollars.

One last question about currencies: Can investment managers increase returns by taking advantage of currency fluctuations — using the volatility as an opportunity to add value to portfolio returns? Is it a good idea to invest in a fund where the manager is both picking stocks and determining which currencies to expose the fund to?

## Do Active Currency Calls Add Value?

Only the most sophisticated and learned managers in the world, those who specialize in currency, are capable of adding a small amount of value on the basis of active currency calls. An active currency call is one where the manager may be invested in US stocks, for example, but hedge some of the US-dollar exposure of the fund back into Canadian dollars, based on her prediction of where the Canadian currency is going. Or to pick a more extreme example, the manager might be invested in Japanese stocks, and some cash, and choose to eliminate the Yen exposure, but take on euro exposure based on the underlying cash holdings, even though she doesn't hold any European stocks. This decision would likewise be based on currency predictions.

Because of the sudden moves in currencies, it has been estimated that the opportunity to add value through currency management is limited to a minority of time periods. Unlike stock picking, the currency markets offer good trading opportunities less than 50 percent of the time. In addition, exchange rates can remain flat for long periods of time, then move violently and suddenly. Currencies are the most "fitful" of any asset class: It has been estimated that the largest currency moves occur in only 5 percent of time periods, whereas most of the big gains from bonds occur in about 30 percent of time periods, and big gains from equities in 5 to 10 percent. The factors that drive currency moves are so numerous that it's hard for a manager to be able to reliably predict their direction. Even an experienced currency manager will only generate an extra 0.5 percent on average each year to returns, but it's easy to lose at least that much with a few bad currency calls. Very few funds in Canada do any sort of active currency management; even hedging is rare and limited, for the most part, to a few global bond funds.

Since active currency calls don't add a lot of potential upside value, yet are vulnerable to equal or greater downside, currency management should be limited to reducing excessive risk rather than trying to squeeze out extra returns. And reducing currency risk is only a concern for Canadian investors who are planning to spend a lot of time outside of Canada, and have most of their money invested in foreign mutual funds that will eventually be sold and converted back to Canadian dollars. The best function of currency management in this situation is therefore a limited use of hedging back into Canadian dollars. With the exception of these extensive travellers, Canadian investors are best served by a portfolio that reduces currency risk with a sufficient weighting of Canadian securities.

# Suggested Reading

- Bernstein, Peter. *Against the Gods: The Remarkable Story of Risk.*
  New York: John Wiley & Sons, 1996.
  *A fascinating history of finance and risk, from the ancient Greeks to today's leading-edge risk management techniques.*

- Dewdney, A.K. *200% of Nothing.* New York: John Wiley & Sons, 1993.
  *An entertaining and light review of innumeracy and "math abuse."*

- Gilovich, Thomas. *How We Know What Isn't So.* New York: The Free Press, 1991.
  *A review of what Gilovich describes as "the fallibility of human reason in everyday life." This book is similar, but a nice complement to,* Innumeracy, *by John Allen Paulos. Gilovich takes more time to explode the myths of supernatural beliefs and the like.*

- Kahneman, Daniel, Paul Slovic, and Amos Tversky. *Judgement Under Uncertainty: Heuristics and Biases.* Cambridge: Cambridge University Press, 1982.
  *This is the original compilation of academic work on behavioural finance. The book is an edited text of numerous studies on the topic of investor psychology, most of which first appeared in the 1970s and are still referred*

*to today. These are many of the original scholastic works that initiated the academic field of behavioural finance.*

- Milevsky, Moshe. *Money Logic*. Toronto: Stoddart, 1999.
  *Professor Milevsky teaches finance at York University. He takes readers through some enlightening discoveries about everyday investing, including a detailed look at guarantees and assessing fund performance.*

- Paulos, John Allen. *Innumeracy*. New York: Vintage Books, 1988.
  *John Allen Paulos coined the term "innumeracy." For that reason alone, among many others, this book is essential reading for anyone interested in how mathematically illiterate most of us really are.*

- Shefrin, Hersh. *Beyond Greed and Fear*. Boston: Harvard Business School Press, 2000.
  *A comprehensive and detailed account of behavioural finance. The book draws on many academic studies to demonstrate the elements of psychology that pervade everyday investing.*

# Index

# Praise for Ted Cadsby's previous book, *The Power of Index Funds*

"Ted's case for indexing is buttressed by a powerful array of facts and figures that would make any fair judge rule: 'Case closed.' Readers who first understand this advice, and then follow it, will be duly enriched."
— JOHN BOGLE, SENIOR CHAIRMAN OF THE VANGUARD GROUP, INC.

"Cadsby offers a wealth of background about indexing and fund investing in general and practical advice on how to create index-based portfolios. It's a keeper for any fund investor."
— TORONTO STAR

"Ted Cadsby makes a strong case for using index funds as a core portfolio holding — and then tells readers exactly how to do it."
— GORDON PAPE

"Canadian readers are going to find that Ted Cadsby has provided a valuable addition to the world of investment finance. This book, on one of my personal favourite topics, passive investing, is well written, thorough, packed with interesting background, and can immediately be put into action."
— ERIC KIRZNER, PROFESSOR OF FINANCE,
ROTMAN SCHOOL OF MANAGEMENT, UNIVERSITY OF TORONTO

"The most likely candidate for Canada's indexing guru is Ted Cadsby."
— NATIONAL POST

"The key to long-term success is to invest wisely and think long-term. Ted Cadsby has given us excellent information on how indexing fits into these important goals."
— DAVID CORK, BESTSELLING AUTHOR OF THE PIG AND THE PYTHON

"Regardless of your philosophical position in the active-versus-passive portfolio management debate, Ted has done an excellent job explaining the significance of indexing. It is a must-read for Canadians who are serious about investing."
— MOSHE ARYE MILEVSKY, PROFESSOR OF FINANCE, YORK UNIVERSITY,
AND AUTHOR OF MONEY LOGIC

"More of you will get richer if you read and follow Ted Cadsby's investment tips."
— TORONTO STAR